Emergency Preparedness and Survival Guide Volume Two

The articles that appear in this book were previously published in *Backwoods Home Magazine*.

ISBN: 978-1-62440-100-8

Cover art by Don Childers

Manufactured in the United States of America

Published by *Backwoods Home Magazine*, Inc.
P.O. Box 712, Gold Beach, OR 97444
www.backwoodshome.com

Table of Contents

Introduction

Welcome to Volume Two of *Backwoods Home Magazine's Emergency Preparedness and Survival Guide*. Volume One was written as a one-stop guide for how to prepare for disasters, whether they were natural, economic, or caused by terrorism.

Volumes Two and Three are written in the same vein and, like Volume One, each contains articles taken directly from *Backwoods Home Magazine*, along with several which are entirely new and were commissioned specifically for these guides.

Volume One was our first preparedness and survival anthology, and an all-round guide. If there is a practical difference between the two new volumes, it's that this volume leans a little toward winter weather, whereas Volume Three leans toward the warmer months.

Like Volume One, this volume and Volume Three are divided into three sections. But there is a lot of overlap, and most of the advice in both volumes is good for any time of the year.

In all of the volumes you'll find various grab 'n go strategies as well as when and why you should stay in place instead of fleeing, and how you should go about preparing to do just that.

The anthology is divided into three sections:

Section 1 — The Threat

In this, Volume Two, we present some overviews, then address some credible threats such as bioterrorism, civil unrest, the possibility of tsunamis along our coasts, the new threat of electromagnetic pulse (EMP), and blizzards.

Section 2 — Immediate Preparation

Among other subjects, this section contains information on treating wounds, dealing with cold weather, starting fires both for cooking and keeping warm, backpacking stoves, impromptu shelters, treating "wild water," selecting and stashing firearms, and various grab 'n go bags for your person and your vehicle.

Section 3 — Long-term Preparation

Among other subjects, this section deals with creating food larders, gardening to feed your family if the supermarkets close, methods of preserving food, how to "bug out" in place, water storage, and even stashing "junk silver coins" for barter if the monetary system fails.

Dave Duffy
Publisher
Backwoods Home Magazine

Section 1
The Threat

"There's no harm in hoping for the best as long as you're prepared for the worst."

— Different Seasons, Stephen King

Chapter 1
The 7 core areas of preparedness

By Patrice Lewis

As I write this article, it's early September. And September, as you may or may not know, is National Preparedness Month, sponsored by the Federal Emergency Management Agency (FEMA). This is the time of year when we are officially recognized for our efforts to prepare for hard times. This is also the month we recognize everyone else who will ignore or poke fun at our efforts until the bleep hits the fan, after which they suddenly become our best friends and want us to share our supplies with them.

The subject of preparedness is so massive that I can barely scratch the surface in a single article, but it's a start. Websites such as Survivalblog.com can provide much more comprehensive information.

In a nutshell, preparedness refers to the stockpiling of goods, supplies, knowledge, reference literature, and other essentials in order to better weather natural disasters, terrorist attacks, economic uncertainty, and other difficulties. Preppers (as we're called) know our efforts will not insulate us from hard times, but will help cushion the blows of regional or national emergencies which are out of our control.

Food is just one of the seven core areas of preparedness. Canning is a valuable skill; take time to learn to preserve food.

By definition, "prepping" means preparing in advance of hard times, not after. This little subtlety — that preparing is best done before rather than after a serious event — seems to escape a lot of people. A typical example is the panic that ensues whenever a hurricane approaches landfall — there is widespread chaos at grocery stores, Home Depot locations, and gas stations as people frantically try to get ready for something they should always be prepared for anyway.

Bakery buckets — the prepper's best friend. These can be obtained free or cheaply from most grocery store bakeries. Ask around every time you shop.

When Hurricane Irene came ashore in August, I asked readers of my blog (www.rural-revolution.com) who were in the path of the hurricane to check in and report how things were going. Many readers wrote about the frantic crowds at grocery stores, of shelves stripped bare, of panicked lines at gas stations.

Three testimonies from my readers stand out:

"It is amazing how people react to the news of a hurricane. There appear to be very few people prepared, which is surprising to me as we usually get a hurricane here once every other year or so. I had to work yesterday, but swung out at lunchtime to top off my car with gas. The local grocery stores were packed! I passed by two other gas stations with lines out of the parking lot. Later after talking to people it seemed that people either fell into two categories, either they were panicking trying to get everything they needed now or they weren't going to bother at all. My most surprising conversation was with a good friend who has two children and doesn't even have a flashlight in her house — let alone water and non-perishable food. Sure is an eye opener."

"I've only been prepping for about a year, but have made significant strides. All I had to do yesterday to prepare was secure things in the yard that could blow away. It was amazing to me how frantic and panicked people seemed to be! I was absolutely calm, no pressure at all. I had food, water, shelter and backup plans if needed. It's good to be prepared, really lowers the stress level. I often wonder why more people aren't prepared."

"This is the first hurricane since I officially became a "prepper" and it totally shocked me. There was almost nothing left to do. We were able to spend all of our time getting our animals set and taken care of. We gassed up the cars midweek. The only thing left for the last minute was to purchase a cooler full of ice and draw up lots of water for the stock. Wow, what a stress-free way to live."

I think everyone can agree: it's far better to be prepared than not. But preparedness comes in a lot of different flavors and intensities, depending on the personal level of concern by the individuals involved.

How you prepare depends on endless numbers of factors. Your location (urban vs. rural), type of home (house, apartment, mobile home, etc.), numbers and ages of family members, health, income — these issues will all affect what kind, and to what extent, you can prepare.

Many people feel it's easier to be prepared in a rural location, and to some degree this is true. Livestock, gardens, space for stored supplies, and a lesser likelihood of roving gangs of looters are all benefits of living in the country. But living in the country is no guarantee that Preppers will escape any problems. And this does not excuse our urban cousins from preparing to handle emergencies as best they can.

This article will focus not so much on the nuts-and-bolts of what to store, but rather on some general things to consider. These considerations must then be tailored toward your particular circumstances.

Short-term preparedness

It's helpful to know what you're preparing for. Preparedness can roughly be divided into two categories: short-term and long-term.

Short-term preps generally are meant to address local and regional events. Here in rural north Idaho we prepare for wildfires, earthquakes, and blizzards. Other locations need to prepare for tornadoes or hurricanes as well. Urban short-term preparedness may consist of all of the previously listed natural disasters, but might also include social unrest and acts of terrorism.

In the short-term, most urban situations can be handled by staying indoors rather than roaming the streets or attempting to bug out to a rural area. When riots or other social unrest erupts, your chances of escaping looters is fairly high if you stay inside and make sure your doors and windows are barricaded or at least patrolled from within.

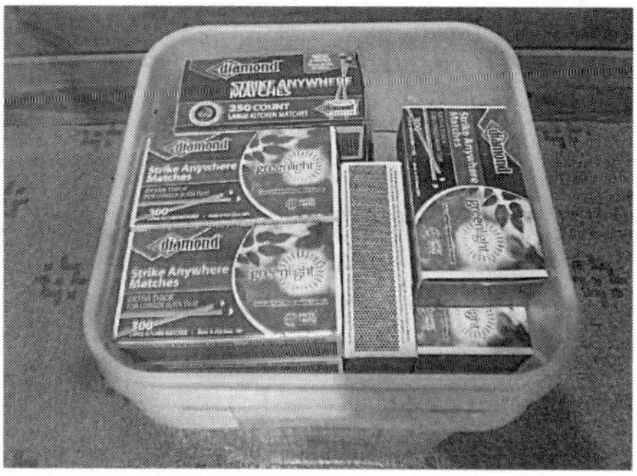

Strike anywhere matches should be a top preparedness item. They're cheap now, but how priceless would they become if they were no longer available?

For short-term preparedness, I recommend having at least three months of supplies in the Seven Core Areas (listed later in the article). Why three months? Under even the most dire regional conditions, things will usually shake out by the end of three months. Outside help will become available, or conditions will otherwise change.

Keep in mind that if things are in chaos for a week or more, your unprepared neighbors may ask you for help. And you should help, if for no other reason than long memories after the crisis is past. It's important not to forget charity and mercy during an emergency.

Long-term preparedness

What conditions would necessitate long-term preparedness? This would mean an interruption of our way of life on a national (or extended regional) scale. Along these lines, I have concerns about two possible scenarios.

The first is that our country will experience an economic collapse, in which case our best "savings account" is what is euphemistically called "tangibles." (In Prepper lingo this is known as beans, bullets, and band-aids.) A collapse of our banking system and its fiat currency could result in massive employment and other financial hardships.

A second possible scenario that concerns many Preppers is the loss of our national power grid either through natural events such as massive solar flares or through terrorism (electromagnetic pulse weapon detonated in the upper atmosphere which will incapacitate the power grid). Our country is no longer capable of functioning without electricity. If you've read the book One Second After by William R. Forstchen, you'll understand the need for additional supplies to handle a long-term interruption of services.

Under these conditions, having adequate supplies in the Seven Core Areas will help people survive in moderate comfort. By "adequate" I don't mean you're living in the lap of luxury; I mean you're not starving, freezing, or sitting in the dark.

Rule of Three

We have some prepared neighbors who abide by what they call the Rule of Three (see Issue #111, May/June 2008). What this means is they have one main and two backup methods of doing whatever needs to be done (in other words, a backup to their backup). Cooking, heating, lighting, and communications are all aspects that need backups of backups in case the primary method(s) are incapacitated.

These neighbors are off-grid, so having that Rule of Three for everyday necessities has allowed them to

Don't forget such things as sewing notions. The day may come when we need to hand-sew clothes.

live comfortably under conditions many of us would find difficult. So in your preparations, think in terms of multiple backups in case your primary source fails.

Bugging out vs. bugging in

The decision whether to bug out or bug in (hunker down) depends on the nature of the emergency as well as your physical location. A few scenarios:

Riots are hitting your urban area: Stay indoors, barricade doors and windows, and hunker down. Do not draw attention to yourself.

A Category 5 hurricane is approaching your low-lying coastal property: Gather your grab-and-go kits and get out.

An economic crash has plunged our nation into a severe depression and resources are scarce: There is no easy answer to this situation. Bugging in (staying in the city) will only work until your supplies are gone or your safety is compromised. At that point, bugging out may be your only option — if you have someplace to bug out to.

Hunkering down (bugging in) is a legitimate option for many people under a number of emergency circumstances. But that doesn't mean you just lock your doors. Hunkering down means you create your bug-out retreat right there at home. That means having your Seven Core Areas stocked and ready.

However, bear in mind that no one can be self-sufficient in an urban apartment. The best you can hope for is to stay safe until the immediate crisis passes.

Bugging out from an urban location opens a whole new can of worms. Unless you have a fully-stocked self-sufficient rural retreat (and who does?), then you'll probably be trespassing on the kindness of rural friends or relatives. How long will you be staying? How long can they support you? It's almost impossible to say, since no one can predict the duration of a major emergency.

All I can suggest in this case is: (a) bring every supply you can possibly cram into your vehicle; (b) be the most gracious houseguest you can possibly be. Remember it's not your home, so be prepared to work for your "rent."

You're not Euell Gibbons

Remember Euell Gibbons? ("Ever eat a pine tree? Many parts are edible…") Gibbons was known for his ability to literally live off the land.

Most of us aren't Euell Gibbons. Most of us wouldn't know an edible plant if it bit us on the butt. So whatever you do, don't think you can "live off the land" if the bleep hits the fan just because you know what a blackberry bush looks like.

One time while lurking on a "green" forum, I posted a question: If you're in an urban area and the bleep hit the fan, what would you do? Do you have any food stored away? I receive the usual we'll-all-join-hands-and-sing-Kumbaya type of answers, but one reply made me blink in astonishment: this person didn't see the need to store any food because he would simply forage for all his dietary needs from wild plants in vacant lots.

This kind of — sheesh, what would you call it? Ignorance? Naiveté? Stupidity? (yeah, that's the word) — always astounds me. Assuming you could even identify edible plants, just how much filthy polluted plantain can you collect in order to keep yourself and your family alive? How will you cook it? And what happens when the vacant lot is stripped bare of everything except broken glass and tin cans? Would you even dare to step outside your apartment and risk meeting roving mobs while you search for wild purslane and dandelion shoots?

And please, don't even get me started on the "mountain-man" hunting scenario. I don't care if you're the greatest recreational hunter in the world — you won't be able to survive off your hunting, especially if you live in the city. Where will you hunt? How will you get there? Will the locals welcome you? (Remember, if people are hunting for survival, you're no longer a visiting cash cow — you're competition for a limited resource.) How will you get your meat back home? How will you preserve it?

There's a reason humans moved from hunter/gatherer societies to an agricultural-based culture: food sources are more secure. To assume you can suddenly move back into a hunter/gatherer mode to survive — while living in a city, no less — is lunacy.

You're not Rambo either

A popular whimsy among some male survivalists is the Rambo fantasy. They have vague thoughts of gunning down any and all threats to their survival. Let a starving mother with a crying toddler knock on the door and plead for a bowl of cereal, and Mr. Rambo will threaten to blow her away rather than treat her with compassion. (That said, my elderly aunt who lives in Louisiana told me how this was a common ploy for home invasion robberies after Hurricane Katrina hit.)

This kind of hyper-machismo is asking for trouble. I firmly believe part of being prepared is being suitably armed, but if you'll pardon my French, don't start talking from your balls. Be sensible in your defenses.

In my aunt's case, after hearing about a number of these home invasions, she refused to answer the door at all. Other people answered the door while fully armed. All I'm saying is, don't go looking for trouble. Just be prepared to handle it if it arises.

Practice, practice, practice

No matter how fully prepped you think you are, you won't know for sure until an emergency arises. But the least you can do is make sure (a) you know where all your emergency supplies are located; (b) your equipment is in working order; and (c) you know how to use it. (You'd be surprised how many people panic-buy generators before a hurricane but don't have the faintest notion how to hook them up.)

If the power goes out, the last thing you want to do is grope around in the dark trying to find your flashlight, only to find the batteries are dead because the kids were playing Spook. Know where your equipment is and make sure it's in working order.

Once you feel you've thought through every contingency and you're reasonably prepared, the best possible thing you can do is shut off the power for a week and prove it. There is no finer way to discover your weaknesses and vulnerable spots than to stage an "emergency." That's why professional emergency services stage drills.

Operational security

This is advice we ourselves have not taken because of our rather public involvement in teaching Prepping and self-sufficiency, but I suggest you practice Operational Security (OpSec). In a word, shaddup. Keep your preps quiet and low-key. Don't talk about it. Don't brag. Don't announce to the world what kinds of firearms you possess and how much food you have stored.

The reason is, there will always be somebody happy to liberate you of your supplies. Nuff said.

The Seven Core Areas of Preparedness

I've listed below what I call the Seven Core Areas of Preparedness. I need to stress that this list is by no means comprehensive. However, if you're prepared in these seven areas, then you can focus on achieving other, more tailored preparations to suit your particular circumstances.

Food

This is obvious. I don't mean you should stuff your freezer with TV dinners, either, because if the power goes out, they're gone. Consider purchasing staples you enjoy eating (rice, beans, oatmeal, etc.) and learn to store and prepare them. These have the added advantage of being dirt cheap. If you want to take the next step, learn to can. Properly canned food lasts years without refrigeration, and canning is a valuable skill as well. Alternately, buy lots of commercially canned food.

Along with storing food, you should have the means to prepare it. Your options will be more limited if you're in an urban high-rise apartment (where you can't install a wood cookstove, for example), in which case your food will have to be pre-cooked (such as MREs) or otherwise edible without cooking. Eating unheated soup or beans right out of a can might not be the most pleasant meal, but at least you won't starve.

Water

Without water to drink and wash, you'll be miserable (or dead). At all times you should have a minimum of 20 gallons stored in your home. Look for options to secure larger quantities of water (roof runoff? storage tank?) as well as ways to sterilize surface water such as bleach, iodine, or filtration.

If you're preparing for a minimum of three months, then your storage space for water will be huge and will probably take up far more space than most people have available. That's why you need the means to purify water. A non-electric water filter (such as Berkey) might be part of your water storage efforts.

Heat

We live in rural north Idaho not far from the Canadian border. Heat is a major concern for us. How can you heat your house if the power goes out? Everyone's circumstances are different – you probably can't install a woodstove in a Manhattan apartment – so think through the alternatives that will work for you.

Be careful about ventilation when considering your heat sources. Endless people have been asphyxiated due to carbon monoxide poisoning because they chose the wrong option to heat their living space. Some buildings have windows which will not open, and this must be considered when thinking through your heat sources.

Lights

You don't want to be in the dark, do you? Everyone can afford an oil lamp or two. Don't bother with those pricey containers of scented lamp oil, either. A gallon of kerosene is less than $10 and works just fine.

While flashlights and batteries are nice (and necessary), you'll go through your battery supplies very quickly if you depend on them exclusively for lighting. Remember your Rule of Three: plan to have backups to your backups. You should have candles, oil lamps, perhaps battery-powered LED lamps, or other light sources.

If you're "bugging in," consider blackout curtains for your windows that will block light. Alternately, a roll of black plastic and duct tape will work (as well as being useful for other purposes). No sense advertising how prepared you are (OpSec!). But remember, sheeting your windows in plastic will trap carbon monoxide, so be careful.

Sanitation

What happens if you can't flush your toilets? If you run out of diapers or feminine hygiene products? If you don't have toilet paper? Think about what kind of reusable alternatives you can substitute for pricey disposable items.

Find reusable versions of disposable sanitary items. Cheap washcloths from the dollar store can act as reusable toilet paper. Use cloth instead of disposable diapers. Try washable feminine napkins instead of disposable. Of course, these reusable versions require a means to wash them, so think through your options. For short-term preparedness, it might be better to stock up on disposables.

If you cannot flush your toilets and an outhouse isn't possible, a five-gallon bucket lined with heavy-duty trash bags and a toilet seat may be your next best option. Wood shavings, sawdust, or ash can be sprinkled in the bucket after each use to help control odors.

Medical

Can you doctor yourself for minor injuries? Do you have a good stock of your prescription medicines? It doesn't cost much to pull together a comprehensive first-aid kit. It might be harder to stockpile prescription medications, so this is something worth discussing with your doctor.

Now may be the time to take a refresher course for basic first aid. You might also stock up on medical items you may not otherwise consider — burn dressings, tape closures, compression bandages, and lots of over-the-counter pain killers.

Safety

What happens when too many people suddenly want to be your best friend post-bleep? What should you do if you live in an urban area subject to rioting and unrest? Some people interpret "safety" to mean they should have an arsenal of guns. Others think they need a secret rural bug-out location. However you interpret it, identify prospective dangers for your circumstances and think of how to mitigate them.

Personally, I believe every family member old enough to handle a firearm should be taught safety factors and target practice. Adult members should also have holsters (either concealed or otherwise) for ease of carry during "bleep" situations. I recently purchased a bra holster which will make concealed carry very simple and comfortable (and invisible).

Safety should be more than just firearms. It also includes such things as situational and strategic awareness, home and property security, communications, and local relations (friends, neighbors, community).

A single magazine article can barely scratch the surface of the preparedness mindset. But as our nation faces an unprecedented number of major threats to our economy, our security, and our way of life, I believe everyone should have the basics of Prepping down cold. Δ

Chapter 2
Balancing your high- and low-tech preparedness needs

By Patrice Lewis

I happen to think *all* attempts to improve one's self-sufficiency are a good thing. But while technology has provided preppers with many wonderful and creative innovations like better water filtering methods, more resistant materials such as Kevlar, higher efficiencies in heating and cooling systems, and certainly better communication options, it's easy to make the mistake that all expensive, high-tech solutions are always superior to the tools and skills used by our ancestors.

Many readers of this magazine live off-grid and therefore have a variety of alternative high-tech amenities already in place (or planned) for day-to-day living. This article is *not* an attack on technology. But there's a difference between having systems in place to provide everyday modern comforts — whether conventional or alternative — and systems meant as backups to carry us through stressful times when modern amenities may not be available.

I love modern technology. I adore electricity. I love having a washing machine. I think the internet is one of the greatest inventions since sliced bread. Clean, running water is absolutely wonderful. Grocery stores? Fabulous. But if these things are taken away, I don't want to be miserable or otherwise unable to function because normally-predictable services are down

Illustration by Jessie Denning

and I have no alternatives to fall back on. That's why we all prep. However, I also don't want to be miserable or unable to function because one or more of my high-tech backups have broken down or run out. The classic and much-maligned (but true) example? The power goes out. No problem! You have endless amounts of canned chili stored away… but only an electric can opener.

The point of this article is to encourage you to keep the KISS principle in mind: Keep It Simple, Stupid. The more complicated the solution, the less likely it is to work flawlessly and forever.

The wood cookstove — an excellent multi-purpose, low-tech tool that cooks, heats water, and supplies heat to the house.

Please don't make the mistake of thinking "simple" means "easy." It doesn't. Using a woodstove in the winter is simple. It doesn't break down, it doesn't require electricity … but let's face it, it's a lot easier to turn a knob to heat your home. Using a woodstove means you have to obtain wood, split it into manageable pieces, stack those pieces out of the weather, start the stove early in the morning, stoke the stove periodically throughout the day, and deal with ash and splinters. None of this is easy. But it's very, very simple.

High-tech Rambos

The Rambo stereotype (of movie fame) is some macho dude whose first solution to any problem is physical, usually in the form of beating the other person to a pulp. Well, high-tech Rambos (called "technophiles") see a problem as an opportunity to indulge in all sorts of pricey, complicated systems —"toys for boys," pardon the stereotype.

Power out? No problem! All we need is a $30,000 solar array, loads of deep-cycle batteries, maybe a windmill, and *voilà*! Our kitchen light works, and we're the envy of the neighbors!

But what if something goes wrong within this complex system? Can you diagnose the problem and fix it? Do you have spare parts? And in a grid-down event, can you obtain more spare parts, and/or hire an expert to rectify the situation at your remote retreat?

Although a combine is more efficient, scything wheat can be done by hand.

Whereas low-tech people, or high-tech folks with *forethought*, simply light an oil lamp. See the difference? Keep it simple.

Too many technophiles resist doing anything the old-fashioned and time-tested way. Pioneer methods are for pansies. The more expensive and technical the solution to our basic needs, the better. But they're missing the big picture. Almost invariably, high-tech solutions are complicated, require continuous maintenance (often by professionals), necessitate specialized parts, and are prone — simply because of their complexity — to breakdowns or other mishaps. For the cost of a solar array or even a generator, I can buy a whole lot of beans, bullets, and band-aids (not to mention a manual can opener or two). If your finances are limited, then it's far more worthwhile to search for low-tech options, too.

I know some people who have spent endless tens of thousands of dollars preparing to keep themselves supplied with all the modern comforts should the bleep ever hit the fan. But last year we had a local power outage and — I'm not kidding — their expensive solar array was incorrectly wired to transition from conventional to alternative power, and they were plunged into darkness along with everyone else.

In our case, we lit a couple of kerosene lamps, cooked dinner on our woodstove, and sat around playing board games. In their case, they had no heat, no way to cook dinner, and they didn't even have candles (they said they didn't need any since their solar array was going to work so well). It took them about 30 seconds to realize that perhaps their high-tech solutions weren't the best solution after all, at least until they could get more bugs worked out. Since they had no low-tech backups (as I said, not even candles), they joined us for dinner and pleasant conversation in our warmly-lit house until power was restored.

Ensure that *you* have multiple low-tech backup options available. While high-tech stuff can be wonderful, you also have to be practical and realistic.

Another thing to think about is that blazing lights and a noisy generator draw attention. If you have the only brightly-lit house — the envy of your neighbors — then you might attract more than envy … and more than neighbors. Just saying.

Our legendary pioneer ancestors

Whenever I address the subject of low-tech living, I make frequent references to our legendary pioneer ancestors. The reason I do this is because I hold them as the ultimate standard to which we should aspire. These are people who created homes and livelihoods out of virgin wilderness with a minimum of hand tools. Sadly, many of their skills as well as their tools have been lost in our modern times. This loss of knowledge is tragic.

They may not be as luxurious, but some of the solutions the pioneers used had the advantage of long-term dependability. If something low-tech broke, they could either fix it or make another. But when's the last time you tried to make or fix a solar array, generator, or computer?

Even chainsaws and log splitters have their limitations, which is why, for long-term preparedness, it's wise to have the backup of axes, mauls, two-person bucksaws, sharpeners, and other tools for providing wood for warmth. But never forget, having these low-tech tools is only half the equation; you also have to know how to use them.

The importance of skills

Oddly, some of the best people to talk to concerning low-tech skills are Living History Reenactors. These are folks whose passion for a particular time period (Medieval, Renaissance, Pioneer, Civil War, Mountain Man, whatever) have led them to extensive research about life during those times. This research extends not only to re-creating clothing and accoutrements, but also recapturing skills particular to that period.

It's not unusual for historical reenactors to learn such skills as blacksmithing, carpentry (with old or handmade manual tools), outdoor cooking and baking, hunting and trapping with handmade equipment, leather tanning, making soap, and fiber arts like shearing, carding, weaving, felt-making, sewing, and needlework. While these reenactors may not be learning these skills with an eye to prepping, this base of knowledge nevertheless gives reenactors a sense of confidence with regards to their ability to survive if the lights go out.

A Civil War reenactor once told me, "We have found that many of the older technologies and tools are actually much better than some of the newer junk made in China. The only caveat is that many of these things require more time to accomplish."

This sums up the reason why so many people are reluctant to embrace low-tech options: they require more time, work, and skill.

The knowledge required to use low-tech tools is often overlooked among preppers. Low-tech living can be a surprisingly difficult prospect, mostly because few of us have grown up learning the necessary skills at our parents'

Food staples such as beans, rice, spices, etc. are versatile and inexpensive.

knees. With rare exceptions (except perhaps among *BHM* readers), modern society doesn't call upon us to sew on a treadle machine, cook on a wood cookstove, milk a cow, cut and split firewood by hand, build without power tools, or repair anything from a shoe to a window screen.

There's no doubt that modern methods are usually highly efficient — a combine harvests wheat far more efficiently than hand-scything (take it from someone who knows) — but it also means there is an enormous wealth of skills that we've lost in the last century.

The problem with these kinds of skills is they take time to learn … and the time *not* to learn them is when the bleep has hit the fan and people are scared and panicky. If you're coping with a long-term power outage and need to preserve the food in your chest freezer before it rots, are you going to wait until then to teach yourself how to can?

Knowledge is of limited use without the proper tools and equipment; but tools are useless without the knowledge of how to use them. Both are important.

Sensible compromises

People also have to balance low-tech solutions against whatever physical limitations they may have. Many low-tech solutions are low-tech because they're labor-intensive, so they won't work for everyone. To someone who is elderly, disabled, or in poor health, owning livestock and maintaining a garden might be beyond their physical abilities, in which case those MREs and freeze-dried foods are a smart alternative.

But physical limitations aside, too often we avoid low-tech solutions because of the workload involved. Even people in robust health often don't think in terms of choosing low-tech options because it's such hard work.

A couple of years ago, we grew a half-acre wheat field as an experiment. While we used a tractor to break up the soil, the rest of the work was done by hand. We sowed by hand, we scythed by hand, we raked by hand, we bundled into sheaves by hand, we threshed by hand, we winnowed by hand, and we ground the wheat into flour by hand (okay, we used a hand-operated grain grinder, but you get the point). It was a tremendous amount of work that gave us a deep appreciation for what early farmers did as a matter of course. It is not an experiment we're anxious to repeat unless we have to.

The point is, not everyone has the physical ability (or, frankly, the interest) to engage in such a tough activities. So don't. Prepare yourself to handle things commensurate with your abilities … but don't overlook the fact that low-tech living is, by definition, harder than high-tech.

Less is more

One of the problems with our luxurious modern society is we will do anything and spend whatever it takes so we will never be deprived of our creature-comforts. If the power is out, we still want our hot showers, bright lights, and flush toilets.

But our pioneer forefathers didn't have those luxuries and they mostly got along. I'm not saying they didn't stink or experience discomfort using an outhouse in freezing weather, but that was just the way things were.

If the time comes when utilities are unavailable and our lives revert (temporarily or long-term) to life without modern amenities, then we can't expect to keep our creature comforts at the same level. Remember this: *Ultimately it's better to learn to live with LESS than to be dependent on MORE.*

I recently spoke to Charley Hogwood with P.R.E.P. (Personal Readiness Education Programs, www.readygoprep.com) about this issue. Mr. Hogwood teaches emergency preparedness and disaster readiness in the southeast. His company also puts on preparedness expos. He admits that high-tech gizmos are seductively attractive. "It can be like a toy store," he says. "When people see the possible things they can get in order to be prepared, they tend to buy stuff because they like it. But *skills* supersede *things*. The more you know, the less you have to carry. But since many people lack skills, they think they can buy their way out of it, and that's not the case."

His focus is to get people away from the superficial, reactive stance and "take the crazy out of prepping." Instead, he teaches people to understand the hazards around them that they might face in their daily lives. And rarely does he advise people to depend on highly technical options when a low-tech alternative will do.

Indoor clothes racks (either standing or hanging) are an excellent low-tech alternative to clothes dryers.

"Our parents and great-grandparents knew how to do stuff," he says, "but today's society has made those older skills unnecessary. It's gotten to the point where it's abnormal for someone to hop off the industrial treadmill. When did it become extremist to be more self-reliant?"

Don't own stuff you can't fix

One of the dangers of Rambo technophiles is they often can't fix the stuff they buy. Of course, I could be wrong — many people are technologically savvy, in which case I recommend a stash of replacement parts for if/when an item breaks. But otherwise, be careful of owning stuff you can't repair.

My husband happens to be a very "handy" fellow who can turn his hand to any number of fix-it projects — construction, plumbing, wiring, carpentry — but anything involving mechanics is beyond him. He can change the oil and make a few adjustments on the car, but when it comes to the more intricate functions of metals and machines, he calls a mechanic. In my opinion, he's smart to know his limits and when it's worth turning to experts to fix a problem.

But what if experts aren't available? If your prepping efforts depend on high-tech things such as generators, solar panels, windmills, pumps, and communications devices — and then something goes wrong — what will you do if service experts or parts aren't available?

We can't be too purist about the notion of only owning stuff we can fix. I don't have the faintest clue how to fix a computer, yet our family owns several. Ditto for the car, the well pump, and the chainsaw. These items are useful and valuable and help make our lives easier and more productive. But they're not critical to our survival. If they were knocked out of commission, we have low-tech backups so we won't be sitting in the dark hungry, thirsty, and unable to stay warm.

Rule of three

Even those currently living off-grid know the wisdom of having the Rule of Three in place — essentially backups to your backups. If your solar panels fail, have a generator. If your generator fails, have a woodstove and oil lamps.

The same applies to lower-tech options: make sure you have backups to your backups, or at least multiple versions of the same useful, dependable item. If your Aladdin oil lamp breaks, make sure you have a regular oil lamp ready to light. Lay up a good supply of candles as well. And don't forget the matches.

Now let's face it, by no stretch of the imagination are oil lamps anywhere near as bright as incandescent bulbs or CFLs powered by solar panels or a generator. But so what? Is it necessary to have home lighting so bright that you're forced to squint? Prior to electricity, the world was a much darker place; but it's better to have a candle to light than to sit around in the dark when your generator runs out of fuel.

The seven core areas of preparedness

In a previous *BHM* article, I wrote about what I call the seven core areas of preparedness: food, water, heat, light, sanitation, medical care, and protection. These are the things that are necessary for physical survival. In a "bleep hits the fan" scenario (storm devastation, extended power outage, etc.) then it's best to have these things be as solid, dependable, and unfailing as possible. In other words, it behooves you to think "low tech" rather than "high tech."

Let's examine a few low-tech options for the seven core areas.

Low-tech food

How, you may ask, can food be high-tech?

There are many people who have no idea how to cook. They live their lives eating boxed, frozen, canned, deli, or otherwise pre-made foods. One of the underrated but necessary skills under hard conditions is the ability to cook food from scratch.

One time we were standing in a checkout line at Costco, a good place to get bulk staples. But it's also a good place to get an endless variety of premade convenience foods. Do you know there are some people who think "homemade pizza" means popping an unbaked Costco pizza into the oven?

Anyway, our 18-year-old daughter was quietly noting the contents of many carts in the checkout line. After we had paid for our items and left the store, she commented on how many people's carts were loaded with convenience foods and how few were loaded with staples.

Scratch cooking is a dying art, it would seem. Faced with a bag of dried beans, too many people have no idea what to do with them. That's why freeze-dried foods and MREs are such best-selling items in the emergency preparedness market — because the thought of cooking beans and rice is intimidating to so many people.

Don't get me wrong — freeze-dried foods and MREs have their place. Certain freeze-dried or

Books are your low-tech friends.

powdered staples also make sense (powdered eggs, milk, and cheese). Scratch cooking requires a *means* to cook (wood cookstove, rocket stove, even a campfire) and if you're living in a 15-story high-rise apartment, those things are unlikely. Also, packing some MREs into bug-out bags is sensible.

But for long-term conditions, bulk staples (and the knowledge of how to prepare them) are not only cheaper, they're superior in taste and nutrition.

Part of your low-tech prepping should include stocking your kitchen with the equipment necessary to create a meal — pots and pans, measuring cups and spoons, bread pans and cookie sheets, etc. (These items can be picked up very inexpensively at thrift stores.) There are myriad excellent cookbooks on the market (hint: avoid Martha Stewart) for beginning cooks that will walk you through the intricacies of the kitchen.

You'll begin to create meals tailored toward your family's likes and dislikes. You'll also acquire a sense of accomplishment as you realize you can take that bag of beans and create a delicious meal out of it.

Sanitation

In an emergency or long-term power-down situation, we can't allow sanitation to go by the wayside. Adding an illness caused by unsanitary conditions to an already stressful "grid-down" situation is unnecessary. And here again, low-tech solutions are often best.

Think through your daily cleanliness needs, everything from lavatorial requirements to a hot shower to feminine hygiene to washing dishes to doing laundry. While you can probably get away with letting dirty clothes pile up for a week or two, certain things like the "monthly visitor" for women and everyday toilet use can't wait.

For those fortunate to live rural, an outhouse can be a wonderful backup. If your groundwater is shallow, then sink a trash can and position the toilet seat over it (a scoop of dirt, ashes, or lime will help with smells and flies). Composting toilets, sawdust toilets, or even (in a pinch) a plastic bag in a bucket with a toilet seat over the top can serve the needs of nature when conventional facilities aren't available.

For women, consider reusable feminine hygiene products. My two daughters and I switched to washable hygiene products over three years ago and have never looked back. Besides the amount of money saved, we never have to worry about running out of critical supplies during a blizzard or other stranding event.

For washing clothes under emergency conditions, a plastic plunger-on-a-stick (known as a "breathing hand washer") works to wash clothes in a bucket. (If you're very dedicated toward hand-washing options, consider a wringer as well.) Even under non-emergency conditions, a clothesline (outdoors) or clothes drying rack (indoors) can save an astounding amount of money. We haven't used an electric clothes dryer for years thanks to our indoor hanging clothes racks (winter) and our clothesline (summer).

Low-tech lighting

Having a generator in place makes sense for people who are prone to frequent power outages or who live where natural disasters regularly occur (hurricanes, ice storms, etc.). But remember, generators are noisy, and only last as long as you have fuel. They also must be serviced, and they require proper installation. If a generator has been sitting in a box for a year or more, you might be in for an unpleasant surprise when you try to hook it up.

Meanwhile, that full kerosene lamp that's been sitting on the mantle merely requires the touch of a match and voilà — let there be light.

Therefore, part of your low-tech backup for lighting should include oil lamps, candles, matches, and fire extinguishers.

Kerosene lamps and/or candles make for intimate light. By "intimate," I mean you really have to bring the light source close by in order to see well. I've seen people get their hair burned (especially women, whose hair tends to be longer) because they leaned too close to a flame while reading.

In our modern society, we are so used to unwavering light that the relative dimness of oil lamps or candles makes things hard to see. Under such circumstances, get any tasks requiring good lighting done during daylight hours, and reserve the darkness for board games, reading, cards, or other pastimes.

In short, don't *fight* the dimmer lighting. Live with it. People have spent thousands of years living with dim lighting. You can too, if necessary.

Hard copies vs. e-copies

Even information has gone high-tech at the expense of low-tech.

We own an extensive library of reference books, including volumes on gardening, food preservation, animal husbandry, small engine repair, homesteading issues, cooking, etc. But there's so much information available online that we've also amassed a considerable amount of reference material on the computer.

It took me a while to realize that this valuable material would be entirely unavailable should power go down. So over the years we've assembled a large binder filled with articles and tutorials on a wide variety of subjects. We are no longer dependent on unreliable technology if the need arises to consult this material. You might call this our "information dirt road" rather than our "information superhighway."

We enjoy the internet and the wealth of information it offers as much as anyone else. This one example of technology has revolutionized our world like nothing before. Our daughters have Kindles (courtesy of a generous uncle) and they're phenomenal little machines. Download a book and it's there whenever you want.

But drop them and they're toast. Drop a book and it's usually fine.

Computers, Kindles, and other marvels can all fail. So can GPS units. How many people can even read an old-fashioned map any more? How many people even have maps of their immediate surroundings, let alone maps that may help them evacuate during a disaster? When it comes to important reference material, I strongly urge printed copies you can consult in a power-down scenario. Think low-tech, not high-tech.

The moral of the story

Since everyone's circumstances are different, it's important to make whatever concessions are necessary depending on your health, finances, and physical location.

It's not easy going low-tech in modern houses. The most obvious low-tech solution for heating, for example, is a woodstove … a solution that's difficult in the suburbs (where will you get your wood?) or impossible in the city (high rise apartments frown on woodstoves).

In our modern culture, and with the vast ignorance we have about low-tech living, the best we can hope for is a blend of high- and low-tech answers. I'm not about to give up the convenience of flashlights (a high-tech gizmo) in favor of a hurricane lamp if I'm trying to find out what kind of predator is harassing our livestock at midnight. But if my flashlight fails, at least a hurricane lamp is available.

The moral of the story is this: Don't indulge *only* in high-tech solutions at the expense of their low-tech alternatives. Even folks who regularly live off-grid understand the need for backups to their backups in the form of kerosene lamps, simple water purification systems, etc.

As you acquire more skills and the equipment necessary to tackle low-tech living, you may discover a lovely side-effect: a sense of accomplishment. Low-tech living is harder, requires more knowledge, and is sometimes messy; but it can also be soul-satisfying, peaceful, and fun. And if you get used to low-tech living now, your learning curve will be less and your pocketbook will thank you.

Prepping isn't a destination, it's a lifestyle. In this high-tech world, I prefer to take refuge in a lower-tech standard of living that will serve us equally well in both normal and emergency times. As someone once said, "Reject convenience and select inconvenience now. It will help in adjusting to life without later." Δ

Chapter 3
Subduction Zone Tsunami
What the residents of the Pacific Northwest have to fear

By John Silveira

I was sitting in my cubicle poring over a map of the Oregon coast—actually, just that part of the coast that is Gold Beach where *Backwoods Home Magazine* is located. Suddenly, I heard a voice behind me ask, "What map is that, John?"

I just about jumped out of my skin. I turned around and there, standing over me, was O.E. MacDougal, our poker playing friend from southern California. He was holding a grocery bag in his left arm.

"Sorry, I didn't mean to startle you," he said.

"It's okay," I said, "I'm just jumpy."

He nodded "I forgot."

"Tsunami Hazard Map of the Gold Beach Area, Curry County, Oregon," he read from the top of the map. "Are you expecting a tsunami?"

"Well, sort of. I mean, I've been told one will happen sooner or later."

"It will!" he said.

I looked at him. That kind of certainty from Mac was unsettling. "You really think so?"

"Well, this area is one big subduction zone, and you know the old saying, 'It's not a matter of if, but when.'

"Really!" I said.

"One of the things that's certain from the geological record," Mac went on, "is that there have been plenty of tsunamis, or tidal waves, on this coast before and you can bet that there'll be more. And the odds are pretty good that it will be a big one, possibly much bigger than the one that hit Asia the day after Christmas six months ago. That was caused by an earthquake on a similar subduction zone. The Asia tidal waves killed 250,000 people."

"You're using both terms, Mac. Is there a difference between a tsunami and a tidal wave?" Dave asked. Dave Duffy, the publisher of *BHM*, had just walked in.

"Hi, Dave. Good to see you," Mac said shaking Dave's hand.

"No difference," he continued. "They're also called seismic sea waves, and sometimes they're called names I'd never say in front of small children or my mother. But that's only when they're barreling down on you."

"How do you like the new office?" Dave asked.

"I like it."

"Want a tour?"

"Sure."

"What's in the grocery bag?" Dave asked.

"I told Ilene I'd make lunch. You guys hungry?" Mac asked.

"Sure," Dave and I said in unison.

"Well, I am too, and lunch is what's in the bag, so let me fix it, then we'll take the tour."

We led Mac from my cubicle to the lunchroom.

He placed his bag on one of the counters and proceeded to go to work.

"What are you making for us this time?" Dave asked.

"Sort of a fish salad."

"Your own recipe?"

"Yeah. I'm sure I'm not the first person to come up with this idea, but I'd never seen one before.

"So, what's with the interest in tsunamis?" he asked.

"I want John to write something about them," Dave said. "I watched a TV program on the *Discovery Channel* that stated our Pacific Northwest coastline has a very similar subduction zone to the one that spawned the tsunami waves in Asia. They said it could happen here."

"It has and it could," Mac said. "In fact, it will happen here." He started to shred some lettuce.

"That's what the program said; it's only a matter of when. Mac, what do you know about tsunamis?"

"Well, most tsunamis are caused by earthquakes and that's what's most likely to cause a big one here. But earthquakes aren't the only cause. The next leading causes are submarine landslides, then volcanoes, and least often they're caused by impacts from celestial bodies—like the one that finished off the dinosaurs. That one probably sent a tsunami clear across the Florida peninsula."

The Cascadia Subduction Zone

"But here the chief danger is *tsunamigenic earthquakes* — they're the earthquakes that most often cause tsunamis. They occur at what are called subduction zones."

"Just *what* is a subduction zone?" I asked.

"It's where one of the tectonic plates that makes up the surface of the earth is moving under another one, as opposed to the plates sliding past each other

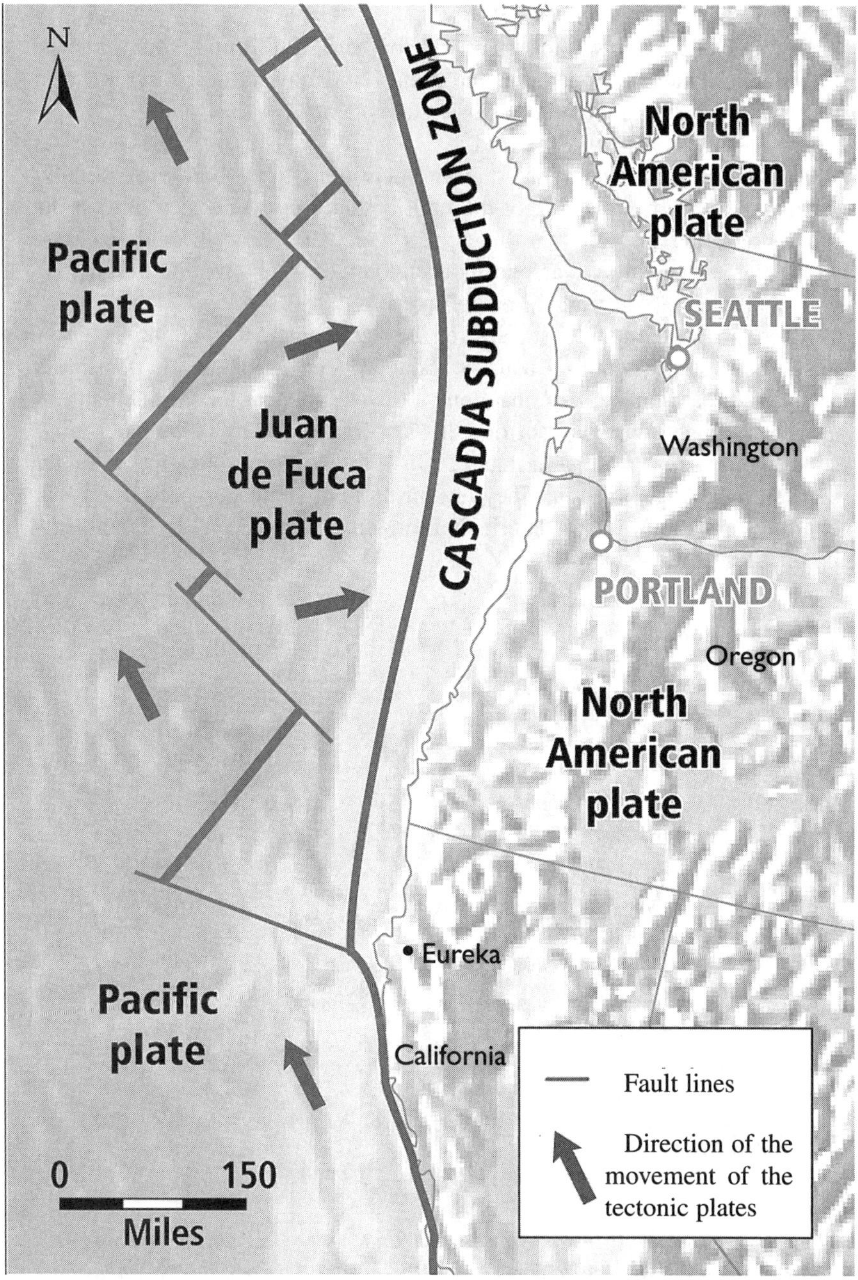

Courtesy U.S. Geological Survey

Where the Juan de Fuca and North American tectonic plates meet they are locked together and form the Cascadia Subduction Zone. Periodically, the plates break apart creating earthquakes capable of generating tsunamis.

horizontally, as they do in much of Southern California. You have the *Cascadia Subduction Zone* here, and it may be one of the worst in the world when it comes to its potential to spawn a tsunami."

"How would it happen?" I asked.

"At a subduction zone, when the fault between two tectonic plates finally breaks, the plate on one side of the fault bounces up while the plate on the other side often sinks. When this occurs under the ocean it creates a huge 'paddle effect' that moves an enormous amount of water creating a tsunami."

"How big could the tsunami be?" Dave asked.

"There are no hard and fast rules for the sizes tsunamis come in. An earthquake-generated tsunami is usually about 30 feet high. But it's possible a really large earthquake, like one along a major subduction zone such as you have here along your coast, or one that's accompanied by underwater landslides, could cause a tsunami that's 50 to 100 feet high. That's much bigger than the ones that hit Asia. They're unusual, but some geologists feel that could be in the future of the Pacific Northwest coastline because of the severity of the *Cascadia Subduction Zone*.

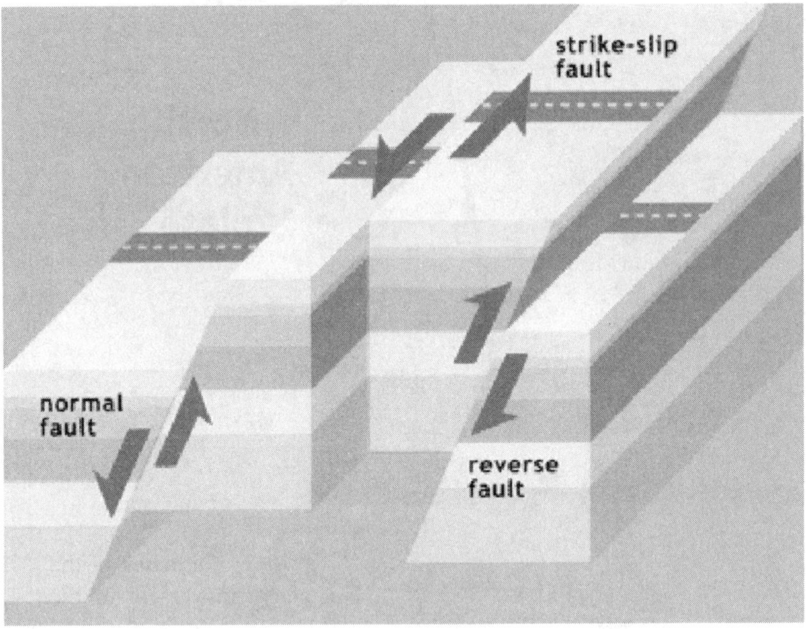

The three basic fault types: the normal fault, where one plate drops down relative to another; the strike-slip fault, where the plates meet evenly and slip horizontally past each other; and the reverse fault, where one plate is thrust up over another. When under water, it is the normal and reverse faults that create the kind of water displacement that can cause tsunamis.

An East Coast tsunami?

"However, they can be even bigger than that. There are scientists who believe a volcanic eruption in the Canary Islands, off the shore of West Africa, could lead to the collapse of the western flank of the Cumbre Vieja volcano on the island of La Palma. It would create a landslide that would drop as much as 125 cubic miles of rock into the Atlantic Ocean and create a tsunami at least 150 feet high—and perhaps as much as 300 feet high—that would hit the East Coast from Florida to Maine."

"What would a tsunami like that do?" I asked.

"It would wash inland for miles and cause trillions of dollars in destruction. But the good news is that it would take nine hours before it reached Boston, New York, and other places along the East Coast, allowing plenty of time for warning. The bad news is that there's no in-place warning system or evacuation plan for the Atlantic seaboard so it's likely there would still be a huge loss of life."

"This sounds like science fiction," Dave said.

"It's not. Two of the scientists who have written about it are Dr. Steven Ward of the University of California and Dr. Simon Day of the Benfield Greig Hazard Research Center at University College London."

"How likely is such an event?" Dave asked.

"It's one of those things that no one knows for sure. Volcano prediction is still in its infancy. But sonar mappings of the seabed off the islands have revealed deposits from a dozen or so large collapses that occurred there in the past. So we know it *can and does* happen there, just like it *can and did* happen here."

"Can we get back to the West Coast?" I asked.

Mac was slicing mushrooms. "Okay," Mac said. "A subduction zone like you have here is much different than the faults you have in, say, Southern California, where the fault lines generally move parallel to each other. When the tectonic plates just slide past each other, horizontally, they usually don't create tsunamis. But in a subduction zone, the tectonic plates move over and under each other, and when the earth under the ocean moves up or down like that *suddenly*, it moves an incredible amount of water that creates a tsunami. And it is also possible that the shaking from one of those kinds of earthquakes could cause an underwater landslide, and that in itself can cause a huge displacement of water that creates a tsunami."

"Can you give me an analogy of all this tectonic plate movement stuff?" I asked.

"Imagine the surface of the earth is like a soft boiled egg whose shell is rife with cracks," Mac said. "Some of the pieces of the shell are big while others are small. But unlike an egg, where the pieces stick to the egg, the earth's shell — the tectonic plates — floats on top of nearly molten rock deep inside the earth. That's where we are, living on these pieces of shell that are literally floating on this nearly molten rock. Some float past each other like barges floating on a river, but others crash head-on, with one trying to go under the other."

"And where they're trying to go over and under each other is called a subduction zone," Dave said.

"That's right. Earthquakes occur because all the plates, whether they're moving horizontally against each other or trying to move over and under each other, tend to hang up on each other along their edges. Meanwhile, the motion of the nearly molten rock beneath tries to keep them moving. The forces that are trying to move them start to accumulate. Eventually, those forces get so strong that something has to give, and the fault literally breaks, and when all that energy is released, wham! That's your earthquake. And here along the Pacific Northwest coast, that's the likely trigger for your tsunami."

"How powerful can they get? Is there a limit to an earthquake's size?" I asked.

"There appears to be. The reason you won't see too many quakes that go much over a 9.5 on the Richter scale is because the rocks just can't hold much more energy without breaking. The largest recorded earthquake in history was the 9.5 Chilean earthquake of 1960. It's possible that one could be a little larger, but there's a limit, somewhere. Maybe it's 10, maybe it's a little higher."

"Exactly what is the Richter?" I asked.

He was cutting up a red bell pepper, and paused as if to search his memory. "It's a scale of measurement invented by two guys, Charles Richter and Beno Gutenberg, for quantifying the magnitude of earthquakes."

The Richter Scale

"But how do the numbers on the scale work?" Dave asked. "I mean, it doesn't seem like there should be much of a difference between an earthquake that's a 4 on the Richter scale and one that's a 7. Yet, there is."

"It's a logarithmic scale," Mac replied, "and first you've got to understand what a logarithmic scale is.

"Using what's called a *common logarithm*, the number 10 is represented by the number 1, the number 100 by the number 2, the number 1,000 by the number 3..."

"It sounds like powers of 10," Dave said. "10 to the first power is equal to 10, 10 to the second power is 100, 10 to the third power is 1000."

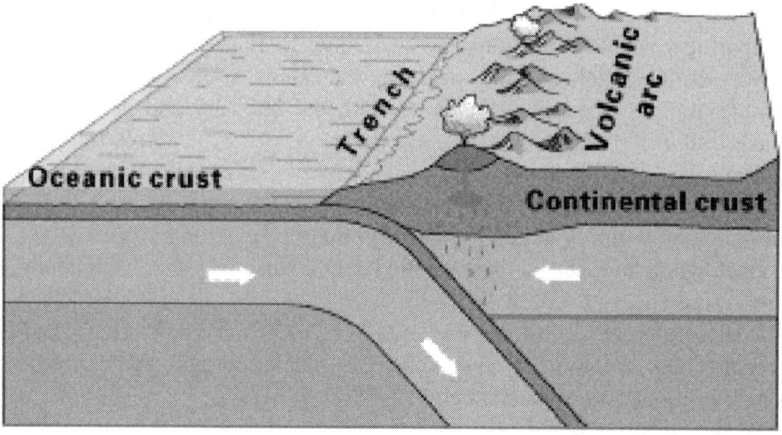

A cross-section illustrating what the Cascadia subduction zone looks like. Where the Juan de Fuca (left) and North American tectonic plates (right) collide, the dense rock that underlies the ocean tries to go under the lighter continental crust. Where the plates collide a subduction zone is formed. The movement of the plates doesn't go smoothly and they hang up on each other forming a "fault." As pressure builds up, the continental plate, including part that is submerged, buckles upward while the oceanic plate bends downward. When the pressure becomes too much, the fault breaks creating an earthquake. Meanwhile, with the pressure gone, the continental plate suddenly sinks lower while the oceanic plate springs up. The up and down actions displace billions of tons of water that create a tsunami.

"You've got it," Mac said. "So, when you go from an earthquake that's measured as a 4 on the Richter scale to one that's a 5, the one that's a 5 is 10 times more powerful than the one that's a 4."

Dave said, "So if you go from a 4 to a 7, it's three powers of 10 making a 7..." He paused for a second and mumbled under his breath, "...10 times 10 times 10 ...

"1000 times more powerful than a 4," he said out loud.

"Right," Mac said.

"So when you're talking about a 9, that's gotta be one *huge* earthquake," Dave said.

"It's a monster," Mac replied.

"It's 100,000 times greater than a 4," Dave said.

"That's right," Mac replied.

"Another mystery cleared up," Dave said. "But I have another question. Is there a nuclear bomb equivalent to the Richter scale? I mean, they're always comparing volcanic explosions and hurricanes to atom bombs."

"Sort of. The Richter scale measures the intensity of a quake. But how much energy is released depends on both the intensity and how long the quake lasts.

"Typically, a 5 on the Richter scale releases about 1½ times as much energy as the atom bomb dropped on Nagasaki. A 6 on the scale is like a one-megaton bomb or about 50 Nagasaki bombs exploding.

"Each whole number increase on the Richter scale translates into about 30 times more energy released.

"The Northridge, California, earthquake of 1994 was a 6.7." He picked up the calculator. "Figure it released about as much energy as a five-megaton bomb, or about 500 Nagasaki bombs."

"Wow!" was all I could say.

"What about the San Francisco earthquake of 1906?" Dave asked.

"That's a tough one," Mac said. "The traditional number assigned to it is 8.25, though it may have been smaller, but we'll go with 8.25."

He pushed a few keys on the calculator. "It released the energy of some 95,000 Nagasaki bombs going off in the ground under the city."

"The numbers are becoming incomprehensible," I said.

"They are," Mac agreed.

"What about the quake in Indonesia?" Dave asked. "I understand that was about a 9.3."

Using the calculator again, he said, "It was like more than three million of those bombs going off in one place. But keep in mind, these are just rough figures."

"Yeah, but it gives me an appreciation for just how powerful earthquakes can be," Dave said.

Mac was now putting a variety of seasonings on the salad.

"Here's another thing about tsunamis. Although the dangerous ones are the ones that are caused by earthquakes at subduction zones, there are some other factors. For example, the more shallow they are, the bigger they are. The really dangerous ones are those generated by earthquakes centered 30 miles or less below the earth's surface, in an ocean, near a subduction zone, and with a magnitude of 8.5 or greater. And they're even worse if they also cause an underwater landslide.

"You said landslides are the second most common cause of tsunamis," Dave said.

Mac put the salad in the refrigerator, then started seasoning a piece of red snapper as we watched. "That's right."

"I presume a landslide causes a tsunami just by creating an almost instantaneous displacement of water," Dave said.

"That's exactly how they do it."

"And it's possible they could get as big as 300 feet high, like the one that could come out of the Canary Islands?" Dave asked.

"Bigger. The highest tsunami on record was caused by a landslide in Lituya Bay in Alaska in 1958. The landslide itself was triggered by an earthquake, but the tsunami was caused by the earth that slid off a mountain and fell into the bay."

"How big was it?" I asked.

"It depends on how you measure it. Some say it was 1720 feet high."

"Yikes!" I said. "That's like a third of a mile high."

"But...the 1720 feet was actually how high it ran up on the mountain on the other side of the bay. The wall of water itself, as it crossed the bay, was anywhere from 150 to 500 feet high. No one knows for sure. We have eyewitness accounts from two of the three fishing boats that were in the bay at the time."

"What about the third boat?" I asked.

"The crew drowned when their boat capsized."

"The other two boats rode out the tsunami?" Dave asked.

"It was a miracle," Mac responded.

"Why didn't it create damage further away? Like across the ocean?" I asked.

"Even though it was high, it was only a few miles wide. When it left the bay and entered into the vastness of the open ocean, it dissipated rapidly.

"On the other hand, an earthquake-generated tsunami is going to start out at least as long as the fault that creates it—the one in Sumatra was some 750 miles long. Waves that broad don't dissipate quickly."

"Is there any danger to us here, on the West Coast of the United States, from landslide-generated tsunamis?" I asked.

He put some olive oil and sesame oil in a skillet he had heating, then added the fish. "There can be. Earthquakes can cause landslides along any of the continental shelves that lie off our coasts. The earthquake wouldn't even have to be that severe. All it would have to do is trigger a large underwater slide and the resultant displacement of seawater could cause a catastrophic tsunami that would be out of proportion to the magnitude of the quake.

"For example, there's a fear that, though the faults in Southern California are not the type that directly cause tsunamis, they may be capable of producing a landslide off the continental shelf that runs along the coast there. And that could cause a massive tsunami that would send a wall of water into Los Angeles and other cities along the coast like Long Beach, Malibu, Oxnard, and Ventura.

"Worse, since the edge of the continental shelf on the West Coast is so close to the shore, the wave could take as little as one minute to rush onto the beaches."

"It would be on top of people before they even had a chance to think about it," Dave said as Mac turned the fish over.

"And you said volcanoes can also cause tsunamis," I said.

"Underwater volcanoes can cause them either by an explosion where the pyroclastic flow explodes into the water, by landslides, or by collapses of an underwater caldera.

"The eruption of Krakatoa in 1883, though above sea level, caused a landslide that generated a 100-foot tsunami that swept up onto the coasts of Java and Sumatra and killed some 34,000 people."

"What's a pyroclastic flow?" I asked.

"Do you recall seeing sequences of photos from Mt. St. Helens when it erupted? Remember seeing an explosive cloud of ash, dust, and gasses that sped across the landscape?"

"Yes," I said. "*National Geographic* did quite a spread on it."

"That's pyroclastic flow. It would expand like an A-bomb going off underwater."

"What's a caldera collapse?" I asked.

"The caldera is the volcanic crater. Sometimes during an eruption, the caldera collapses. This happens both above and below sea level. But when it happens below sea level, the almost instantaneous displacement of a huge amount of water can generate a tsunami. When it happens above sea level, it can cause a landslide that falls into the ocean.

"It's also thought that an explosive volcano could expose enough hot magma to cause an underwater explosion as the seawater rapidly turns into steam. This actually has a name; it's called a phreatic explosion.

Dave said, "You said the biggest tsunamis of all can be created by..."

"...meteors," Mac said. "It's suspected that a comet or an asteroid could cause a tsunami that's both high, like those that can be generated by landslides or caldera collapses, and massive like those created at faults. Some scientists estimate that the asteroid that is thought to have driven the dinosaurs into extinction, when it created the Chicxulub crater in the Gulf of Mexico, sent a 400-foot tsunami that was miles thick into the Florida peninsula. It may well have swept all the way to the Atlantic. Incidentally, today there is no point of land in the entire state of Florida that's over 345 feet in height."

"So, if that happened again..." I asked.

"There'd be no high ground to run to."

He turned the fish over one more time and it was done. He took it out of the pan and let it cool.

"So, are we in any real danger here in Oregon?" Dave asked.

Mac smiled without humor. "The Cascadia Subduction Zone is a fault that lies about 20 to 100 miles off the northwest coast. It's real close here, in southwestern Oregon. It's about 680 miles long and runs from roughly Cape Mendocino, in California, to Vancouver Island in Canada's British Columbia.

"A *major* break in the fault along the Cascadia Subduction Zone would cause the sea floor on one side of the fault to bounce some 20 feet, maybe more, while the other side sunk, and this will create huge ocean waves, some of which will rush into shore here. You'll have less than 30 minutes to get out of their way. Actually, I heard one geologist say that here, in southwestern Oregon, you may have as little as five minutes."

"Will the quake itself be a big one?" Dave asked.

"Possibly as big or bigger than the one they had the day after this last Christmas in Indonesia. It'll last about five minutes, and if the whole fault goes it's likely to be a 9 or better on the Richter scale. So, when the shaking stops, be ready to head for higher ground. The waves will be hitting the shore before you know it."

"Five minutes of shaking and the waves may get to shore in five minutes?" I asked. "Do you mean the shaking may stop just as the tsunami hits?"

Mac nodded with a sardonic smile. "It's possible."

"And did you say 'waves'?" Dave asked. "*Plural?* As in *more than one?*"

"Yes. I should have said it earlier. Tsunamis are actually trains of waves. There could be four, five, maybe more. And they'll be anywhere from 15 minutes to an hour apart. And there's no way to know ahead of time which ones will be the biggest. Worse, if there are major aftershocks in the days following the first quake, they may be accompanied by even more tsunamis."

"I guess our consolation is that we'll at least get some warning of the approaching tsunami from the shaking caused by the earthquake itself," I said.

"Most likely, but that's not a certainty either. Sometimes, an earthquake may not feel like much to those on land because so much of the energy released is absorbed by the seawater. In that case, with the ocean absorbing most of the energy, the resulting tsunami can still be huge even though the ground doesn't seem to have been shaken much at all. It's thought that that's what happened in Nicaragua in 1992. The earthquake was generated at a subduction zone, like the one you have here off the coast, but it was barely felt by people on land. However, it was followed by a tsunami that surprised everyone and was catastrophic."

"And, from what you said, a minor earthquake could cause an underwater landslide off our coast, and that could spawn a tsunami too," Dave said as if in deep thought.

"Right."

"Good grief," I said. "Do you know how much trouble I'm going to have sleeping tonight? I only live a few hundred yards from the beach."

"Move," Mac said.

Dave laughed. Then he said, "So we should head for high ground with even a tiny earthquake."

"If you live on the coast, you should really consider it."

History of Cascadia fault

"Have there been big quakes here before?" I asked.

"We know from the geologic records that earthquakes have taken place along the Cascadia fault, irregularly, about every 500 to 600 years, for the last 10,000 years."

"What do you mean 'irregularly'? Dave asked.

"It's not a 500 or 600-year 'cycle,' it's an average. They run from about 100 years apart to about 1,000 years apart. And each was accompanied by tsunamis that swept ashore."

"How can the geologists tell there've been earthquakes here in the distant past, when there's no written history about them?" I asked.

"What they're doing is radiocarbon dating of organic material in the layers of sand, called turbidites, that come from underwater landslides the earthquakes cause. From that they know there have been about 20 major earthquake events off the coast here just in the last 10,000 years."

"When was the last big one?" Dave asked.

"On January 26, 1700, the whole 680-mile Cascadia fault let go. There were no writers in this part of North America at that time chronicling the event, though there are legends of that quake that come down through the local tribes. Then, a few years ago, geologists in Japan informed their counterparts here in North America that there had been a quake of at least 8.5 magnitude, and probably greater than a 9, that occurred the evening of January 26, 1700. They know the date because the Japanese have kept records of tsunamis since the 1500s and one hit their shores January 27, 1700, with waves more than 15 feet high. American geologists studying tree rings knew an earthquake had happened around that time. Suddenly they had the exact date. Estimates are that the first waves took about 10 hours to get from here to Japan, a distant of about 5,000 miles."

"That's like 500 miles an hour," I said.

He took the salad out of the refrigerator and broke up the cooled fish into it. Then he added some olive oil and vinegar dressing. He was thinking.

"It's done," he said.

We scooped some of his salad out into plates and tasted it.

"Holy cow," Dave said. "This is good."

"Let's go back to the office," Dave said.

Just then, Ilene, Dave's wife and the magazine's business manager and managing editor, came into the kitchen.

"It's ready," Mac said to her.

"Good, I've been waiting," she said as we left.

Back in the editorial part of the magazine I said, "So, the only tsunami danger to the East Coast is one coming from the Canaries, right?"

"Relatively speaking, they're in less danger. Some 75 percent of all tsunamis take place here in the Pacific. But on the East Coast, they're still in danger from tsunamis from other sources. One is the Mid-Atlantic Ridge, a chain of underwater mountains that runs up the middle of the Atlantic Ocean. It's seismically active making it another possible source of underwater landslides that could trigger tsunamis that could endanger North and South America, Europe, and Africa. And there's the danger of landslides off the edge of the continental shelf there.

"There's also a subduction zone in the Caribbean Sea. Earthquakes that originate there could trigger tsunamis along the Atlantic and Gulf coasts. In 1946, an earthquake-generated tsunami killed at least 1800 people in the Dominican Republic.

"There's the potential for tsunamis that comes to us from Europe. A tsunami generated by the great Lisbon earthquake of 1755 reached across the Atlantic and was felt in the Caribbean Islands and even the northeastern coast of South America. But, for some reason, there's no record of it hitting the Atlantic Coast of what was to become the United States."

"Why wouldn't it have hit here?" Dave asked.

"I don't think anyone knows. But it may have been something as simple as the Mid-Atlantic Ridge I just talked about. It reaches all the way from the Arctic Ocean to the southern tip of Africa, and in some spots it's above sea level. The ridge may serve as a barrier in some places, or even a mirror of sorts, reflecting most of the tsunami back to Europe. If you look at the Azores, they rest on an underwater plateau and are in a line between the part of Europe where Lisbon is located and the East Coast of the United States. So that plateau may have blocked most of it; if a small amount of the tsunami reached here, it may not have been enough for chroniclers of the time to have made note of it. But that's just speculation on my part."

"So, where we are in the Pacific Northwest, particularly here in Gold Beach, what kind of danger are we in?"

"Danger is a relative term. On any given day, your chances of dying in an auto accident or any one of scores of other ways is greater than your danger of getting killed by a tsunami. That said, a tsunami is still going to strike here."

Tsunami from afar

"It could come from a distant source, or one right off your coast."

"How far can the ones that form across the Pacific reach?" Dave asked.

"The Chilean earthquake of 1960 sent a tsunami from the southern hemisphere to the northern hemisphere that reached Hawaii after 15 hours where it killed 61 people. It continued on and reached Japan after 22 hours where it killed twice that number."

"That fast?" I asked.

"Figure a tsunami travels at 450 to 600 miles per hour in deep water—about as fast as many commercial jetliners."

"How will we know if one's coming from far away?" I asked. "It's not like we're going to feel an earthquake in China."

"There's now a tsunami warning system in the Pacific. If a tsunami originated from Asia or Alaska, we'd know it and have hours in which to evacuate to high ground."

"But that's not the one we're really worried about, is it?" Dave said.

"No. With the Cascadia Subduction Zone just some 20 to 100 miles off your coast, you may be an eyewitness to the largest tsunami in recorded history. It could be as big as 100 feet."

"Yikes!" I exclaimed.

"What happens when it hits the shore?" I asked.

"It'll stop just long enough to ask directions to your house," Dave said.

Mac laughed and I have to admit, I did, too.

"It will slow down," Mac said. "When a tsunami enters shallow water, it slows down, but it also gets higher."

He looked at Dave and laughed again. He shook his head. "Ask for directions to John's house," he muttered under his breath. Then he continued. "A tsunami wave that is a few inches to a few feet high in the deep ocean can get to 50 feet high, or even higher, when it hits the beach. No longer doing 600 miles an hour, it's now going about 30 miles per hour. You'll never outrun it without a humungous head start."

"Why do they get so high near shore?" I asked.

"In deep water, these waves reach from the top of the ocean to the ocean floor. In mid-ocean they may be just a few inches or feet higher than the ocean's surface. But when they come into shallow water, all that displaced water—a column of water that may reach 12,000 feet from the ocean's surface to its bottom—gets funneled into a smaller and smaller space. That huge column represents energy. When the energy is compressed, the wave correspondingly expands."

"How far are you above sea level, John?" Dave asked.

Fleeing a tsunami

I didn't answer. "So," I said, "if the Cascadia fault goes, the evacuation must be essentially complete within just a few minutes."

"Well..." Mac paused, "...possibly a little bit sooner. It depends on how the wave comes in. Significant inundation can begin well before the peak of the wave hits."

"I guess I'll just hop in my car and scoot," I said.

Mac smiled that humorless smile again. "I don't mean to rain on your parade," he said, "but one of the problems is that if the tsunami is caused by a major earthquake in the Cascadia fault—one that's an 8.5 or bigger—it'll drop buildings, power poles, and live power lines onto the road. It may also make driving difficult enough to cause accidents that block the roads. But, more so, it's pretty likely that it will tear up the roads so badly that you won't be able to drive away from it. Driving is likely to be out of the question."

"So you may have to leave on foot and literally run for your life," Dave said.

"Run for high ground," Mac said.

"Oh, that's cheery," I said. "Now I've got to find out where the high ground is in my neighborhood."

Dave suddenly looked up at the ceiling as if thinking. "You know," he began, "I remember seeing something on TV about how tsunamis are preceded by a big outrush of water from the beaches. Sometimes it moves out so fast that it leaves fish flopping in the mud."

"Any time you see the water rush out to sea, exposing seabed you've never seen before, you can bet it's coming back in as a tsunami," Mac said. "So you've got to get to high ground immediately. It may be the only warning you'll get.

"But not every tsunami is preceded by the water going out. So if you feel the ground shaking or you hear a tsunami alert, and you're not already on high ground, get there as fast as you can. Don't wait to see what the ocean's doing."

"What determines whether or not the water rushes out or not?" I asked.

"The side of the fault you're on. In a subduction zone, when the fault breaks, one side will suddenly sink and the other side will bounce up. The wave radiating from the side that sinks will start out as a trough or a 'negative' wave. If it's headed for the shore, the tsunami will start with the water rushing out to sea. When the trough hits the shore it's called downdraw. The outrushing of water may be your only warning that the wave's crest is coming in right behind it. Usually, the continental side of a subduction zone will get the trough first because it's the side that's been buckling up, and now it will suddenly sink.

"The wave generated on the other side of the fault will start out as a crest, or a 'positive' wave. When the crest hits the shore it's called run-up. Other than the quake itself, there will be no warning except for the arrival of a wall of water."

"Which one do you think will arrive here in Gold Beach first?" I asked.

"From the looks of it, it'll be a negative wave."

"So, the water will rush out, first," Dave said.

"That's the way it looks," Mac replied. "Then it will be followed by a massive wall of water."

"Won't the quake itself kill most of the people?" I asked.

"Maybe not. In the recent earthquake in Asia, most of the people who died were killed by the tsunami spawned by the quake. The same could happen here, with most deaths by tsunami instead of earthquake."

"Let's say the quake happens," Dave began. "If the highest wave we can expect to see from one generated out here on the Cascadia Subduction Zone is a 100-footer, is anyone above 100 feet elevation safe? I mean, does John just have to figure out where there's a point near his house that's 100 feet above sea level and go there if there's a quake?"

"No. That may not be enough. There are other factors that figure in. For example, the topography of the land below the waterline can change a wave's height. Underwater canyons can channel the wave—it's called 'focusing'—and a wave that should be just 30 feet high may get focused and come ashore as a 60- or 100-foot wave. And, of course, that means that other spots on the shore would necessarily receive smaller waves.

"It's one of the things about coastal cities: more often than not they're founded where there are good harbors formed by underwater canyons. Those canyons can focus the wave.

"Another thing that can change the appearance of a tsunami are changes to the tectonic plate you're standing on. When this Cascadia Subduction Zone gives, this side of the fault is expected to sink anywhere from two to eight feet, so a tsunami, regardless of its height, is going to appear to be higher just because the land will have sunk."

"Does that mean parts of the coastline here are going to be underwater after the quake?" Dave asked.

"Most likely."

"For how long?"

"Until more pressure builds up and buckles the plate again, bending it up."

"The airport here in Gold Beach is just above sea level," Dave said. "So, for all intents and purposes, it could be underwater for years after a major earthquake."

"If this shore falls far enough, it will."

"How far inland can a wave go?" I asked.

"Depending on the size of the wave and local geography—like how flat the area is that gets hit—a large tsunami could wash anywhere from a few hundred yards to a couple of miles inland.

"On the other hand, because tsunamis will also wash up rivers, river cities several miles from the ocean can be struck by tsunamis. It would depend on how the wave hit the river and the geographical factors.

"It's worth noting that the tsunami from the 1964 Alaskan earthquake was detected 100 miles up the Columbia River. Not that it did damage that far upriver, just that it was detected there."

"Is there any way to know how far the waves might go locally?" I asked.

"If you put 'Oregon tsunami maps' in an Internet search engine it'll take you right to a website that has the historic tsunami inundation boundary. But keep in mind, you may be looking at old maps with inundation boundaries expected for a 30-foot or so wave. Right now, for the Northwest, they're preparing maps for larger waves. They should be up on the web soon. Nonetheless, until they do put them up, the maps they're publishing now show elevation contour lines that are useful in trying to guess the boundary of larger waves."

"Well, now that I know I may not be able to drive away at the first signs of shaking, I'm out of my house and up the hill at the end of my street," I said.

"No you're not," Mac said. "If the whole fault lets go, the ground is going to move with .7g acceleration."

"What's that mean?" I asked.

"Well, 'g' is the acceleration of gravity, 32 feet per second per second; .7g is about 22 or 23 feet per second per second. In other words, the ground will be moving back and forth underneath you with about three quarters the acceleration of gravity. And everything—your house, the roads, the trees—will be going back and forth with it. So, don't bet on being able to stand, much less run, for several minutes. That means the furniture in your house is going to start moving around. So, if you've taken refuge under a table, hold on to it and try to move with it; otherwise your cover is going to slide away and you can get hit by falling objects."

"How should you prepare?" Dave asked.

"First, keep you glasses near your bed. I know that sounds dumb, but you don't want to be looking for them when the shaking starts. I'd keep them where you can find them in the dark.

"Second, keep shoes next to your bed, too. When the big one hits, things will be falling and windows will be breaking. You won't want to get up and be stepping on glass in your bare feet, especially if the power has gone out and it's the middle of the night.

"You should also have a survival plan that includes food and fresh water to last you at least several days. If the Cascadia fault goes, rescue workers may be tied up in the bigger cities. In the little town of Gold Beach and in its rural surroundings, people could be isolated for weeks. You should also have something like a three-day survival pack you can grab. You should have a medical kit. You should also have one for your car, just in case you can drive away."

"We've had stuff like that in the magazine," Dave said.

"And keep in mind, wherever you go, every foot farther from the shore, and every foot higher in elevation, helps.

"What's the likelihood of another earthquake here, in the Cascadia Subduction Zone?" Dave asked.

"It depends on how much time into the future you're talking. I can say, with virtual certainty, there's going to be another one someday, but the scientists who do this stuff figure that in the next 50 years there's a 10 to 20 percent chance you'll have a big one here. The further into the future you figure this, the more likely one will occur.

"But seismology is an inexact science. Scientists are trying to find some way of predicting or forecasting them. At this point, there are certain things they expect to see before the Cascadia fault does go, and right now they're not seeing many of them."

Just then, Ilene passed through the office. "Mac, that's the best salad I've ever had."

"Thank you," he responded.

"I want the recipe."

I'll write it down," he said, and she left.

"I think I'll have some soup," Dave said. Δ

Chapter 4 The threat of electromagnetic pulse!

By John Silveira

I like "doomsday" scenarios — even ridiculous ones, such as the supposed Mayan calendar prophecy for 2012 or what had been Y2K doom-and-gloom leading up to the year 2000. Of course, there are some genuine doomsday threats to worry about, such as the possibility of another flu pandemic like the one of 1918-1919 or other pandemics health officials worry could be caused by drug resistant "superbugs" that could kill tens of millions, if not hundreds of millions, worldwide.

There are also unlikely but *plausible* catastrophes I like to mull over, such as the eruption of one of the world's super volcanoes, the impacting of a large asteroid, or the onset of another glacial age, all of which are going to happen — *eventually* — and, if one of those happened now it could wipe out as much as 90 percent of humanity, and we're powerless to stop them.

But what if there was a well-documented, but preventable threat, that could bring this country to its knees and kill as many as a quarter of a billion Americans, yet we were doing nothing to prevent it. In fact there are fixes we could put in place now to lessen the consequences — but the media and our nation's leaders not only ignore it, Congress has even cut money from the budget that could provide the means to deal with it.

The threat is called electromagnetic pulse (EMP) and it could come about as the result of detonating one well-placed nuclear device high over the United States. In fact, it could happen even without a nuclear attack as a result of a naturally-occurring solar flare from our own sun.

What is EMP?

According to a government website, an EMP is: "The electromagnetic radiation from a nuclear explosion caused by Compton-recoil electrons and photoelectrons from photons scattered in the materials of the nuclear device or in a surrounding medium. *The resulting electric and magnetic fields may couple with electrical/electronic systems to produce damaging current and voltage surges.*"

All you really need to pay attention to is the last sentence. EMP is an electromagnetic surge that would follow the high-altitude detonation of a nuclear bomb. It could turn the United States into a Third World country.

Without going deep into physics, an EMP caused by a nuclear bomb has three components. The first, designated E1, is the result of electrons being stripped from atoms in the upper atmosphere in the aftermath of a high-altitude detonation. As they travel downward through the earth's magnetic field at near-relativistic speeds, they produce a massive, though momentary, electromagnet pulse. You won't feel it, but the electronic equipment all around you will. In the old days of vacuum tubes and relay switches, most equipment would likely have escaped damage from the E1 component of the pulse. But today's microchips and delicate electronic devices, though incredibly convenient and efficient, will be fried by the pulse. Things like modern automobiles and trucks, computers, radios, televisions, cell phones, pacemakers, and anything else dependent on computer chips, whether plugged into the power grid or not, will short out and simply stop working. *Kaput!*

This also includes aircraft in the sky. Unless their avionics are "hardened" (and commercial aircraft and most military aircraft are not hardened against EMP), they will simply cease operation and the thousands that are in the air at any moment are going to simply fly into the ground with everyone onboard. Almost all microelectronic components damaged by the E1 component of an EMP will be *unrepairable*.

The E2 component resembles the surges caused by lightning and are less likely to be damaging to most equipment. But if protective equipment such as surge protectors are damaged by the E1 pulse, it may now allow the E2 pulse to cause further damage.

The E3 component may be the worst. It is caused when a nuclear explosion distorts the earth's magnetic field. As the field distorts, then tries to regain its original shape, it induces currents into long metal conductors — like the power lines and such that crisscross the country. The longer the conductors, the more current will be produced. It is this component of EMP that will overload the nation's power grid and fry *everything* connected to it, from your laptop, which is plugged into the wall recharging, to the transformers at the power stations.

The 370 or so largest transformers connected to nuclear, hydro, and fossil fuel-burning power plants around the country are what make the electricity these plants generate usable, but they will be destroyed by the pulse. Without these transformers, the country will go dark. And they cannot be easily replaced. The size of a building, they are *no longer* produced in the United States and current procurement time is three years.

What will happen?

Without electric power, radio and TV stations and phone services won't work, so there'll be almost no communication. Water systems will cease to function, gas stations won't be able to pump fuel, banking transactions (including ATMs) will fail, and the network for distributing food will collapse. Perishable foods and medications that require refrigeration or freezing will spoil in a day. Emergency services will be unavailable, including those necessary to fight the tens of thousands of fires that will start from short circuits on the grid.

The inability to produce or distribute proper medications would doom many needing cancer treatments or suffering from heart disease, Type I diabetes, and other ailments.

Most farmers won't be able to plant, fertilize, irrigate, or harvest, but even if they could, they won't be able to get their products to market because there will no longer be transportation. What is harvested won't be preserved since there will be no power to run refrigeration and none to run the factories that ordinarily can our food.

Supermarkets typically have just a few days' supply of food and are being resupplied continuously every 1-3 days. Once the power goes out, the supermarkets will quickly be emptied and it could be months before they're resupplied.

Imagine the great metropolitan areas of this country: the corridor from Boston to Washington, DC, which includes the great cities of New York and Philadelphia among them, and has a population of about 50 million people, the Chicago area with its millions, the Los Angeles to San Diego corridor, Seattle, Portland, etc., and suddenly there's no food coming in, the water is turned off, and sewage facilities no longer carry away and treat our daily waste.

In no time at all cities will become quagmires of hungry, thirsty people living amid filth, squalor, and disease.

From an enemy's point of view, a single large device exploded 250 to 300 miles above Iowa would disrupt the entire United States. But getting a missile that far inland could be a problem for them. On the other hand, because the radius of destruction of one high-altitude explosion is very large (as much as 1400 miles), three missiles, launched almost straight up, from freighters off the Pacific, Atlantic, and Gulf coasts, should just about cover the lower 48 states with EMP surges that would all but incapacitate our nation.

Recovery time, if it happened, would take years but more likely a decade or more. In the meantime, deaths in this country would be *at least* in the low millions.

All of this would seem to be the fodder for fiction and, in fact, a scenario involving an EMP attack is played out in a book by William Forstchen titled *One Second After*. Though he's populated the book with rather two-dimensional characters, the events described in the book are credible and thought-provoking and make it worth a read.

The problem with an EMP event is *not* news. We've known about nuclear weapon-induced EMP since 1945. Enrico Fermi anticipated it prior to the detonation of the first atomic bomb, called Gadget, at the Trinity test site in New Mexico. The media and the American people briefly became aware of it after a high-altitude detonation of a hydrogen bomb during the Starfish Prime Test of 1952 when effects of it were felt in Hawaii (900 miles away from the test), where the resulting voltage surges blew out 300 street lights and damaged a microwave link. This was with a weapon that wasn't even designed to maximize EMP and it was detonated back in the day of vacuum tubes when electronic equipment was more robust than today's highly efficient but sensitive computer chips which can be fried by even *modest* current surges.

Solar flares

Even if someone were able to convince me no one would ever launch a nuclear weapon over the United States, I would not rest easy. Nuclear weapons are not the only things that cause an E3 pulse. A giant solar flare caused such a pulse on September 1, 1859. Back then, there was no electronic infrastructure, but telegraph lines acted like antennas and transmitted the energy along their wires, causing shocks to many telegraph operators and, in some cases, causing fires. A large solar flare of this sort is now called a Carrington Event, named after the British astronomer, Richard Carrington, who first described it.

Solar astronomers and many engineers feel that with the United States (and most of the rest of the industrial world) now crisscrossed with power and communication lines, a solar flare with the magnitude of the one that occurred in 1859 would blow out power station transformers and plunge this country and much of the rest of the world into the dark for years. (Imagine trying to build transformers if there's no electricity at all!) It could also cause fires across the continents as circuits overload, overheat, and arc.

The 1859 event is not the only time solar flares have wreaked havoc. It's happened many times since, only on smaller scales because the flares were much smaller. The 1859 solar flare happened at the dawn of the electric age. Had it happened a few decades later when the world was more electrified, we'd probably now take the threat seriously and we'd have been "hardening" the grid to EMP all along. But it didn't, and we haven't.

Solar astronomers are positive it's only a matter of time before there will be another Carrington Event. They just don't know when. However, next year is one of the prime times it may happen. NASA says the solar cycle we're entering now is about the same size as the one that produced the original Carrington Event.

With a major Carrington Event, all the things that could follow a nuclear weapon-induced E3 strike may happen, except it won't be just a local event but one that affects the entire world.

The solution

The lowest estimate I've seen for the projected cost of a recovery for just the solar disruptions is $1 trillion, but most estimates run into the many trillions of dollars. However, the FBI projects the cost of hardening transformers that service major metropolitan centers at about $200 million. That's $1/5000^{th}$ of the smallest estimates of the cost of damage. In fact, it's less than $1/2000^{th}$ of the job package President Obama recently proposed. And hardening the grid wouldn't just make the country more secure, it would provide meaningful jobs, unlike the kinds government spending usually create.

There are voices trying to call attention to the problem. The Heritage Foundation has been calling for a national EMP recognition day to raise awareness of the threat.

An EMP attack will be the most catastrophic event to happen to our nation in its history — more devastating than 9/11, more devastating than Pearl Harbor, in fact, more devastating than all of the wars this country has ever fought.

It's about time for the mass media to talk about it, and for Congress and the President to address it. This is a real-world problem with a relatively inexpensive fix. Δ

Chapter 5
A quick tour of hyperinflation and the possible consequences for America

By John Silveira

"No one can predict the future," I heard a voice say as I walked into the offices of *Backwoods Home Magazine*. The speaker went on to add, "But there are a lot of reasons to believe we are in danger of entering a period of hyperinflation of the dollar."

I hesitated because I knew the voice and I followed it to Dave Duffy's office. Dave's the guy who publishes this magazine. But the speaker I was hearing was none other than our poker-playing friend from Southern California, O.E. MacDougal.

I walked into Dave's office and there was the pair of them, Dave and Mac, drinking wine and talking. After greeting me, their conversation seemed to drift to the subject of the steelhead that were making their way up the Rogue River just north of town. But I wanted them to get back to what I'd heard them discussing when I first came in. So I cut in.

"Hey, I heard you saying something about hyperinflation. I know I've seen references to it on the Net, but what exactly is it?"

Before Mac could answer, Dave interjected, "Inflation is when prices go up, hyperinflation is when they go up beyond all reason."

"But how do you know when you've gone from inflation to hyperinflation?" I asked.

"There's no hard and fast rule," Mac said, "and no exact number for determining when we've gone from one to the other—or bad to worse. But it's been said that inflation is reported annually while hyperinflation is reported more often, like monthly, weekly, or, in extreme cases, daily. It's not a bad rule of thumb. But let me make a quick comment about what Dave just said.

"It may sound like I'm nitpicking," he said to Dave, "but I'm not. Inflation isn't so much that prices go up—because that would imply that groceries and stuff like that have somehow become more valuable. Inflation is when money becomes less valuable so it takes more money to buy a sack of potatoes, a gallon of gas, or hire a babysitter. It's a distinction most people don't seem to get.

"In fact, in cases where commodities become more valuable, it's usually a case of supply and demand. When there's increased demand for something, or the supply of something we typically use runs short, the price of it goes up. For example, if a bad winter wipes out much of the citrus crop, oranges become more expensive that year. When the crop returns to normal, the next year, the price of oranges returns to where it usually is.

"Inflation, on the other hand, is an increase in the money supply that exceeds the expansion of the goods and services available to buy."

"That sentence sounds like a mouthful," I said. "Give me an example I can actually understand."

"Let's use an analogy," he said. "Imagine a bunch of us are stranded on a desert island with a set of poker chips. Our first year there, we decide the poker chips are going to represent the total of goods and services on the island because we want to use them as money. Say some of us harvest coconuts and we decide each coconut should cost five white chips. Next year there's a bumper harvest of coconuts. If there are too many coconuts, each one is going to be worth less than they were in the previous year because the people harvesting them are going to have a harder time dumping them all, so the price may fall to three white chips apiece to encourage people to buy them. On the other hand, if there's a bad harvest, it's going to be harder to buy them, so if consumers want them they're going to be willing to pay more for them and the price will go up. Maybe they're going to be seven or eight white chips each. But we expect the cost of a coconut to hover around the average price of five white chips we pay for them in a normal year."

"What you're saying is the cost of coconuts depends on supply and demand, surpluses and shortages," Dave said.

Mac nodded.

"I can see that," I said in agreement.

"Now," Mac continued, "let's take the same island and a raft drifts in with another set of poker chips that's the same as the first set. So, we effectively double the money supply on the island. What happens to the value of everything?"

I thought a second. "Well, if we accept the second set of chips as part of our money supply, with no increase or decrease in the number of coconuts, the cost of each coconut is going to be doubled because there's now twice as much money—or poker chips—on the island."

"That's right. And think about this: Anyone who's been saving his poker chips for a rainy day is going to suddenly find his stash of chips have half the purchasing power they used to have. That's inflation: an increase in the chips or, more generally, in the money supply and a decrease in the value of each poker chip or dollar."

"So, as more chips are introduced, not only do prices go up, but it discourages saving," Dave said.

"That's correct," Mac said.

"Then tell me if this is right," I said. "If instead of more chips showing up, half the chips on the island suddenly fall into the ocean and are lost for good, each remaining chip would now have twice the purchasing power they previously had and coconuts would cost half as much, because we said the number of chips represent the value of all the goods and services on the island, including the coconuts. That's deflation; a decrease in the money supply makes each chip more valuable."

"You've got it," Mac said. "By the way, a recent real-world example of prices going up due to supply and demand, and not inflation, was caused by a mandate created by Congress a few years ago. It stipulated that a certain amount of our energy had to come from ethanol. To comply with this mandate, fuel producers started buying a large portion of the grain harvests to make fuel. That took grains out of the market and created a shortage of grains available for human and animal consumption. The result was an increased demand on them without a commensurate increase in supply and we wound up with five-dollar loaves of bread as well as more expensive chicken, milk, and steak because it also cost more to feed the animals those grains."

"So that jump in grain prices at that time had nothing to do with the money supply, but with how much grain was available to make fuel," I concluded.

"Right again, and later on the cost of grain went down based strictly on market forces. But a lot of people labeled the price jump inflation when it wasn't."

"What should it have been called?" I asked.

"There is no convenient word or words in our language to cover the rise and fall of prices based on supply and demand, so we use the word 'inflation' indiscriminantly."

"Has this country always had inflation?" I asked.

"This may surprise you, but we've only had long-term inflation since the Federal Reserve was established in 1913 and they got control of our money supply. They have steadily increased the money supply faster than than the increase in the amount of goods and services that that money will buy. The result is that money has become worth less and less until, today, a dollar has about the same purchasing power as four cents had in 1913."

"Are you kidding?" I asked.

"No," Mac replied.

"But that means that a penny in 1913 had the same buying power as a quarter, today."

He nodded.

"What about before that?" Dave asked.

"Prior to the Federal Reserve, our currency had an amazing amount of stability for more than 100 years because it was based on gold. That is, prices remained pretty steady for over a century. The only thing that really happened is that prices went down as one technological advance after another made life easier, crops more plentiful, and businesses more efficient. There was a blip of inflation during the Revolutionary and Civil Wars, but those passed when those wars ended."

"People like Congressman Ron Paul want to go back to the gold standard," I said. "Why's gold so special?"

"Because it's rare, pretty, and useful, and we've agreed it's valuable," Mac said. "All the gold ever mined in the world would form a cube that was only 50 feet on each side. So there's a limited supply and if money was based on it, currencies couldn't help but be stable."

"But consider this," he added. "If someone suddenly found a pile of gold as big as Mount Everest, the price of gold would plunge until it was all but worthless because it wouldn't be rare anymore, though it would still be pretty and useful."

"I don't mean to cut you off," I said, "but why do we inflate our money?"

"Oh, there are economic theories that say it's good, but basically we do it because governments like inflation."

I was surprised. "Why?"

"Governments like to tax us and inflation is a tax. Most people simply do not understand that."

"How's it a tax?" I asked.

"Let's go back to the analogy of the island. As I said, if a second set of poker chips arrives, as they're introduced into the island's economy, the prices of everything on the island will begin to rise to reflect the number of chips. But before they do, the person who found the chips gets to spend them while the prices are still low. In effect, they're stealing the value out of everyone else's chips.

"In the same way, when the government increases the money supply, without a corresponding increase in the amount of goods and services, they devalue everyone else's dollars—they're worth less and buy less as prices begin to go up. But government gets full value with this newly created money because they spend it first."

"So, with inflation, they're stealing value out of every bill I have in my pocket," Dave said,

"Stealing is exactly what they're doing. Keep in mind that if introducing more money were harmless, the government wouldn't care about counterfeiters."

"So inflation amounts to legalized counterfeiting," Dave concluded and the three of us laughed at what he'd said.

"You're catching on," Mac said.

This concept clearly intrigued Dave.

"What's worse," Mac continued, "is that the same people who would scream at a tax hike or a new tax imposed on us, blithely ignore inflation because they don't understand that it's caused by the government and it's another tax. It's the ultimate withholding tax because it comes out of everyone's pocket even if you're in the underground economy. But the worst thing is that it discourages saving and investment, the things that made this country great."

"But it would still seem prudent to save even in an inflationary economy, wouldn't it?" I asked.

"We should try to invest our money somehow," Mac said. "But consider the effect inflation has on some types of savings, say a savings account, a certificate of deposit, or a U.S. Savings Bond. The interest paid on any of these is low. In fact, they're often lower than the rate of inflation. On that basis, the more you save the further you fall behind in purchasing power. But what makes it worse is that the interest paid is also taxed, that is, part of the imaginary gains you've made are taken away from you by the IRS. So, saving that way becomes a loser's game. The more you save, the further you fall behind.

"Over the long run, even putting money into precious metals is a loser's game—that is, if you do it honestly."

"How's that so?" Dave asked.

"If you invest in gold or silver, it's a nonproductive investment; it doesn't even earn you interest. What gold and silver really do is respond to the value of the dollar and other currencies. The price of those metals will go up with the inflation rate so, over the long run, if you hold onto them you should theoretically break even in purchasing power. The problem is that when you sell your gold or silver the IRS sees your gain as a 'real' gain and takes a chunk of it by taxing you. Thus, even precious metals are a losing position—unless you don't report the sale."

"So you're against holding gold or silver," I said.

"Oh, no. As a hedge against inflation they're terrific, but they're not making you money in the way stocks, bonds, or savings accounts would in a stable and noninflationary economy."

Hyperinflation in the past

"Other countries have already experienced periods of hyperinflation," Dave said. "The result of Germany having to pay war reparations after World War I led to that country's hyperinflation, and the hyperinflation led to Hitler's rise to power."

Shown is Zimbabwean currency, including the one hundred billion dollar bill shown here and one trillion dollar bills issued later. They all became worthless.

"The war reparations certainly contributed to Germany's inflation," Mac said.

"Were they intentionally inflating it to pay the war debt off with cheaper money?" I asked.

"No. Part of the Armistice agreement said the reparations had to be paid in gold or another stable currency, not the German mark. So inflating their currency didn't help them pay off the reparations at all. But paying the reparations did create part of the shortfall the German government had in its budget so they tried to make it up by letting the presses at the mint run, and it destroyed the German currency.

"However, hyperinflation alone wasn't the reason Hitler came to power. His ascendency was sort of a political perfect storm made up of the convergence of several important events, none of which, alone, was likely to produce a dictator. There was Germany's losing World War I coupled with the terms of surrender, the hyperinflation, the Great Depression, and other factors. There are those who want to say hyperinflation in this country could result in a Hitler of our own. But, again, it would take more than one event to make us that crazy. Not that it couldn't happen, but it won't just because of hyperinflation.

"Besides, Germany's hyperinflation was only one of several hyperinflationary periods that happened in many countries around the world during the 20th century, and none of those others led to the rise of another Hitler."

"How bad was Germany's inflation?" I asked.

"The German mark started losing value so fast that people were getting paid two and three times a day and they'd leave work each time so they could spend it before it lost even more value. They'd buy anything: Food, hard goods, knickknacks, who cared? If you didn't spend it right away, it was going to be worth a lot less in just a few hours. It got so bad that people not only spent their money as fast as they could, they often didn't bother taking their change."

"You're kidding," I said.

"You know how stores today have those little penny trays on the counter near the cash registers? 'Take one; leave one?' You buy something for a dollar ninety-nine and give the clerk a two dollars. He gives you one penny change and you drop it in the tray because a penny is close to worthless, nowadays. Suppose in a hyperinflationary period the price of a loaf of bread goes up to $19,900, something not at all inconceivable, and you've given the clerk two $10,000 bills. He gives you back a hundred dollar bill. That hundred dollar bill now has the purchasing power the penny used to have. It's easy to leave it on the counter and leave, especially because in a few hours it'll be worth even less."

"I know what you're saying is true," I said, "But I'm having a hard time wrapping my head around it."

"In October of 1923," Mac said, "prices in Germany went up over 40 percent a day. Money was so worthless you couldn't buy heating fuel with it, so to keep warm many people took to burning the paper bills instead."

"Wow!" I said. "Can it get worse than that?"

"Believe it or not in Hungary, just after World War II, the Hungarian pengö lost its value even faster. Throughout July of 1946, prices tripled everyday. What cost 1000 pengö one morning cost 3000 the next and 9000 the morning after that."

"People must have been outraged," I said.

"I agree, but the circumstances also honed their senses of humor."

"Is this a joke?" Dave asked.

Mac kind of smiled. "There are stories about incidents during hyperinflationary periods that may or may not be apocryphal, but they give you a good idea of how people can find humor even in dire situations.

"The first one involves a man in Germany, during the post World War I hyperinflationary period of the Weimar Republic. He is said to have paid his fare upon boarding a bus. When he reached his destination, he was informed he'd have to pay more to get off the bus because the fares had gone up during the trip."

"Can they do that?" I asked.

"Who knows?" Mac replied and he looked at me as if I was crazy for asking. "Like I said, I don't even know if it's true, but it reflects how people felt about the rapidity with which their currency was being devalued."

"It sounds like the old Kingston Trio song, Charlie on the MTA," Dave said. "Charlie couldn't get off the trolley because the fare had gone up a nickel and he didn't have one on him." Both Mac and I thought that was funny because we're familiar with the song.

"Another story...and keep in mind, John, these may not be true...involved a student in Hungary who went into a coffee shop during their hyperinflationary period and ordered a cup of coffee. After he finished it, he ordered another cup. When he went to pay the bill, it was for more than he'd expected. When he complained, he was told he should have ordered both cups at the same time because, while he was finishing his first cup, the price went up on the second one."

Dave glanced at me as if expecting me to ask, "Can they do that?" again. But I'd learned my lesson.

"But to me," Mac said, "the funniest story is about a man in Germany in 1923. This one may be true. He put his money in a wheelbarrow and headed off to the store to buy a loaf of bread."

"All he was going to get for a wheelbarrow full of money was one loaf of bread?" I asked.

"Listen to the story," Dave said.

"Yes," Mac said. "It got so it took a wheelbarrow of money to buy a loaf of bread. But when he got there, the store was closed. He left his wheelbarrow outside the door, figuring he'd come back when the store opened, knowing the bundles of money in it weren't worth enough for anyone to steal. And he was right. When he came back, the money was still there, dumped on the ground, but someone had stolen his wheelbarrow."

That story was funny in a perverse kind of way, so funny that, for some inexplicable reason, I wanted to believe it was true, but I didn't say anything.

Zimbabwe hyperinflation

Mac continued, getting back to actual historical accounts. "Today, Zimbabwe is undergoing hyperinflation. Their hyperinflation started when the country's president, Robert Mugabe, took land away from the former white landowners to give to blacks who, unfortunately, were unfamiliar with agricultural practices. Crops failed and Zimbabwe began having problems feeding itself. As a result, food prices jumped and Mugabe started to run the presses to keep up with the price increases. Coupled with that was his decision to quadruple the pay of the police and the military, without putting it in the budget, and the presses had to run even faster and longer to make up for these and other budget shortfalls."

"I'm guessing he increased their pay to keep their allegiances," Dave said.

"That's my guess, too," Mac responded. "Of course, each jump in inflation sent all prices further skyrocketing and the presses were run to keep up with that, so prices climbed even higher..." He raised his arms as if he were lifting the prices himself.

"It becomes a vicious circle," Dave said. "Prices go up, so you print more money so the government can make purchases, but that makes prices go even higher, and so on."

Mac nodded. "There was a time when the Zimbabwean dollar was worth more than the American dollar. Today, it's possible to find 100 trillion dollar

Zimbabwean notes, but no one wants them. You can't even bribe a Zimbabwean official with Zibabwean money."

"A 100 trillion dollar note? I'd love one," I said dreamily. "I'd be a trillionaire."

It may have been because of the wine, but they both laughed.

"Yeah, imagine the girls that would want you then, John," Dave said. "I'm going to get you one of those bills."

"Many South American countries," Mac went on, "Argentina, Brazil, and Bolivia among them, experienced hyperinflation in the late part of the 20th century. All of it was the result of government overspending; when the bills came due, unable to pay them with taxes, the respective governments ran the printing presses and got caught in that same vicious circle."

"Do you think it could happen here?" I said thinking back to the comment I thought I'd heard him make as I was coming into the building—that we may be headed for hyperinflation.

He thought about my question. Then, he said, "In the past, common causes of hyperinflation have been war, when governments couldn't raise money fast enough through taxes or the sale of bonds to pay to keep its war machine running. But, that's changed. As you can infer from the examples I gave, nowadays, whenever governments have accumulated extreme debts that they are unable or unwilling to raise the money to pay off, either with the sale of bonds or the raising of taxes, they often resort to simply printing more money by running the presses, whether it's the paper presses or the virtual electronic presses of the computer age that create electronic credits.

"Governments have streams of commitments, and more often than not they're political promises politicians make to voters to keep themselves in power. And for them it's often only about staying in power. But, having made those promises, they often can't renege, even if there's no money in the treasury to keep them."

"Such as what happened to Mugabe in Zimbabwe," Dave said.

"So they order the presses to run and print money, oodles of money, to pay the bills. That's what happened in Germany, Hungary, Zimbabwe, and, in last third of the 20th century, several South American countries. They all experienced runaway inflation because they borrowed too much and couldn't pay off the debts, and they continued their high-spending practices.

"Do you see where this is going?" he asked.

"Their solutions were to let the presses at the mint roll," Dave said. "So, neither inflation nor hyperinflation can exist without the government having a hand in it," Dave said. And before Mac could answer, he added, "In fact, from what you're saying, government is the cause of both inflation and hyperinflation."

"Ah. If only the American electorate could understand that, we'd throw all the bastards currently in Washington, DC, out and get officials who care about this country. Well, throw out all but Ron Paul, of Texas, who is the only one there who both knows and cares about what's going on."

Neither Dave nor I said anything. We both know of Mac's respect for Paul.

"At some point, the politicians may try to blame it on the 'greedy bankers,' speculators, and black marketeers, but none of them can run the presses," Mac added.

"What ends hyperinflation?" Dave asked.

"First, they've got to stop creating money out of thin air. Second, a new currency has to be established. Generally, issuing a currency backed by something tangible, like gold, will prevent the inflation of the currency in the future. Third, the government has got to get its spending under control. A balanced budget is the way to do it."

"What about the Federal Reserve?" Dave asked. "That's not a part of our government, but it manages our money. Are they doing a good job?"

"The Fed may as well be part of the government because Congress could dissolve it tomorrow, if it so wished. And is it doing a good job? As I said before, the dollar now has the purchasing power four cents had when they started out.

"But let's get back to whether hyperinflation could happen here. Consider our unfunded debts. These include the costs of Social Security, Medicare, national healthcare if it passes, the trade deficit, and the bailouts—for which trillions were manufactured out of thin air in a way a Zimbabwean strongman could only dream. We owe trillions in loans to foreign governments, most notably China. The responsibility for paying all of this off is being thrown on the backs of the young and those yet unborn.

"There's no way we can keep this up. In fact, when the younger generations of voters come of age and they realize what we and the other older generations of voters have voted ourselves, and that we've saddled them with the onerous task of trying to pay off these unpayable debts, they may just welcome hyperinflation and screw us the way we've been screwing them, for example, by making our savings and Social Security payments worthless.

"But not only do we have all this debt, a lot of our currency is overseas. Foreigners have been willing to hold American dollars for decades because it's been universally recognized and it's been considered stable. But, if all those dollars were to come back here and were spent in a short time, it too might lead to hyperinflation."

"It would be like the raft with a duplicate set of poker chips suddenly showing up on the island," Dave said.

"That's right."

"You mentioned Social Security," I said. "But in the beginning, Social Security was a good idea and it was self-sustaining. Right?"

"Actually, it was never self-sustaining. If any insurance company were to set up such a plan, the stock holders would revolt and the government would throw the officers in jail. In fact, in the early 1950s, several insurance companies approached Congress and showed them that Social Security, the way it was conceived, was unsustainable and offered to manage the system and turn it into something other than the Ponzi scheme that it is. You know what a Ponzi scheme is, don't you?"

Dave said, "It's a financial scheme where the people getting in early are paid off with money put up by later ones, rather than from some kind of profits, in order to encourage more people to come in and take bigger risks. And it falls apart when too many people want their money back and it's shown to be insolvent."

Mac seemed to be surprised Dave knew this. I know I was.

"At the beginning," Mac said, "when Social Security was set up, there weren't many people collecting, so the millions and millions of contributors had no problem supporting them, and only a little came out of each person's paycheck to keep it going. But, as the number of people collecting increased, and as Congress kept voting bigger slices for those who were collecting, those getting in later had to give up a bigger portion of their paychecks to support them.

"In the future it's going to reach a point where the amount taken out of workers' checks is going to be horrific and, ultimately, the system will start running in the negative. Young people coming into the workforce will be forced to pay huge amounts of their incomes to keep it going, with no chance of collecting anything meaningful when it comes their time to retire. Long before that point, I wouldn't blame them for revolting and it will be these younger generations that may welcome hyperinflation to pay the debt off."

"It sounds like we're bankrupting our country," Dave said, "and if we don't stop, the only way out of it may well be to let hyperinflation happen."

"But what happens if we do that?" I asked.

"There will be winners and losers," Mac said. "The prime winners may be future generations, including those not yet born, with whom we've been trying to saddle all these debts. You must keep in mind that the last few generations, including our own, have been the most selfish in American history. We've voted ourselves all kinds of benefits that are going to have to be paid by the young. But there's going to come a time when the young realize it. We can't hide it forever. And when they see what's happened, they're going to do something about it at the polls. As a result, it's likely to be the older people who are going to be hurt."

"Including our generation," Dave said.

"In almost every country where inflation has gotten out of control, many who had spent their lives providing for themselves with investments and savings found the purchasing power of their retirement nest eggs wiped out by the hyperinflation, the value of their savings stolen by a government. And those who watched their retirement disappear overnight had to return to the workforce in their old age."

"But won't young people be hurt, too?" I asked.

"The young are resilient and have their whole lives ahead of them. They may be better off if hyperinflation manages to wipe out the debts we've been trying to saddle them with."

"I heard hyperinflation might help a lot of homeowners who are behind on their mortgages because it would allow them to pay their mortgages off with inflated dollars," I said.

"Keep in mind," Mac said, "that the recent bailouts went through despite polls showing the public was against them. It's because Wall Street and the bankers have Washington's ear. So, for better or worse, Congress is likely to step in and make laws saying mortgages and other loans, such as car loans and credit card balances, would be inflation-adjusted."

"That would be tantamount to another bailout," Dave said.

"Isn't there a way to keep prices down despite inflation?" I asked.

"You mean like wage and price controls?" he asked.

"Yeah."

"They don't work. At best they do nothing, at worst they destroy businesses and jobs. By instituting wage and price controls, policy makers force sellers, under penalty of law, to sell their goods and services for money that is worth less and less every day. They force workers to work for less and less of a living wage. The result is that sellers may wind up selling goods at a loss and may go out of business while workers struggle because they can't pay their bills. So we have scarcity of goods, lost jobs, and a burgeoning black market. Even if the prices stay down temporarily while the controls are in place and the government threatens penalties, once the controls are lifted, the prices shoot up to where they should be. If you'll recall, this is what happened when Nixon tried to impose price controls in the early '70s.

"Price controls also force businesses to either withhold their products from the market or they force them to sell on the black market in order to survive. Goods including food and clothing often disappear from the shelves, and people walk away from their jobs to work under the table. Politicians are against black markets because they expose political policies for what they are—shams—and they can't tax them."

"What could we have done differently to have prevented this?" Dave asked.

"We could have voted differently."

"Voted differently?"

"It can't be that simple."

"It is. It's the Democrats and Republicans we've been voting for for the last several decades. They created the debts that may lead to hyperinflation, and the American electorate chose not to stop them and kept reelecting them year after year."

"How were we to know what was coming?" I asked.

"You should have turned off the sitcoms you watch, turned off the football games—just a few nights a year—and gotten yourself informed. The problem with the American electorate is that it doesn't want to inform itself of what's going on in the world, but it still wants the right to vote."

"I see what you're saying," Dave said. "Ultimately, we're responsible because we let it happen. Is there anything we can do now, before it happens?"

"Go back to the Gold Standard—it kept our money stable for over a century—and start paying our debts and stop expecting the as-yet-unborn to pay them for us."

"That's not likely to happen," Dave said. "Sooo..." and he paused, "What is O.E. MacDougal doing to protect himself?"

"Well, if we're lucky, we'll watch our currency inflate slowly and we can get rid of our dollars and turn them into hard assets. But I'm already hedging my bets. I buy hard assets, everything from junk silver coins and ammo for the guns I own to food and wine. I have lots of food, lots of wine. It's also good if you can get your hands on some stable foreign currencies like the euro. But, if not, the junk silver coins will be good, maybe better, because they'll be universally recognized as good currency because of their silver content."

"There was some gas station over in Medford, Oregon," I interrupted, "that was selling a gallon of gasoline for a quarter that was made prior to 1965. Those are the silver ones, right?"

"Yes, and we may see a lot more of that in the future," Mac said. "Especially if inflation is running rampant. You'll be able to buy a bag full of groceries for a few silver dimes while people are getting a mere loaf of bread for a thousand inflated dollars. Then you'll get another bag of groceries, a few days later, for the same number of dimes, while the price of bread has gone to $2,000 in almost worthless currency."

"So, you think it will happen," I said.

Mac smiled. "Like I said earlier, no one can predict the future. But let me add, it's prudent to hedge your bets." Δ

Chapter 6
Killer blizzards

By John Silveira

Winter storms and blizzards can occur any time from late fall to early spring, and in some northerly regions or high elevation they can happen all the way into April.

What is a blizzard and how does it differ from a typical winter storm?

The National Weather Service (NWS) defines a blizzard as having the following conditions that persist for more than three hours:

- A lot of snow either falling *or* being blown around
- Winds of 35 miles per hour (mph) or greater
- Visibility below ¼ mile

If snow has stopped falling but persistent winds continue to blow snow around, reducing visibility, the conditions are sometimes referred to as a *ground blizzard.*

How blizzards form

Three things are needed to create a blizzard:

- Cold air (below freezing)
- Moisture in the air
- Warm, rising air

Cold air. There must be one weather system in which the air must be cold enough at high altitudes for snow to form and cold enough near the ground to keep it from melting before it hits the ground. If only the upper air is warm, the storm will start out as rain and may turn into sleet. Sleet is somewhat reminiscent of hail. On the other hand, it may fall as rain and become "freezing rain" as it hits the cold earth and other surfaces and freezes. Freezing rain makes for particularly hazardous driving conditions. (See driving article by Don Fallick in Issue #26, which is in *A Backwoods Home Anthology, The Fifth Year*.)

If the upper air is cold and air near the surface is warm, what begins as snow at high altitudes will become rain before it reaches the ground.

Moisture in the air. The way blizzards form is when warm wind blows over a large body of water, such as the ocean, and picks up moisture. So, there must also be a weather system with warm air. This is how Nor'easters develop as warm air over the Gulf or the Atlantic gets saturated with moisture and moves north where it will run into a cold-weather system.

It has to be *warm* air simply because warm air holds more water vapor than cold air. In fact, if it gets too cold, snow won't form at all because the cold air will not hold enough moisture. It is from this that many old-timers came up with the phrase, "It's too cold to snow."

Warm air rising. While warm air is required to hold the moisture that goes into making snow, it's also needed because warm air rises and where it rises over the cold air, a *front* is formed. It is at the front where the moisture-laden air turns to snow. As the moisture in the air condenses, it also releases an incredible amount of energy. Part of this energy is turned into wind, and without wind we won't have a blizzard.

The fiercest winter storms and blizzards occur in the "Snowbelt," which stretches from Minnesota to New England. But, they also occur outside this zone with devastating consequences simply because more southerly parts of the country are less prepared for heavy snowfalls.

If you live in a Gulf Coast state and get a heavy snowfall, you may think you just had a blizzard. In all likelihood, you didn't. However, the Southeast and the Gulf states, though unaccustomed to snow and freezing conditions, are not immune to winter storms. When these storms sweep though the South, local municipalities may find themselves unprepared, as they usually do not have equipment for either snow removal or for salting or sanding the roads.

Also, though blizzards seem more often to be phenomena in the eastern states, blizzards and bad winters also occur in the West. It was an early winter blizzard and severe winter that led to the legendary trapping of the Donner Party near today's Truckee, California.

Can we prevent blizzards? Like all weather phenomena, there is little we can do with current technology to prevent or even moderate blizzards.

In the meantime, even if there is global warming, blizzards are likely to remain a part of our future. In fact, they may even become worse because as the air over the Atlantic and the Gulf of Mexico warms up, it'll carry even more moist air north than it does now. And when it collides with late-season cold fronts hovering over the Great Plains and Canada, even bigger blizzards are likely to occur.

The effects of blizzards

Blizzards are not new. However, to the first Europeans who settled this continent, they were. They knew snow when they left Europe, but they had rarely, if ever, seen anything like the winter weather they discovered in the New World.

An impromptu lean-to, coupled with a fire and a reflecting wall, will never have all the comforts of home, but it may be enough to keep you alive.

If we look at historical blizzards, several things become apparent. Until late in the 20th century, blizzards could come as complete surprises. Major cities were often isolated from the outside world as both communications and transportation broke down in the face of heavy snowfall, fierce winds, and freezing temperatures. People caught off guard were stranded away from home, some away from any kind of shelter. People died as a direct result of the storms.

Because of the presence of warm air that frequently precedes blizzards, the weather can sometimes seem unseasonably warm before a storm strikes and people get lured out into the outdoors wearing less than they should. It's the reason that during the Armistice Day blizzard of 1940, so many hunters died. They had simply gone out underdressed into the path of one of the worst storms ever to hit the Midwest.

As time has passed, some things have changed, but some have remained the same. With each passing year, because of satellites and improvements in computer technology, weather forecasting has become better. So, the storms have become more predictable—though the severity of an encroaching storm is not always obvious.

Communications continue to improve, and with today's wireless communications, people are more apt to be able to stay in touch with loved ones,

Greatest snowfalls in North America

	Place	Date	Inches
24 hours	Silver Lake, CO	April 14–15, 1921	76
1 month	Tamarack, CA	Jan. 1911	90
1 storm	Mt. Shasta Ski Bowl, CA	Feb. 13–19, 1959	89
1 season	Mount Baker, WA	1998–1999	1,140
1 city	Buffalo, NY	1976-1977	199

Courtesy U.S. Army Corps of Engineers, Engineer Topographic Laboratories

rescuers, and the outside world even if away from home, and even if other lines of communication are down.

On the other hand, improvements in transportation seem to make it more likely many people will be stranded away from home. Sometimes, they will be stranded at jobs, sometimes they will be snowbound on roads while making a bid to make it home, and sometimes people will try to make grocery runs at the last moment thinking they can make the round-trip in no time at all, unaware of just how *fast* a blizzard can come up and strand them.

Records of blizzards go back to the days of the earliest settlements in North America, including "The Great Snow of 1717," which was really a series of four snow storms that occurred between February 27 and March 7. And one of the most notable, the "Blizzard of 1899," created record low temperatures from New Orleans to New England, some of which stand today. It would be 94 years before a storm comparable to that one wracked the country, and that was the Blizzard of 1993, the so-called "Storm of the Century," which we *will* talk about.

Let's look at five historic blizzards and see what happened to the people who endured them, and see what can be learned from them.

Historic blizzards

The blizzard of 1888, sometimes called the Great White Hurricane (March 11-14, 1888). This is the blizzard against which *all* other blizzards in the United States are measured. It has become a legend in the annals of winter history.

For almost everyone who endured it, the greatest blizzard on record came without warning. There were no satellite photos as there are today to see it developing or to warn the cities in its path when it began to move. And, when it hit, no one knew how bad it was going to get until it was over.

It was March, the weather was warm for that time of year, frequently rising into the 50s.

And this is our first lesson about blizzards: They can come in what seems like beautiful spring-like weather and catch even the most self-reliant people by surprise.

On the 11th of March it began to rain heavily. On the 12th, a Monday, the rain turned to snow as temperatures plummeted and the wind picked up. The combination of falling and drifting snow started to choke the Northeast.

There have been storms with heavier snowfall, and there have been storms that have been colder, but the Great White Hurricane was a combination of bad weather conditions not seen before nor in the 118 years since.

The storm spread over an area from Washington, D.C. to Maine and brought the nation's capital, along with the cities of New York, Philadelphia, and Boston, to their knees. Businesses closed, fire stations closed, and hospitals were inaccessible. More that 200 ships ran aground in the gale-force winds and whiteout conditions with a loss of more than 100 seamen, and there were at least 300 other deaths directly attributable to the storm.

That particular combination of events couldn't happen today. But in 1888, people afraid of losing their jobs went out into the storm that Monday morning, and many of them died later in the day trying to get home.

In rural areas, people who left that morning were stranded away from their homes for as much as two weeks as families and friends, bewildered by the catastrophe, had no idea what had become of them.

Measured snowfalls were up to 50 inches in New England and 40 inches in New York and New Jersey, and severe winds created snowdrifts that were as much as 50 feet deep.

The only means of electronic communication at the time were the telegraph and telephone. When those lines went down, which they did under the weight of accumulating snow and ice buildup, that entire part of the country was out of touch with the rest of the world for days.

Not only were streets and roads blocked, but drifting snow actually rose high enough in some places to block the elevated trains. The transportation crisis created in New York City led to the decision to build that city's subway system.

Armistice Day Storm (November 11-12, 1940). Fifty-two years after the Great White Hurricane, another deadly blizzard of epic proportions hit. This one was in the Midwest.

Like the 1888 storm, the weather preceding the blizzard had been unseasonably warm. In fact, gardens were still producing in the orth country well into October. It was a beautiful fall, the kind you like to savor.

Then, on Armistice Day (now called Veterans Day), November 11, 1940, with temperatures still in the 60s, a storm moved into the Midwest from over the Rockies. It had started in the Pacific Northwest, and, when it arrived in Minnesota it met warmer, wet air that had been travelling north through the

Among clothing items I carry in my vehicle year-round, are (clockwise from upper left) a "hoodie," some quilted shirts, a spare set of old but still wearable shoes, a clean shirt, socks, and jeans. Spare underwear is good, too, but I didn't want to photograph them.

midwestern states from the Gulf of Mexico. Along with that was a cold front that was moving down from Canada. The three weather fronts were about to collide.

Duck hunters, out to enjoy the great fall weather, found themselves in some of the best hunting in memory as ducks flooded into the Mississippi Valley. Survivors said shots could be heard from all directions as hunters were bent on easily filling their limit. What they didn't and couldn't know was that the ducks were fleeing the storm that would soon create a life-and-death struggle for hundreds of hunters and thousands of others as well.

Then it began to rain. Unconcerned, the hunters stayed out. Soon, the rain turned into sleet...then snow. Then, with the rising winds, the conditions for a blizzard were set, and hundreds of hunters realized, all too late, they were trapped—and poorly clothed for what was to come.

In the meantime, as occurred in the 1888 storm, telephone and telegraph lines were soon downed, putting many towns out of touch with the outside world. Almost every road across several states was closed as snow piled up faster than any highway department could remove it.

With any blizzard today, this can still happen: You can expect power lines to fall and roads to be blocked.

Meanwhile, because of whiteout conditions, an engineer driving a freight train missed a track-side signal, and he was unaware that the track he was on was also being used by an oncoming passenger train. So, instead of pulling into a siding, he lumbered on into a disaster—and his own death—as the two steam locomotives collided in a head-on wreck.

Winds as high as 80 miles per hour created snowdrifts of more than 20 feet. Other trains on other tracks were slowed down by the deepening snow until finally almost all rail traffic in the northern Midwest ground to a halt, and they were snowbound with their crews and passengers.

Farmers who had left their rural farms for a day of shopping and provisioning in the nearby towns found themselves unable to get home for days.

The storm created a 1,000-mile swath of death and destruction though the Mississippi Valley and sunk boats on Lake Michigan, where at least 66 sailors died.

At least 80 other people died because of the storm, most of them the unprepared hunters who had left home without adequate clothing that morning and were stranded in the outdoors with no means to keep themselves warm.

One young hunter, who may otherwise have died of exposure, found a novel way to keep himself warm: He started running. He ran around and around a tree on the island where he'd been stranded. He ran, and ran, and ran. When rescuers reached him the following morning, there was a well-worn path in the snow around the tree, but he was otherwise healthy and safe.

Economic losses from the blizzard were difficult to assess, but they included thousands of cattle and more than a million Thanksgiving turkeys that were being groomed for the upcoming holiday.

The Blizzard of 1978 (February 6-7, 1978). There were two blizzards in 1978, one in New England, the other in the Midwest.

The New England storm was the more severe. It was the result of three air masses, one moving in from Pennsylvania, a second from Georgia, and a third from over the Atlantic. The storms converged over Connecticut, Rhode Island, and Massachusetts, forming one huge storm.

This new storm packed winds of 65 miles per hour. Unlike the typical Nor'easters that hit New England and pass through in 6 to 12 hours, this one stalled before a high-pressure area that hovered in Canada, and for 36 straight hours it poured its snow onto and tore the states with its high winds. It was even accompanied by unusual winter thunderstorms.

An advantage of the German military surplus entrenching tool is that it can be opened at a 90° angle to expose a pick that is handy for digging or breaking through crusty snow.

There are numerous kinds of lean-tos you can make if you need shelter from snow. They can be constructed using branches, boughs, and even lined with trash bags. Remember, all you're trying to do is stay sheltered and dry for a day or two, so beauty & durability are not important.

Despite the steady improvements in weather forecasting, the severity of this storm still caught many New Englanders by surprise.

Once again, people were stranded away from their homes. Some died in their cars from carbon monoxide inhalation, unaware that snow blocked their exhaust pipes as they idled their engines in an attempt to keep warm.

Transportation broke down as some roads were buried, and many became difficult or even impossible to plow because of the abandoned vehicles. Other roads became difficult to plow simply because they ran out of spaces to push the snow. In Boston, with no place else to put it, the snow was often loaded into trucks and dumped directly into Boston Harbor.

When it was over, more than 3,500 cars were found abandoned on major roads and highways, and countless others were found abandoned on side streets.

People who found themselves trapped in their homes were lucky. Many others found themselves trapped at work and were unable to reach their homes. Some couldn't even leave the buildings they were in because snow drifts as deep as 15 feet blocked the exits.

How bad was the storm as compared to other storms? For the first time in years, New York City schools were closed. Ordinarily opened in even the most severe weather conditions (remember, the breakdown in transportation during the blizzard of 1888 was one of the reasons the New York City subway was built), the blizzard of 1978 succeeded in closing them. And one of the only means of transportation, such as getting the ill to hospitals, was the use of snowmobiles on the city's snow-choked streets.

Superstorm of 1993—also dubbed the "Storm of the Century" (March 12-15, 1993). This is an example of a storm they saw coming. Yet, despite all the advances in meteorology and the use of satellite photos, the fact that the meteorologists saw the storm as it was developing, days in advance, wasn't enough to prevent it from being catastrophic. Nor was it enough to keep people from getting stranded.

What the meteorologists saw was an extremely low-pressure weather system loaded with moisture as it moved north from the Gulf of Mexico. This warm, wet front was on a course to collide with an arctic high-pressure cold-weather system moving in from the Great Plains. That cold-weather system was being forced further south than it ordinarily would have been for that time of year by the jet stream. Meteorologists say such an event happens only once in 500 years.

When the two fronts met, they created perfect conditions for a blizzard.

Beginning March 12, snow fell from as far south as Alabama, and north to New York. (Remember, March 12 was the exact day the snow started to fall, 105 years before, during the Great White Hurricane.) As snow accumulated, winds picked up, temperatures fell, and fully one-third of the country was affected as roads became impassable and literally millions along the Atlantic seaboard and further inland lost power. Because airports couldn't plow the snow off runways fast enough, a quarter of all the air traffic in the United States was disrupted for the next two days.

Fully 26 states and eastern Canada were affected. In the South, where heavy snowfalls are so rare that it makes no sense for municipalities to make heavy investments in snow removal equipment, transportation broke down. In the North, despite winter preparedness, automobiles and trucks were, once again, abandoned on major thoroughfares, people were stranded away from their homes, and power outages left people cold and in the dark.

Because of record snowfalls, roofs on factories not designed to withstand accumulations of standing snow, collapsed, as did the decks and porches of many homes.

Extreme low temperatures for that part of the year followed the snowfall. Records were set in more than 70 locations in the East on March 14, and 75 more record lows were set on the 15th. Wind gusts of 144 miles per hour were recorded on Mount Washington in New Hampshire.

Though meteorologists say this type of storm can only happen once every 500 years, no one really knows.

Still, this was not the worst blizzard of record, by any standards. Yet, some 300 people died.

What is there to learn from such a storm? If you hear one coming, don't go out, don't drive, stay home, keep warm, and wait it out.

Blizzard of 1996 (January 6-12, 1996). To New Englanders, the storm of record in the 20th century is the Blizzard of '78. And other parts of the country may feel other storms were greater in their area. But for the amount of snow that fell over so wide an area, nothing beats the Blizzard of '96.

In fact, from a meteorological standpoint, this wasn't a blizzard at all. It was actually three separate storms that lay siege to the eastern United States from January 6 through the 12th. High winds, freezing temperatures, and massive snowfall combined to shut down much of the Middle Atlantic States. More than a foot of snow fell in parts of Ohio, while two-foot and two-and a half-foot accumulations were common all along the seaboard from Virginia to Boston.

Many roads, though plowed, were quickly closed again by drifting snow driven by the winds.

The federal government was virtually closed down. In some counties, as many as 50 percent of the residential neighborhoods lay unplowed for days, and for a week after the storms many people found themselves on streets that had not yet seen a snowplow.

To compound the problems, after the three storms passed, temperatures shot up causing massive snow melts that resulted in flooding.

This storm killed at least 50 people.

Preparing for a blizzard

According to the United States Search and Rescue Task Force, about 70 percent of "winter deaths" related to ice and snow occur in automobile accidents directly attributable to weather conditions.

Another 25 percent occur to people caught out in storms. This includes hikers, hunters, people who have abandoned their cars, and anyone else with or without good reasons to be out in the storm. Of those who die as a direct result of exposure to the cold, half are over 50 years old, and 70 percent are male.

If you are going to be caught out in a storm, the overwhelming chance is that it will be when you're out in your car. So, what can you do? What can you carry in your car to improve your chances of survival? It would be wise to take the advice of Jackie Clay and have a survival kit in your car. (See article in Issue #55, which is in *A Backwoods Home Anthology, The Tenth Year.*) But, in addition, in the trunk of my car I always have a military surplus entrenching tool (folding shovel). If you can find one made for the German Army, they're better built and more versatile than the American-made versions. The ones made for the commercial market are usually flimsy.

I also carry a spare set of clothes: Footwear, socks, flannel shirt, and a couple of quilted flannel shirts. One of the things I keep telling women, particularly women with office jobs, is to carry a pair of walking shoes in their trunks.

I also carry a few butane lighters and some of the treated fire-starting blocks. I even carry a few full-sized heavy-duty trash bags. They make impromptu but effective rain panchos.

It's all cheap stuff, and it takes very little space. I wouldn't drive around without a spare tire, so I don't drive around without stuff that could save my life when I'm in the North Country during winter.

Another item I carry is a pair of military-style ground mats. They're great to lay on for prone-position shooting, but they'll also insulate you from the cold ground or even snow if you have to sleep outdoors.

Blizzards today will be met with a whole new set of tools. With today's cell phones, loved ones are less likely to be "missing" for weeks at a time, as they were in the aftermath of the Great White Hurricane. With today's weather technology, including satellite photos and up-to-the-minute reporting, more will be known about impending storms. Still, there will be a surprising number of individuals who will venture out into the storms anyway, and not unsurprisingly many will become victims.

What to do if you're caught out in a blizzard

If you're caught in a storm, find shelter. If you have to, build a lean-to. Trash bags make excellent coverings for a lean-to.

Keep dry. Cold water can suck all of the life-giving heat right out of you. Cover every exposed part of your body. In particular, keep your head covered. (As much as 20 percent of your body's heat is lost through the top of your head.)

Unless you've built one before, don't expect to build a snow cave to save yourself. For one thing, they're not easy to build. For another, you're likely to get wetter from sweating and from melting snow trying to build it. Cold and wet are a deadly combination in a blizzard.

If you can, build a fire. A fire not only provides heat, it draws attention. Rocks around a fire will absorb and reradiate heat. A wall, even a makeshift wall (another use for a trash bag), will reflect heat. But if you're near trees, beware of snow in overhanging branches. Snow suddenly falling from overhanging branches can suffocate a hard-built fire.

Unless you absolutely have to, do not abandon your car. Rescuers will find it easier to find a car than they will a hiker stumbling around in the backcountry. However, be careful. Cars do not retain heat well, though they will keep you dry. It's a good reason to keep blankets in your trunk. But also keep in mind that cars can get buried in snow drifts.

If you run your engine for heat, make sure the exhaust doesn't get covered because, instead of dying of exposure, you may kill yourself with carbon monoxide poisoning.

Finally, if you get thirsty, **don't eat ice or snow**. The amount of energy required to melt ice or snow is greater than you think. If you're cold now, the ice or snow you ingest will lower your body temperature even further with possible fatal consequences.

A story that sticks with me is one I read years ago. A couple in the Northwest, taking advantage of some early spring weather, went with their newborn into the mountains. A freak storm came up, stranding them. Though they were lightly dressed, they were afraid they wouldn't be found, so they abandoned their car and began walking. The mother was nursing. She felt compelled to eat snow so as to produce enough milk to feed her baby. The father didn't.

But as a result of ingesting the snow, coupled with the fact that they weren't wearing warm clothes, the mother's body temperature fell dangerously. When rescuers finally reached them, the woman was dead, her husband and baby were still alive. The tragedy is that the baby, though uncomfortably hungry, could have weathered the hunger just fine until help arrived, and all three could have survived.

Again, if thirst becomes overwhelming, and the only source of water is ice or snow, don't eat it. Find a way to melt it first, and don't use your body's heat to do so. Use a fire, use the sun, or even the heater in your car.

In fact, if you can find a heat source to melt it, get it as warm as possible. Drinking the water warm is an even better way to ingest it when you're cold.

Last, avoid alcohol. Alcoholic drinks are diuretics. They will not quench your thirst, and they can contribute to a reduction in your body's temperature.

If you live in the North Country, blizzards are a fact of life. Learn to live with them. And learn to survive them. Δ

Chapter 7
Wind chill factor

By Tom and Joanne O'Toole

Checking the temperature is not always a reliable indicator of how cold a person will feel outside. There are many other determinations. One important guideline is the wind chill factor.

After many years the U.S. National Weather Service has changed the wind chill temperature index, and the new formula is now being used throughout Canada and the United States. The old index calculated wind speed in terms of how quickly water freezes at 33 feet above ground (the typical height of an anemometer), while the new replacement index is based on readings at a height of five feet above ground (average face level) and determines freezing temperatures on people's faces.

Originally developed by Arctic explorers and the military, wind chill is nothing more than an "equivalent temperature." It describes the chilling effect of various combinations of moving air, at different temperatures, across exposed skin.

There are a number of definitions for the wind chill factor, but simply put, it combines air temperature and wind speed to come up with a reading of what it really feels like outside.

Wind moving past exposed skin during cold weather increases the body's heat loss. The body pumps warm blood to the extremities in an attempt to maintain the proper body temperature. However, if the temperature is low, and the wind is strong, the body often cannot keep up with heat loss and the skin temperature decreases. While the usual effect of the wind chill is just plain discomfort, freezing of exposed portions of the body can result.

A scientific definition to that elusive characteristic of the weather known as "cold" was first put forth by Antarctic explorer Paul A. Siple and his colleague Charles F. Passel in 1939. Some of the tests used water-filled plastic cylinders to measure the speed at which water freezes at different air temperatures and wind speeds.

Siple coined the term "wind chill" to describe their concept of the relative cooling power (or heat removal) of the human body with various combinations of wind speed and low temperatures.

Army researchers devised the basis for the wind chill index in the 1940s to help the military develop clothing for soldiers.

Wind chill has gained popular acceptance because it is easy to understand. Weather forecasters throughout Canada and across the northern tier of the

United States routinely refer to the wind chill. The U.S. National Weather Service across the southern states computes the wind chill factor whenever temperatures dip below 40° F and wind speeds rise above 10 miles per hour (mph).

On a calm day (no wind) with a temperature of say 10° F, the temperature as it relates to the body is that same 10°. But when the wind starts blowing, the temperature affecting exposed skin drops dramatically. If the wind is a relatively slow 5 mph, the wind chill factor is already down to 1 degree F. If it's blowing at 15 mph, the wind chill plunges to 7° *below* zero.

The stronger the wind during a given temperature reading, the lower the wind chill factor. It's the relationship between wind speed and the actual temperature that produces the chilling effect. A further concern is for outdoor activists who create their own wind or increase the existing wind—skiing, snowmobiling, and running, for example. Their movement magnifies the air flow, so they should be especially aware of wind chill.

When someone says the wind is "penetrating," what actually happens is the air movement evaporates moisture from the exposed skin, decreasing the temperature. In the summer this feels great (a reason fans are so popular) because it has a cooling effect on an overheated person. Heat is lost in the evaporation process. However, this same experience can have serious consequences during cold weather when hunters, fishermen, backpackers, and other outdoor people want to retain as much heat as possible.

Through physical exertion the body heat production rises, perspiration begins, and heat is removed from the body by vaporization. Any part of the body touching a cold surface also takes away body heat (conduction), as does breathing cold air that results in the loss of heat from the lungs. So, the wind chill chart isn't strictly accurate because it doesn't take into account all the possibilities of heat loss, or the preventive measures against it.

Thus, the temperature of the air is rarely a reliable indicator of how cold a person will feel outdoors. Other elements of the weather such as wind speed, relative humidity, and sunshine (solar radiation) also exert an influence. The state of health and metabolism of a person, along with the type of clothing worn, will also affect how cold one feels.

Frostbite and hypothermia

Two serious wintertime afflictions of wind chill are frostbite and hypothermia. Both are dangerous to those who do not know how to handle them, or become unable to cope with their effects. While frostbite is seldom fatal, hypothermia can be life-threatening.

Frostbite is tissue damage caused by exposure to intense cold, and usually occurs when wind chill temperatures fall below -25° F.

The early stages of frostbite are a burning or stinging sensation in the affected parts. The skin will be bright pink at first as ice crystals begin to form under the surface. Numbness sets in as the skin turns to pale white, with a hint of gray or yellow spotting.

When actual frostbite occurs, parts of the body begin to freeze. It usually starts with the extremities—nose, ears, fingers, and toes—spreading to the cheeks of the face, and on to the hands and feet.

Medical attention is essential. Until help arrives, or the victim can be taken to the nearest treatment center, outdoor companions should give whatever aid they can and keep the affected parts as warm as possible. Fingers are usually frostbit first, and they can be slipped under the arm pits, inside the upper thighs, or in the mouth for warmth. You can also make the temperature rise by flexing fingers and toes. Without assistance—and sometimes even with it—the consequences are gangrene, severe infection, and possible amputation.

Another result of wind chill is hypothermia, the rapid cooling of the body's inner core to below its normal temperature of 98.6° F. Some of the symptoms are violent shivering, slurred speech, exhaustion, drowsiness, disorientation, and impaired judgment. (See the following article on hypothermia.)

Hypothermia is sneaky, gradually overcoming a person who has been chilled by wet clothing, low temperatures, or brisk winds. The important thing to remember is, temperatures do not have to drop below freezing for this condition to set in.

Few people consider that smoking, drinking, prescription drugs, and narcotics present added dangers in wind chill conditions. All of these dull your sensitivity to the circumstances, and have physical effects that will make you more susceptible to frostbite and hypothermia.

Alcohol dilates the capillaries of the skin, increasing the heat loss of the body. Nicotine smoke absorbed by the blood causes the capillaries to constrict, thus restricting the blood flow to the earlobes, fingertips, and other areas of the body. Medication can have side effects too, which might mean you shouldn't venture outside during extraordinary weather.

With winter always offering the possibilities of extremely low temperatures, those who enjoy the outdoors have a responsibility to be aware of the wind chill factor and what it can mean.

Wind chill charts for regular reference are available wherever outdoor equipment is sold.

When you venture out in winter, dress for both the weather and the wind, wearing loose-fitting, lightweight, warm clothing in several layers, which can be removed to prevent perspiration and subsequent chilling. Snug mittens are better protection than fingered gloves. Δ

Chapter 8
Hypothermia: a real winter danger

By Tom and Joanne O'Toole

Hypothermia is a deadly enemy. It steals body heat and kills more outdoor enthusiasts every year than anything else.

Hypothermia is the rapid and drastic chilling of the body's core temperature (normally 98.6 degrees F) during adverse conditions, and begins when the body loses heat faster than it can be replaced. As the body temperature drops because of exposure to cool air and cold water, things begin to happen in a predictable sequence. Left unchecked, it affects one's mental condition and physical reactions, and can result in unconsciousness. The ultimate result is death.

While cold rain or wet snow, combined with a brisk wind, create classic conditions, hypothermia is not exclusive to northern winter weather and bitter cold. When water temperatures are 50 degrees F or less, and air temperatures as high as 60-70 degrees F, hypothermia is possible. Given the right set of circumstances, it can (and does) occur anywhere.

Skin, surface fat, and superficial muscle layers act as insulation for the vital organs—heart, liver, kidneys, lungs, and the like. As hypothermia takes over, the internal temperature is dangerously lowered creating an extremely serious condition. It quickly leads to mental and physical collapse.

There are two types of this debilitating condition—chronic (long onset) and acute (rapid onset).

Chronic occurs when one is exposed to a cold environment for an extended time, and usually develops in air temperatures between 30 to 50 degrees F. It is commonly associated with winter hikers and backpackers, but can creep up on hunters, cross-country skiers, snowmobilers, and others.

Acute hypothermia happens from sudden immersion in cold water, and depending on the water temperature, can develop from within a few minutes to several hours. Boaters, ice fishermen, skaters, trappers, and those at or on water are often affected by this hazard.

Moisture is the worst enemy in the fight against hypothermia, and gets its start when victims become wet from their own perspiration, a sudden shower, or from an accidental plunge into water.

Protecting yourself

If you slip into cold water from a boat, it is best to get back in or cling to the craft. Staying as far out of the water as possible maintains more body heat, and postpones advanced symptoms. If getting out of the water is impossible, you should be wearing your Coast Guard-approved personal floatation device (PFD) that doubles your chances. A PFD not only helps insulate the body from cold water (reducing heat loss), but lessens the need to move in order to stay afloat.

You can also greatly extend your survival time by assuming the Heat Escape Lessening Posture (HELP) or fetal position—sometimes called the self-huddle. To do this, cross your ankles and bring your knees up toward your chest to protect the trunk of the body. Wrap your arms around your legs just below the knees, cross your wrists, and hold tight.

The greatest heat loss is from the head and neck, and these areas should be kept as high out of the water as possible. The other "hot spots" that lose heat most rapidly are the groin and the sides of the chest. These areas need to be protected the most.

Under hypothermic conditions, avoid the drown-proofing technique as it requires putting your head in the water, and causes you to cool faster than if floating with your head held high.

If there are several people in the water, use the "huddle" method to help each other preserve body heat. Lock your arms around one another and stay side-by-side in a circle.

Swimming to shore can be a deadly decision. The general advice is to stay with a disabled boat. Distances are deceptive, and rescuers can more easily spot a capsized boat than a lone paddler. Swimming burns up body heat, and in 50 degree F water even the best strokers could not make a mile.

Because cold water draws heat from an individual indefinitely, any activity drains the body's stored energy. Thrashing around creates swirling water, which steals heat from the body more rapidly than still water. Even treading water brings on complications faster. Remaining motionless just about doubles the time a person can endure.

You might be surprised to know hypothermia is the leading cause of death in boating accidents.

The historic sinking of the *Titanic* in 1912 is a dramatic example of hypothermia's effect. When the great ocean liner started sinking, passengers put on their PFDs and headed for the lifeboats. When rescue ships arrived two hours later, most of the people in the lifeboats were alive, but none of the almost 1,500 people floating in the 32 degree F water (still wearing those life jackets) lived.

Progressive hypothermia

There are degrees of hypothermia, and you can determine the state of the victim by recognizing the symptoms. If you want to categorize the stages, consider:

Mild Hypothermia (98.6-95 degrees F): Conscious and alert; sensation of cold; pain and numbness; teeth chattering; vigorous shivering; normal speech; increased heart rate; and some loss of manual dexterity (fingers and toes).

Moderate Hypothermia (95-90 degrees F): Conscious, but mentally cloudy; diminished shivering; stumbling; non-coordination; slurred speech; weak; confused; and drowsy.

Severe Hypothermia (90-85 degrees F): No shivering; inability to follow instructions; mental confusion; staggering and frequent falling; unusual behavior; blurred vision; unintelligible speech; and possible unconsciousness.

Profound Hypothermia (85-80 degrees F): Unconsciousness; rigid muscles; greatly lowered blood pressure; decreased heart rate; diminished respiration; dilated pupils; and appearance of death.

The colder the water and air surrounding a victim, the more sudden and severe the hypothermia. While water will conduct heat away from the body 25 times faster than air of the same temperature, when it is choppy or there are swift currents, along with a blowing wind, the body's heat will be pulled away 35 times faster. Water chill is much greater than wind chill.

Everyone differs greatly in their ability to survive. Large people with ample body fat cool slower than small, thin people. Women cool more rapidly than men, and children cool the fastest. Of course, health, resistance, and the will to live are all contributing factors.

Treating hypothermia

Any person pulled from cold water or found on land when the classic conditions exist should be presumed to be in trouble. As one's temperature drops, the heart begins to slow, and the victim becomes weak and confused as less oxygen is delivered throughout the body.

Once the affliction begins, many people are unable to counteract the process by themselves. When the blood to the brain is slowed, the mind fails to function correctly. There are many symptoms, but it is usually the other person who recognizes them in someone having the reactions. Frequently the person experiencing the tell-tale signs becomes too disoriented to realize what is going on.

Ignore protests that everything is okay. Denial of being cold is common, and a hypothermic may truly believe nothing is wrong. Their judgment is impaired. They become drowsy, and usually want to drift off to sleep—but to sleep is to die.

Victims can range from appearing drunk or in a delirium, to acting desperate or combative.

Any of these reactions are probably a signal someone is suffering from hypothermia: difficulty with simple tasks (clumsy actions); dull eyes; listlessness; slurred speech; incoherency; confusion; forgetfulness; fatigue; an inability to control the hands, arms, or legs; stumbling; slow breathing; cold, stiff muscles; uncontrollable shivering or trembling; the stomach cold to the touch; apparent exhaustion; or someone dozing off and being hard to arouse.

Advanced stages of hypothermia render a person unconscious, the skin turns bluish-gray, muscles are rigid, breathing is shallow, and the pulse is weak. Rewarming is crucial, and medical assistance is necessary.

Do's and don'ts

What to do? Too often people try to help, and invariably do the wrong thing for someone who is hypothermic. There are certain "common sense" things you must **not** do:

- don't massage the arms or legs
- don't raise the legs
- don't put the person in hot water
- don't allow any type of exercise
- don't give alcohol or drugs
- don't administer hot drinks or hot food

What you should do is promptly get them out of the elements, cover the head and neck to prevent further body heat loss, remove wet or damp clothing and replace it with dry garments, keep the body warm to maintain the vital organs, and handle the person gently. Gentle handling is extremely important so as to not cause ventricular fibrillation—a condition when the heart quivers but does not pump blood.

Once it is determined a person is becoming hypothermic, it is essential others offer aid to prevent additional body heat loss. Skin-to-skin contact is an excellent way to transfer body heat. A field measure for rewarming is to remove all clothing and place the victim in a sleeping bag or in a blanket with one or two rescuers who have also removed their clothing.

If this is not possible, build two fires and put the person between them. Even better would be four fires, to surround them with heat.

If the victim appears dead, continue trying to restore body heat. Often hypothermics appear lifeless. Yet, their vital organs continue to function—but at a much lower rate—and they are alive. The medical adage is, "No one is dead until they are warm and dead."

Ever hear of "after drop?" This occurs with deeply hypothermics after they are moved to a sheltered spot. As a person is rewarmed, the stagnated and cold blood from the extremities returns to the core of the body, dropping the internal temperature even lower. Just as recirculation is started, death may occur.

When this happens, the official cause is frequently listed as something other than hypothermia. Those in cold water lose control of their arms and legs and drown, while those on land die of heart failure. Sometimes death is listed as "due to exposure," yet the real reason was hypothermia.

Prevention

Instead of hoping you'll be clear-headed enough to recognize the symptoms, know enough to prevent them. There are a number of things you can do.

When heading outdoors during questionable weather, dress properly. Several layers of loose clothing are better than tight clothes, and wool clothing traps body heat even when wet. Mittens are always warmer than gloves. Because much of the body's heat is lost through the head, a hat, cap, or stocking pullover will trap heat and allow your body to send more warm blood to your hands and feet. Most important, stay dry and change clothes if they become damp or wet.

One of the best safeguards against hypothermia is to eat hot meals and drink warm liquids before going out. This provides the nutrition and fuel your body needs to stay warm. In the field do not allow yourself to become dehydrated, and keep nibbling on high-energy snacks to help maintain body heat.

If weather conditions worsen, seek shelter wherever possible, and protect yourself from the wet, wind, and cold.

The best preventive maintenance against hypothermia is awareness. Everyone should put on rain gear before getting wet. For insurance, an extra set of clothing should be with you, in the camper, or at least nearby.

Outdoor enthusiasts—who frequently believe they are tougher than the other guy—should be able to recognize in advance the conditions that lead to the problem, and take the necessary precautions to avoid trouble. The savvy person also must be able to spot the warning signs in others in their group.

You don't have to be in the wilds of Hudson Bay, on the Alaskan tundra, or in a Montana blizzard to succumb to hypothermia. Given the right circumstances, you can become a victim in the Everglades of Florida, on the southwest deserts, or in (or out of) a rowboat on a favorite lake.

Hypothermia doesn't just happen to the other guy. We all need to know the danger signs. Δ

Section 2

Immediate Preparation

"The more you know, the less you have to carry.
The less you know, the more you have to carry."

— Mors Kochanski, Canadian bushcraft and wilderness survival instructor

Chapter 9
Impromptu shelters

How to stay warm and dry in an emergency

By Charles Sanders

Remember, emergencies happen. Whether you are camping, hunting, fishing, hiking, boating, or just traveling, there may come the time when you are thrust into a real survival situation. As a self-reliant type of person, you probably realize that there are times when we can not depend upon getting help exactly when we need it and must rely upon our own wits and skill to get the job done.

As a part of the Survival Basics Program that I present occasionally, I stress the importance of remembering the Rule of Threes. Generally speaking, an average human can go:

3 minutes without air
3 hours without shelter
3 days without water
3 weeks without food
3 months without companionship

In this article, I am going to deal with the second factor, namely, shelter.

In a survival situation, you have roughly three hours to find shelter. While this depends upon your location, your activity, the weather, and other factors, it is a good rule of thumb.

If you're hiking, or lost, or stranded and the sun is about to set, you want to make sure you have a good shelter to protect you from the cold. Even in warm weather, the nights can get cool and a windbreak or other shelter is very helpful. If you are sweaty or wet, heat loss will be compounded.

Make your shelter just large enough to accommodate you and not much else. This is important, especially in cold climates, because your body heat may well have to heat it.

Be extremely careful if you are going to use fire to heat the shelter, as most natural shelter materials are flammable.

Plan ahead, and use common sense. If you are hiking in a desert, you'll want a shelter to provide shade. If you are in a remote area, a small survival kit can be important.

Survival shelter items don't take up much space in a pack.

Most of the time, though, you'll be trying to keep warm. Use everything you can think of for insulation. Crawling inside a big pile of leaves or pine needles is actually pretty warm and comfortable (do not attempt this near a fire). The more, the better, as your goal is to create as much dead air space as you can to help insulate you from the cold and help reduce heat loss. A large pile of fresh pine sprigs is not only a springy mattress, but is good insulation from the ground. Again, the goal is to provide insulation. In this case, from the cold or damp ground.

If you have access to any lumber, limbs, poles, or the like, a simple wooden framework can be covered with a tarp, boughs and limbs, and even snow to provide protection from the wind and elements, as well as to help retain body heat.

Remember, shelter can include tents, tarps, old buildings, or automobiles. Even clothing is a type of shelter. Crawl in under a rootwad, a rock ledge (check for snakes), or old shed. Let's look at several other types of shelter that can be carried, worn, improvised, or otherwise created.

Clothing: This topic alone could fill the pages of a book. Suffice it to say that you should dress for the location, activity and expected weather conditions that you might encounter. Remember to dress in layers so that you don't overheat. You can add or remove clothing as your activity and the temperature warrants.

Poncho: The poncho is a fairly familiar type of shelter. They come in a wide variety of materials, sizes, and colors. From the inexpensive plastic ponchos found in the big stores, to those of lightweight rip-stop nylon, you should be able to find one that suits you. In my view, one of the best is the military style poncho. It is of ample size, has a drawstring hood, and has grommets and snaps around its edges. The grommets aid in securing it with lines when used as a shelter. The snaps allow two of them to be put together to make a larger shelter.

Space Blanket: The original Space Blanket® is a quality item. It is durable and offers a shiny, heat-reflective silver side with highly visible international orange on the other. It can be fashioned into a lean-to, a pup-tent-type of shelter, or simply used as a wrap to roll up in to retain body heat. It is hemmed and has grommets along its edge to aid in securing it as a shelter. I definitely recommend one of these for your kit. They cost around $20.

Mylar blanket: These inexpensive sheets are very handy to have in your G.O.O.D. (get out of Dodge) bag or other carrier. They are not much larger than a deck of playing cards and offer some protection from rain as well as providing some reflection of body heat. They can be found at just about any store that carries camping supplies and run only a couple of dollars apiece, making it easy to have several on hand.

Wool blanket: I still prefer wool as one of the best providers of warmth in a blanket, clothing, or covering. Wool is a natural fiber that can help keep you warm even when it's wet. Keep a surplus wool Army blanket or two stashed in a trash bag in the trunk or storage area of your vehicle.

Contractor garbage bag: These durable bags are simply made of heavier weight plastic and are much larger than those we use in the house. They can be used in a variety of ways including making an emergency poncho. Years ago, while fighting wildfires in the rugged mountains of Idaho, I had the occasion to utilize one of the heavy 50-gallon bags as an improvised rain poncho when a storm descended upon us. Yes, it does rain, even while fighting wildfires! By cutting a face-sized hole in one corner of the bag, it worked well and kept me and my gear dry. They don't take up much space, and one for each person in your party can easily be stashed in your Git-Kit.

Jungle Hammock: The venerable military jungle hammock deserves consideration as an emergency shelter. One of my uncles, who was also my wildcrafting mentor, once spent a summer living in a remote river camp where his only shelter was a jungle hammock. It served the purpose, but at summer's end, he did order a canvas wall tent for the next season.

The old jungle hammock is another piece of gear where we are seeing the old becoming new again. There is increased popularity among some hikers and campers of using hammocks instead of tents or other shelters. These trendy, new hammocks are made of lightweight nylon fabrics and weigh only ounces. They can fit into a pint-sized stuff sack with no problem.

Lean-to shelters: There are as many different types of lean-tos as there are people making them. Every situation has different challenges and conditions, and each offers different materials to use in constructing a shelter. Always remember to do the best you can, with what you have, where you are.

A lean-to can be constructed by draping a piece of plastic over a sapling or tree that you have cut nearly down. A cut pole can be lashed between a couple of trees and evergreen boughs can be laid, in shingle fashion, to help

These shelters are built low to help retain heat. The large log helps to reflect heat from the fire and serve as a windbreak.

A tarp made using a hiking stick for a center pole. Practicing in the backyard doesn't hurt.

create a roof of sorts. Be sure to start at the bottom and work upward with the tips of the boughs pointing downward. This will help direct any moisture down and away from the occupant.

Debris shelters: By debris shelter, I am referring to using leafy or vegetative debris commonly found in the woodlands. In a survival situation, these shelters can provide that slim margin needed. I have not used them much and must rely on mostly anecdotal accounts regarding their effectiveness. I realize and appreciate that a huge pile of leaves can help to retain body heat and would not hesitate to crawl into a big leaf pile if need be. Similarly, a shelter made by piling leaves atop a toppled evergreen or similar form could also serve as a survival shelter. While it could definitely protect a person from falling snow, I would not count on it being very effective in the event of rain.

Regardless of the type of shelter you construct, it's a good idea to add as thick a layer of leaves as you possible can. They will go a long way in insulating you from the cold or wet ground.

Snow caves: Other than making the rare igloo in the front yard for the kids, I must admit that I have no experience in constructing or using a real snow cave. We just don't usually get that kind of snow here in Southern Indiana. I have studied them somewhat though and believe that they are effective when constructed properly, preferably with a mounded up sleeping bench to keep you up and out of contact with any melting snow. In addition, the snow cave should have a ventilation hole to allow for some movement of air. As with other types of shelters, the key is to get out of the wind and minimize heat loss. Δ

Chapter 10
Start a fire in any weather

By Charles A. Sanders

Most of us living in the backwoods are comfortable with utilizing fire as a tool. We use fire to heat our homes, burn brush, power our forges, help clear land, smoke meat, and cook our hotdogs at picnics. My grandma used to use kerosene-soaked corncobs to get the fire going in the kitchen range each morning.

But we also know that we may someday be in a situation where our ability to build a fire might determine whether we live or die.

If you often trek the backroads or travel to the backwoods while hunting, fishing, trapping, camping, or hiking, the ability to build a fire under any condition is a necessity.

Fuel

There are three types of fuel: tinder, kindling, and larger wood (sticks, limbs, and logs).

Fuel to start a fire needs to be dry. Most of the time, this is not a problem. It's easy get a fire going on a nice sunshiny day, but what about on a cold, windy, rainy, miserable day? I taught my kids to always look on the lower branches of small cedars and pines for the tiny, dry, dead twigs needed to start a fire. Even in snowy or rainy weather, these lower limbs are much drier than most other fuels available. In my area, Sassafras is another good choice for getting a fire going. It ignites quickly, and burns hot, albeit fast.

Tinder

Tinder is the material used to get the fire going initially. It can be tiny twigs and sticks, wood shavings, or even a mouse's nest. The important thing to remember is that the smaller the fuel, the easier it is to ignite. The tinder has to be dry. This obvious fact can become a real problem on a rainy or snowy day.

One easy solution is to use a "fuzz-stick" to help get the fire going. A fuzz-stick is made by simply taking a dry stick and cutting into it with your knife — making shavings along the length of the stick, but leaving them attached. Make several of these and lay them in place in preparation for lighting your fire.

Birch bark is an excellent fire-starting aid. If you are in birch country, simply peel off several of the loose pieces of bark. The stuff ignites easily and burns with a black smoke that indicates its oily content.

Kindling

Kindling is best described as wood larger than the tinder and up to thumb size or so. Again, find the driest wood you can. Any limbs that are up off the ground will be your best bet. Those can be dead limbs on trees or fallen limbs that have gotten hung up in shrubs and brush on the way down. If you gaze across a piece of woodland, you can easily spot limbs and small wood that is up off the ground. Gather all of it you can.

Trees like this red cedar usually have plenty of dead limbs and twigs on the lower portion of the tree for use as fire-starting fuel.

Larger wood

Cut or chop into the innards of a large piece of dead wood and you'll find plenty of dry fuel to help get your fire going.

Softwoods such as conifers will usually ignite easily and burn quickly — good for getting a fire going.

Hardwoods such as oak, hickory, and birch are harder and denser than softwoods. They are more difficult to get going, but they will burn longer. These types of wood make good "night fuel" when you want the fire to burn for a long time and leave a bed of hot coals.

Although some woods are better for burning than others, in a must-have-a-fire situation, look for *any* type of dry wood.

Laying the fire

Back when I was a Boy Scout, I learned three or four different ways to "lay the fire," or arrange the tinder, kindling, and larger wood prior to igniting it. Experience has taught me that this is one of the most important parts of fire building.

My preferred method is to use a small chunk of wood (three or four inches in diameter) as a back log. I usually try to place it so that it breaks the wind as I start the fire. Directly in front of this piece, I place the tinder. Next, I pile on small twigs and sticks. I pile them with one end on the wood chunk, slanting on and over the fine tinder. Then I add pencil-sized sticks and have the rest of the kindling and fuel wood standing by.

Once you have the tinder going, blow to further ignite the fuels. Long, gentle puffs will encourage the flaming tinder. With practice, you will learn exactly what "gently" means in the context of fire building.

Add kindling and progress up to larger sticks and limbs.

In situations where you must use damp wood as fuel, be sure to put it on a well-burning blaze and remember to add just a piece or two at a time, so that it can dry a bit and ignite before piling on more damp wood. It takes a lot of the fire's heat to dry the wood to the point where it will ignite. That also causes the smoke associated with burning damp wood. A fire made with dry wood will give off practically no smoke.

Fire starters

Matches

The first and most common method of igniting a fire is with an ordinary kitchen match. I keep pill bottles of them stuffed in my pockets — at just about any time, I have a container of kitchen matches on me somewhere. Buy the "strike-anywhere" matches and not the "strike-on-box" type.

Alternative fire starters

Trappers, snowmobilers, and others who travel in cold or wet weather usually include some type of fire-starting aids in their kits.

- A tuna can filled with a long coiled strip of 1-inch-wide cardboard with paraffin poured over it makes a good fire starter.
- Dip cotton balls in petroleum jelly and carry several in a 35mm film can or pill bottle. They burn easily and will last for several minutes each.
- Ordinary snack chips contain huge amounts of oil and can help get your fire going. They will burn by simply holding a match to them.
- Alcohol-based hand sanitizer can be used to start a fire. The higher the alcohol content, the better it will burn.
- Fusees or road flares can help in really tough situations. Backwoods motorists often keep several of these in their vehicles for emergency signaling and fire starting.
- Carry a half dozen or so of the light-with-a-match charcoal briquettes in a plastic zip bag. These little chunks are impregnated with charcoal lighter fluid and will light easily.
- Place a paper toilet paper roll in a ziplock bag. Inside the cardboard tube, stuff some dryer lint. The cardboard tube will ignite easily, as will the dryer lint. Both are lightweight and easy to pack.

I also keep several books of "damp-proof" matches left over from MREs stashed in my pockets as well. These are easy to keep tucked in a pocket or pouch. You won't know they're there until you need them.

Magnesium

An excellent fire starter is a variation on the old flint and steel method. The modern version, called a Metal Match, is simply a small rectangular chunk of magnesium with a flint-like striker on one edge. Use a knife to scrape a small pile of shavings off the magnesium block onto a piece of paper, a leaf, or a similar object. Then, use the knife to scrape the striker, creating a shower of sparks. When the sparks hit the magnesium shavings they will ignite and burn furiously for several seconds, long enough to ignite the tinder you have prepared. These devices are available in generic form as well. They cost around five dollars, so it is easy to keep one stashed away in your vehicle, your get-home pack, and your hunting coat.

> **Tips**
>
> - Fine, dry fuel will get a fire going fast. The dead and dry lower limbs and twigs from cedars, pines, and other conifers work well. With fire building, smaller is always better, at least at first.
> - Gather only dead wood that is up off the ground. Wood absorbs a great deal of moisture when in contact with the ground.
> - Be redundant — keep a variety of fire starters available.
> - Practice building a fire under a variety of conditions. That way, you'll be prepared for the worst.

Disposable lighters

I also keep a few disposable butane lighters in backpack pouches and in survival kits. These are inexpensive, waterproof, and dependable.

Magnifying lens

Just for practice, I have used magnifying lenses to start campfires. On a bright day, you will be surprised just how quickly you can get fine fuels blazing with a little magnifying glass.

It's a good idea to keep two or three different fire starters in your pack or kit. In fact, it is wise to have some tucked away in different places. That way, if you lose one pack or pouch, you will have alternative fire starters available in a different location.

Conclusion

Practice your fire building skills *before* they are needed. Get out in the snow and try to start a fire. Head out during or after a rainstorm and perfect your pyrotechnic know-how. The ability to build a fire under adverse conditions or in bad weather is just another part of backwoods living. Δ

Chapter 11
The fire wick fire starter

By Len McDougall

When my hunting buddy Dar met me for lunch at our rendezvous point, he said he doubted we could make a small cookfire on the wet, snow-covered ground. After a hot meal of canned pork-and-beans and instant coffee, our innards were rewarmed, and he was very interested in the tinder I'd pulled from my daypack.

In a wilderness environment, no ability is more likely to save your life than fire-making, regardless of latitude or season. Air temperatures below 98.6° F steal body heat, especially with the added cooling effects of wind and rain; smoke repels insects, and can be seen from a long distance; flames are a fearsome thing to most animals; and the ability to cook wild flesh (never eat raw fish) insures that any parasites are dead. In one respect or another, fire is vital to human survival, and when not being able to make one might equal dying, every trick in the proverbial book is fair.

The fire starter my friend had been impressed by employed the simplest technology to create a cheap, waterproof, easily-lighted tinder that has been part of every survival kit I've owned for the past two decades. In my youth I'd employed the classic woodsman's trick of using a candle to ignite damp tinder materials, but while the technique worked as well for me as it had for Kit Carson, it became evident that an entire candle was overkill. All that was really needed to get even wet tinder flaming was a candle wick saturated with enough paraffin to make it burn hotly for the minute or two needed to create a self-sustaining fire.

The most basic type of "fire wick" consists of nothing more than thick cotton laundry or packaging string that has been saturated with molten paraffin, allowed to cool and harden, then cut to the desired lengths. The string used must be cotton, never nylon or any other type of synthetic, because these not only don't burn well, but emit noxious fumes while burning. Cotton string is usually found in the housewares aisle, priced at about two dollars for one hundred yards.

In the simplest process, a ten-foot length of cotton string is lowered carefully into an old saucepan containing a pound of paraffin (canning wax) that has been heated to a liquid by a camp stove or hotplate. Paraffin is sold in supermarkets for about one dollar per pound. Or you can melt down the stubs from used candles, which works just as well for making fire wicks, but imparts to them whatever scents or dyes were in the candle wax.

Shown here burning atop hardpack snow, fire wicks might be the best fire-starting tinder available — but you have to make them yourself.

Always take sensible precautions when melting paraffin; do the job in a well-ventilated place where there is little risk of fire and plenty of fresh air. Wear heavy gloves (not latex or rubber) when handling molten wax, and never allow the paraffin to get hot enough to smoke, because this is a warning that it is about to catch fire. If the melting pot does burst into flames, don't panic; the flaming wax is still safely contained. Simply cover the pot with a loose-fitting lid, which will smother the fire, and turn off the heat. Even with the heat off, the wax will remain liquid for a half hour or so.

The next step is to pluck one end of the string from the melting pot using pliers (wear your gloves, too)—always do this in a place where you won't mind a few wax drippings. Pull the string outward in a straight line, allowing it to drag over the rim of the pot, until the entire length has been extracted. Hang the wax-soaked string over a convenient nail or rail until it cools and hardens—usually about 15 minutes. The cooled strings will be stiff enough to lay across a cutting board and cut into sections using a sharp knife, or with sharp scissors. I package the completed fire wicks into "tinder bottles" adapted from pill bottles, 35mm film canisters, or just zip-lock bags, and scatter the hundreds I generally make at a time throughout my gear. My backpack and survival knife sheaths carry fire wicks, but you'll also find them in my kayak, my vehicle's glove box, and next to my wood-fired smoker grill. I even carry them in the toolbox, where they've come in handy for re-lighting gas furnaces and other pilot lights.

In most instances, a single-strand fire wick is all that's needed, but sometimes I prefer a thicker, longer-burning tinder. To accomplish this, I use a twist-lock doubling technique that has been used to make rope from plant fibers since primitive humans discovered that skill. Just twist the string in a single direction until tension causes it to coil around itself when pull from either end is relaxed. Hold the twisted string taut while folding it in half to bring the two ends together. Slowly ease tension on the doubled string, allowing it to wrap evenly around itself like a small rope. This doubled (or quadrupled if you repeat the twisting process again) cord can then be dipped into molten paraffin, cooled, and sectioned to make thicker fire wicks that burn twice as long.

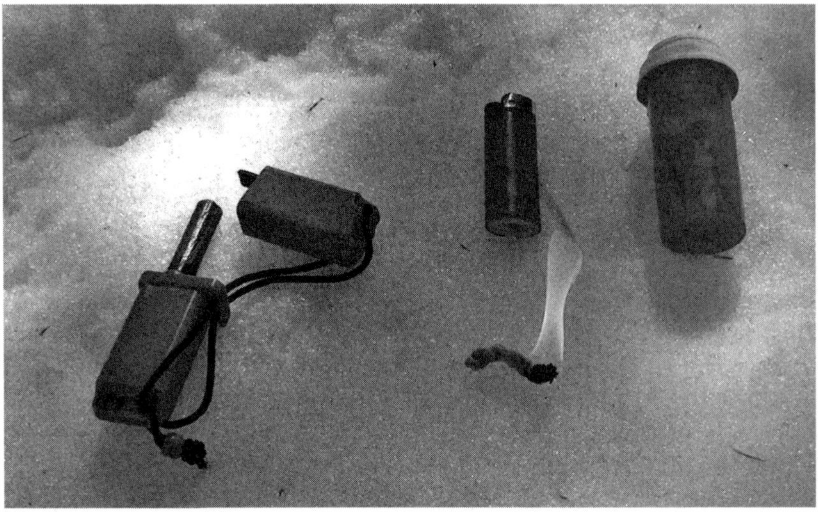

The Strike Force flint-and-steel, a butane lighter, and fire wicks kept together in a container; throw in a little fire-making know-how, and this pocket-size kit virtually guarantees fire in any weather.

A good alternative to cotton string is wool felt weatherstripping, or old felt pac-boot liners cut into sections. Fire wicks made from felt produce longer-burning fire because they absorb more paraffin, and ignite nearly as well as those made from cotton string. Again, use only felt made from pure wool, because some is comprised of synthetic fibers that not only don't burn well, but emit soot and toxic gases.

To use a fire wick, you'll need an initial source of combustion. A butane or liquid-fuel lighter is recommended survival gear at all times, but I've had little trouble igniting a well-frayed fire wick using only sparks from the Strike Force flint-and-steel in my knife sheath. The trick is to fray one end of the fire wick into a small airy mass that flames at the touch of a lighted match. Lay the lighted fire wick onto a small platform of sticks to keep it from being hampered by evaporating ground moisture, add more fire wicks as needed, and slowly build a tepee of pencil-thick dead twigs around its perimeter. Add larger sticks as the fledgling fire grows, until you've achieved a crackling blaze.

Considering the value this simple yet very effective fire starter has had for me through many years of survival classes in pouring rains and heavy snowstorms, when not having fire is simply not an option, I'm surprised that no company is manufacturing fire wicks. Until someone does, I'll keep making and using my own because the fire wick has earned a place as a must-have item in my own never-fail fire making kit. Δ

Chapter 12
The poor man's ultra-light dual-fuel backpacking stove

By Rick Brannan

For as long as I have been venturing into the backcountry, which is a pretty long time, I have been on a quest for the perfect backpacking stove. I have tried everything from the ultra-light micro stoves that run on butane to the cumbersome and messy white gas stoves, none of which I really liked. On a long hike I inevitably run out of fuel for my camp stove and have to hike off trail to restock or spend the rest of the trip eating granola bars and jerky.

The campfire is still best for cooking, but there are times when a campfire is not practical or legal, like during fire season in the national parks.

The wood burning stove

While surfing the internet, I finally hit upon a solution. *Bushcraft Northwest* had an article by Mike Lummio that shows how to convert a folding Sterno stove into a wood burning stove.

The advantage of the Sterno stove is that it's light and folds as flat as road kill. When folded out it has a luxuriously large burner grate that will support an eight-inch frying pan. The conversion was simple too. Bend the prongs, which are designed to hold the can of sterno, out straight to hold dry kindling. Place a sheet of aluminum foil under the stove and load it with pine cones and dry twigs. Let it burn for a few minutes, adding to it, until you have a nice compact bed of coals, then flip up the lid and cook away.

Now, no matter how long my trek is, I have a ready source of fuel for the stove that I don't have to lug on my back. It burns hotter than any butane or propane stove, and the wide cooking surface gives a broader heat distribution under the pan making it cook more evenly and faster.

The alcohol stove

But I decided I wanted a dual-fuel stove. Several websites I found showed how to make an alcohol stove out of pop cans. Apparently, a lot of through-hikers on the Appalachian Trail use these. I gave it a try, but was only marginally impressed. It barely put out enough heat to boil a cup of soup.

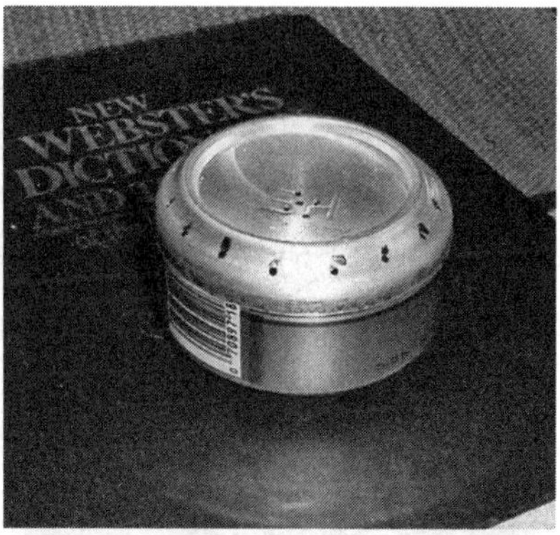

From top, left to right: Rotate the beer can against the razor blade for an even cut. Drill holes evenly around the edge of the second beer can, then drill a few fill holes in the center. Place a piece of fiberglass insulation inside the bottom can before pressing the two halves together. The stove puts off plenty of heat to boil a cup of soup.

After some trial and error I was able to improve upon the idea and ended up with a great little stove for the price of a couple of beers, which of course I consumed while making the stove.

The best can I found for making an alcohol stove is a 25-ounce Foster's beer can. This can has the largest circumference of any other can I have found, and it holds a significant amount of beer. You may want to invite someone over to help with consumption, since it does require two cans.

Another improvement is the type of fuel. Rubbing alcohol doesn't burn as clean or as hot as I like, and can be difficult to find if you are popping into civilization only periodically to re-supply. Methyl alcohol burns clean and hot and is available whereever you find an auto parts store or gas station.

The completed stove

Even most convenience stores carry it. It comes prepackaged in plastic bottles under the name "HEET," and is used to de-ice fuel lines.

I also carry a 3-inch-long 2x4 block of kiln dried wood to set my alcohol stove on to get it closer to the pot. Kiln dried wood is light, and I shave it for some instant tinder when I burn wood in the stove.

This little stove combination is compact and only weighs about 15 ounces, including the 2x4 block. I carry about 1/3 less fuel, since I can usually burn wood instead of alcohol. It burns hotter and is more stable than the micro-stoves which are precarious when trying to balance a pot of boiling soup on their tiny little burners. And with this stove, there are no spent fuel cans to pack out and dispose of, just a little ash to scatter.

Now, when I wander off the trail back into civilization I often find I don't even need to buy fuel since I haven't had to use any alcohol. But there are times, after a long day of trudging through the rain, when I don't feel like scouting around for dry tinder, so I just fill the alcohol stove and cook up a cup of soup while under my rain tarp.

The total cost is 12 to 15 bucks, plus the price of a couple of beers.

Make it

two 25-ounce Foster's beer cans
drill and 5/64-inch drill bit
razor knife blade
a large heavy book
strip of fiberglass insulation

1. Drain one of the beer cans. Place the razor in the book as shown and hold the can against the razor as you turn the can. This will ensure an even cut all the way around. Don't try to cut through the can on the first pass. Just keep light pressure and cut the can like a pipe cutter. This piece will be the bottom of your stove.

2. Take the cut piece and push onto the bottom of the unopened beer can. Work it around to expand the mouth of the bottom piece. This will make it easier to insert the top of the stove which is what you will make next.

3. Now you can go ahead and drink the other beer. When it's drained, but before you cut the can, invert and drill holes around the perimeter of the can. Next, drill five fill holes in the center. No need to measure. Eyeballing it is close enough.

4. Cut the second can as before but make it about 1/8 inch taller since this piece will slide into the other and you want the lip of the bottom to be below the top of the burner.

5. Once cut, place a strip of fiberglass insulation around the bottom piece. You can now carefully slide the top inside the bottom. Once you get it started, rotate as you squeeze the halves together with your hands. It will snap each time you squeeze, which lets you know to rotate to the next position. When it stops snapping and it looks like it's all the way on, it's done. Some of the internet demos show sealing it with JB Weld, but it isn't needed. You couldn't get the halves apart if your life depended on it. You can now fill the stove with HEET and fire it up. Make a dish out of foil and dribble a little HEET around the burner. This will heat the burner and it will self-start. It doesn't take much, so be frugal. Δ

Chapter 13
Treating wild water

By Robert Van Putten

I used to be one of those outdoors men who never filtered or treated water at all. When I happened upon a wilderness water source where a fellow traveler was industriously pumping away with a filter I'd march right up, chug lustily directly from the source, and joke about drinking from muddy hoof prints as I filled my canteen. In decades of backpacking, canoeing, and cycle touring America and a few other countries I've never had any problems. Not everyone is as lucky or resistant. On a recent trip my wife contracted Giardia and it took two courses of antibiotics to rid her of this tenacious parasite. It was time for me to take a good hard look at treating "Wild Water."

For more than 20 years I worked as a project engineer at a systems integration company specializing in municipal water and wastewater. I'm familiar with large scale equipment but knew nothing of portable water filters.

So I did some checking. These things come in a bewildering variety at a wide range of prices. The top of the line can filter down to .02 microns (a micron is a millionth of a meter, the period at the end of this sentence is about 500 microns across) and actually meet the EPA "Purifier" standard. Reasonably priced filters might strains things down to .2 microns, 10 times larger, and at the bottom of the price range are a few one micron filters, with pores fifty times bigger than the top of the line units. Some operate at high pressure with complicated pumping systems, some use gravity, and some you suck water through. Some are easily damaged by freezing, some have silver particles bonded to the filter, some have layers of charcoal or iodine resins, and many tend to be heavy, bulky, complicated and sooner or later suffer from clogging and mechanical failure. Which to get? Time to consider

What's in the water

Naturally there are hordes of mini-monsters lurking in every drop of water. Most are of no concern but there are a few bad guys that can cause trouble. The largest would be some of the Nematodes which are one of the most prolific lifeforms on our planet, with over a million species. The ones to watch out for are the various round worms, liver flukes, and tape worms. These things don't get smaller than about .3 millimeter, so are easy to filter out. Next down are the single celled protozoans. There are strains of Acanthamoeba everywhere. Mostly harmless, but for the rare case of amoebic encephalitis, and one strain can infect your cornea if you clean your contact lenses with tap water, much less wild water. Some amoeba host Legionella bacteria, which causes legionnaire's disease. These blob-like critters run as small as 15 microns, still easy for any filter to catch.

The two primary threats to wilderness travelers in America are the protozoan intestinal parasites Giardia and Cryptosporidium. These critters live in the guts of many animals and produce millions of cysts or eggs which find their way into water where they are consumed by others in what is known as the "fecal-oral cycle." Giardia has been known for about 200 years and used to be considered harmless. According to the World Health Organization as many as 20 percent of children in day care centers may carry Giardia and excrete cysts without symptoms. But, as my wife can confirm, it can be a real gut-wrencher. Cryptosporidium is the new kid on the block and he's moving fast. Discovered to infect humans in 1975, waterborne infection was confirmed for the first time in 1984 and in 1993 it caused the largest outbreak of waterborne disease on record, when more than 400,000 people were infected by the Milwaukee water supply. There are other species that cause trouble in other countries. The good news is none of these cysts are smaller than about 4 microns, and most are rather larger. The cheapest filters on the market catch all of the above easily. So why bother with the finer filters?

Well, next down in size are the bacteria. To many to list them all, some of the highlights are; Good 'ol E. Coli (turista), Shigella (bacillary dysentery), Salmonella (typhoid), and Vibrio Cholera (cholera). This last bug was a 19th century import from the Ganges delta in India and has killed thousands of city dwellers in America. It's the reason we started treating municipal water with chemicals, and is unusual in that it has very few hosts, just some brackish water plankton, contaminated shellfish, and us. No doubt it was introduced by humans eating raw shellfish, as my Dad used to do. Some of these bugs are more usually associated with person to person contact and contaminated food but all have been known to take advantage of the waterborne fecal-oral cycle as well. Roughly speaking, bacteria runs about .2 to 4 microns, and this is why the .2 micron filters were invented.

But wait, we're not done yet. Viruses are the smallest lifeforms known, and technically run as small as .004 to as big as .1 micron. Some of the more dangerous are the various strains of Hepatitis, Poliovirus, and Rotavirus. These are not a big concern in American waters (yet) but are real bad news in places like India, Nepal, parts of Africa and South America. These things are so small that filters traditionally offered as much protection from viruses as did straining the water through your front teeth. Yet we now have filters that are so fine (pores of about .02 microns) that they can catch many dangerous viruses. OK, now we know why filters come in the sizes they do. But before choosing one it may be wise to take a look at

Other methods of disinfection

Bringing water to a rolling boil for 10 minutes will kill almost all lifeforms within, every time. (Various spores, such as the clostridium spores, which cause botulism will *not* be killed. However, the spores will pass right through you. However, do not expect to can with the water unless you also intend to pressure can or can high-acid foods.) Considered to be an awkward method at best because of the time and fuel needed, I've inadvertently done this a great many times as I'd boil a quart over camp stove or twig fire and toss in a tea bag for my afternoon brew-up.

One disinfection technology that has recently become available to backpackers is Ultraviolet Radiation. You stick a long narrow UV bulb into your water bottle, close your eyes (don't look!) and turn on the light for 30 seconds. Disinfecting water could hardly be easier, and UV radiation has been used for decades in some large scale systems. The deal breaker for me is the battery life of these devices which limits their use to short trips for a single user. Then there is chemical disinfection. Three chemicals are used, Chlorine, Chlorine Dioxide, and Iodine. The good news is that all three kill bacteria and viruses at low concentrations of the disinfectant chemical. The bad news is none of them work well against the bomb-proof protozoan cysts and very high concentrations are needed for even partial effectiveness against the likes of Giardia and especially Cryptosporidium.

Chlorine is used by municipal systems, but not by campers because it has serious drawbacks. In dry form it is considered too perishable, in liquid form too bulky and inefficient as it is mostly water, and its effectiveness is limited by turbidity, organic material in the water, low temperature, or high pH. These factors can be monitored in municipal systems but not in the field. Because chlorine produces numerous nasty chemical by-products it is wise to use as little as possible to get the job done. For municipal systems the EPA recommends a level of .25 ppm (Parts Per Million, which is the same as milligrams per liter) and municipal water systems I've worked with run about that or less, and try not to get above .4 ppm or customers complain of chlorine fumes in the shower and pool-water taste. For emergency use, the CDC recommends two drops of unscented household bleach per quart which results in a chlorine concentration of somewhere between .5 to 1.5 ppm. Pools are supposed to run 1.5 to 2.5 ppm of chlorine. The EPA lists an "MRDL" of 4 ppm for chlorine. This is the "Maximum Residual Disinfectant Level," the highest concentration of this chemical allowed in drinking water. To be effective against protozoan cysts in cold water and at a high pH value, 8 ppm of chlorine is needed, twice the maximum legal level. Lower levels are effective at warmer temperatures and lower pH.

Chlorine Dioxide is widely used by backpackers but by very few municipal systems because it is expensive. It does not produce nasty by products and is less affected by temp and pH. Available in pill and liquid form, when used as directed it produces a concentration of 4 ppm, and it needs four hours to kill protozoan cysts. Four hours is a long time to wait for a drink, but that's not my main concern. For this chemical the EPA lists an "MRDL" of only .8 ppm. In other words, when used as directed we get a solution with 5 times the maximum legal level of this chemical.

Last is the old standby Iodine, which is not used in municipal systems because it accumulates in the human body, and the EPA does not list an "MRDL" for it. 1-2 ppm of iodine is considered adequate for bacteria and viruses with a ½ hour contact time. Iodine pills produce a concentration of about 8 ppm when used as directed, and even then it is generally not considered effective against Cryptosporidium. Some people are allergic to iodine, and it isn't recommended for pregnant women or people with thyroid problems. It isn't considered safe for long term use at high levels, and will eventually produce swelling of the thyroid gland. It can be deactivated after the proper contact time by adding ascorbic acid (vitamin C), which converts it to iodide and precipitates it out of solution, and iodine and ascorbic acid tablets are sometimes sold together. Note that many drink mixes contain ascorbic acid, so don't add them until well after the recommended contact time.

Iodine is not affected by pH, organic materials, or ammonia and thus may be a better choice for some sources. Importantly, it can also block the uptake of radioactive iodine (can you say Fukushima?).

My choice

By now you've probably reached information overload. After considering all of the above I made my choice.

As my wife and I are chiefly concerned about protozoan intestinal parasites, an inexpensive one micron filter is all we need. I bought one sold by Coghlan's for eleven dollars. Should it ever be necessary in an emergency to dip water from a less than ideal source I'll also use a low concentration of chemical disinfectant. I picked iodine tablets for their long shelf life (when unopened. Replace every season if you open the bottle) and for the ability to block the uptake of radioactive iodine.

Hiker's friend

I didn't get the water pump that goes with it because I figured that for less coin I could make something more reliable, lighter and versatile, called a Hiker's Friend.

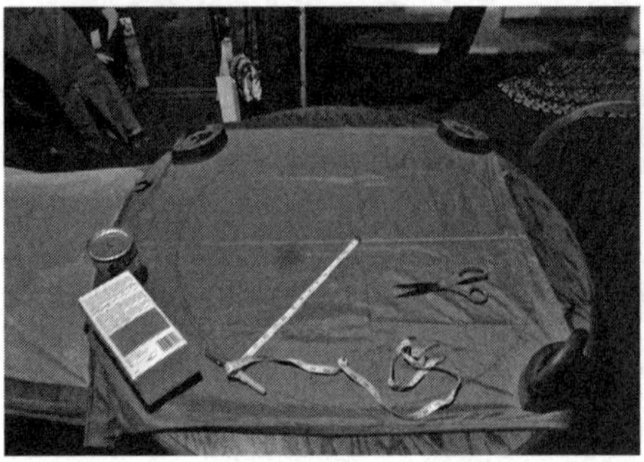

Laying out the circle

Adventurer Ray Jardine invented this system in 1987 and describes how to make them in his book *Trail Life*. Like all of Ray's ideas, it's light, easy to make, and works well. It's nothing more than a hanging water bag, a filter, and a length of hose. I made mine from waterproof nylon taken from the door flap of a worn-out tent. Start by laying out a 30-inch circle on the fabric. Cut it out, sew eight little web tabs around the edge and thread six feet of paracord through them to gather the circle into a bag and hang it. Don't bother to hem the cut edge of the circle, but you can use a cigarette lighter to flame the edge. Next I attached seven and a half feet of ¼-inch soft plastic tubing to the outlet of the filter. Done! A more elaborate waterproof bag isn't needed, and would be heavier and take longer to dry. Total weight, just under six ounces. To use, fill the bag with water and hang. It holds about two gallons. Put the filter in the bag and suck on the end of the tube to start the water flowing. Lower the tube and siphon away. The filter will tend to float but I find that it doesn't matter. Be sure to leave a bend in the tube below the mouth of the container you're filling so that any drips of unfiltered water that run down the outside of the tube do not enter the container. The flow rate is about a quart every two minutes.

After use it's a good idea to back flush the filter by blowing the water left in the tube back through the filter. Spread the bag out on a bush or rock to dry, and wrap the filter and tube up in it when done. I carry it in a mesh pocket on the outside of my pack where light and air can get at it to further drying. A wet filter weighs almost two ounces heavier, and it takes at least four days in a warm and dry environment for it to drop back to its original weight. This raises the concern of bacteria growth in a dark, wet and warm filter cartridge, and is why some have silver particles inside. So be sure to dry it out completely after a trip. To add chemical disinfection to this system, fill the bag with about two gallons of water and add a single iodine tablet for a concentration of 1 ppm, and wait at least a half hour before filtering the water out. The longer you wait the better, especially with cold water. In the event of a serious nuclear disaster, block the uptake of radioactive iodine by dissolving two tablets in a quart of water, and drink two quarts daily (four iodine tablets a day in water, never, ever swallow a tablet!). Continue this dose for at least seven days but not longer than 90. The Hiker's Friend has other uses as well. It can be used as a carrying bag for extra cargo or groceries when

The Hiker's Friend in use

visiting a trail side store, the tubing is ideal for use in a solar still as is the circle of waterproof fabric which can be used to catch the condensate, and of course the paracord has plenty of uses.

There are commercial gravity filters on the market but this one is cheaper, lighter, and has a higher flow rate because of the "coarse" 1 micron filter I used, which nevertheless removes the bugs I'm worried about. All filters quickly clog with silt, so use water only from clean sources. Remember that just because one has a filter, this does not mean you can drink from anything with impunity, and highly polluted sources should be avoided if at all possible. Stagnant water collects a high level of contaminants as does water downstream of industry, population centers, and heavy agriculture. Livestock in particular is notorious, and water downstream of livestock will be heavy with protozoan cysts and coliform bacteria. Agricultural runoff contains fertilizers, pesticides, herbicides, and feedlot wastes, and should always be avoided. Some filters have layers of activated charcoal that can bind with some chemicals to remove them from the water, but all filter systems have their limits.

One last concern I must mention is that the freedom of the hills shouldn't include freedom from personal hygiene. On every trip I come across clumps of used toilet paper close to water sources and surrounding popular camp sites. For goodness sake, please go 200 feet from water or camp and scrape out a shallow hole when answering the call of nature. Take along not only toilet paper and maybe something to dig with but also a water bottle and soap to wash with. Open the soap and water before you squat so you don't fumble them with dirty hands. Some of the primary vectors of both protozoan and bacteriological infection is person to person contact (never shake hands with a filthy backpacker) and by eating with dirty hands. It is ironic that when sojourning in the wilderness and during disasters the first thing forgotten is hygiene, yet this is precisely when good hygiene is most important. Anyway, the system I came up with does what we need it to, and at less than half a pound and under $20 it can find a home in every backpack, bug out bag, and survival kit. Δ

Selected Resources

• Jardine, Ray.
Trail Life: Ray Jardine's lightweight Backpacking.
25,000 miles of trail tested know-how.
AdventureLore Press, 2009

• The Center for Disease Control and Prevention
A guide to drinking water treatment and sanitation for backcountry and travel use
www.cdc.gov/healthywater/drinking/travel/backcountry_watertreatment.html
Many links and information covering a wide range of topics

• World Health Organization
Guidelines for Drinking-water quality.
Fourth edition, 2011
An excellent 564 page report. If you read the chapters on Microbial Aspects and Microbial Fact Sheets you'll drink nothing but beer for the rest of your life. Can be found by following documentation links, along with lots of other good info, from here www.who.int/topics/water/en/

• National Primary Drinking Water Regulations, Table of Regulated Drinking Water Contaminants
United States Environmental Protection Agency
www.epa.gov/ground-water-and-drinking-water/table-regulated-drinking-water-contaminants
This handy chart shows all contaminants the EPA tracks, (including disinfectant chemicals), possible sources and potential health effects. Also lists the National Secondary Drinking Water Regulation, and lots of other good info can be found at the EPA web site.

• Homer J. Lemar, William J. Georgitis & Michael T. McDermontt
Thyroid adaptation to chronic tetaglicine hydroperiodode water purification tablet use
Journal of clinical endocrinology and metabolism, 1995, vol 80, no.1
www.ncbi.nim.nig.gov/pubmed/7829615
Studies the long term use of iodine tablets and documents blocking the uptake of radioactive iodine.

• Edward L. Jarrol, Alan K. Bingham & Ernest A. Meyer
Effects of chlorine on Giardia Lamblia cyct viability
Applied and Environmental Microbiology, Feb, 1981
www.ncbi.nim.nih.gov/pcm/articles/pmc2437201/
How to kill Giardia with chlorine.

Chapter 14
Ten day survival pack for your vehicle for just $25

By Jeffrey R. Yago, P.E., CEM

It seems like every winter there are news stories of people getting stranded for weeks in bad weather while driving through the many remote areas of our country. In fact, this past winter, our nation held its breath waiting for news of James Kim and his family who got lost traveling the snowy roads of Josephine County in Oregon, not far from where this magazine is published. While his wife and daughters, who stayed with their vehicle, were eventually found alive, he succumbed to the cold as he hiked through snow looking for help for his family. And there are also many cases of people trapped for days in their vehicles after skidding over a bridge embankment, even though they were only a few hundred feet from a busy highway.

I have written many articles about how to prepare your home for a power outage or national emergency, but today I want to address how to be prepared for an emergency when traveling in your car or truck.

Keeping warm and safe

Warmth, of course, is a major concern in cold climate and snow emergencies. Since you'll be with your car, you'll have that as protection against the elements. but extra clothing (preferably wool), some blankets, and a sleeping bag will keep you warm if you arc stranded for several days. Store these items in a plastic trash bag in your trunk or behind the seat of your pickup. I recommend wool clothing because it sheds moisture, just in case you have to leave your car during wet or snowy weather. It's no fun being stranded *and* cold, and hypothermia is a real danger in cold weather.

If stranded, you may not want to run your vehicle heater for very long so you can conserve gasoline. But if you do run your car engine to operate the car heater, be sure you aren't breathing in carbon monoxide fumes from the exhaust. In a snow emergency, you must make certain that the car's exhaust pipe is not clogged with snow, and be sure the exhaust is not being sucked into the car through an open window at the rear of the vehicle. Opening a front window a bit will help admit fresh air into the passenger compartment. You can't smell carbon monoxide, so don't rely on your nose.

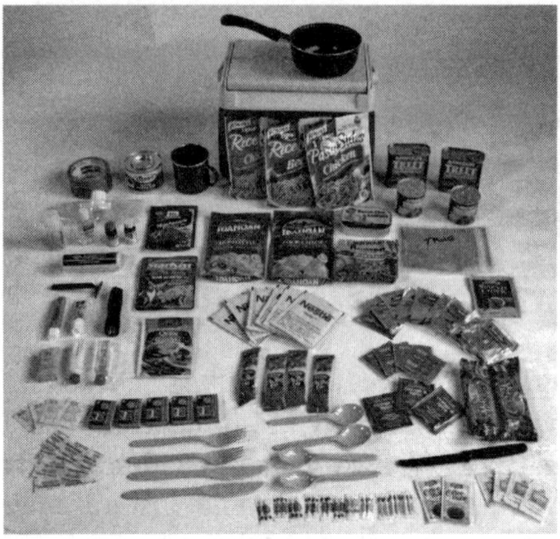

A 10-day supply of dehydrated food and drink mixes, medical supplies, and cooking equipment fits easily in a small plastic cooler.

Finding supplies

Once you've ensured you and your family will be warm during a car emergency situation, you need to ensure you'll have enough food and drinking water. I realize that not everyone lives near a camping or sporting goods store stocked with all kinds of really great fold-up and lightweight camping equipment. Substitutes for many of the specialized camping equipment and freeze-dried foods you will need can be found in most grocery stores, if you know what to look for.

The two biggest complaints I hear from people when it comes to buying emergency supplies are the high cost for items they may never actually use and the need to replace out-of-date food that was never eaten. Yes, those tasty freeze-dried, ready-to-eat meals from most camping stores are expensive, and yes, many may never actually be used. But that is also true of buying a fire extinguisher, as you don't intend to ever actually use it either, but it's a real life saver if you do.

To address these high-cost concerns and the difficulty to locate camping stores that stock hard-to-find survival equipment, I decided to assemble a 10-day emergency food supply by shopping only in a typical chain grocery store, and I kept the total cost under $25. This is very cheap insurance if you travel through areas where you would not want to be stranded, and you will not be out that much if you have to occasionally replace items that have reached their expiration date.

Drinking water supply

A person can actually live many days without any food, but your body must have drinking water. This is easy to solve by tossing a few plastic gallons of bottled water in your vehicle's trunk, but these will not last long during an extended crisis, so an additional source of water is available by using purification tablets to treat any available surface water. For less than $5 you can purchase a bottle of tablets that will completely transform almost any water source into safe drinking water.

Unless you are stranded in a desert, you can usually find water somewhere, even if it's from a drainage ditch, creek, lake, or melting snow. You can use one of the empty gallon water containers to hold the collected surface water while you add the tablets, which will kill off all the bacteria and harmful organisms in about 30 minutes.

Select only dehydrated foods that can be prepared by adding hot water.

Food and drink mixes

When it comes to stored emergency food, you want meals that are easy to prepare, use little or no cooking equipment, and tastes good. Since you could be injured or trapped, you want to keep it very simple. You may have limited trunk space and may have to carry this emergency food supply some distance if you must leave your vehicle, so you want to keep its size and weight to a minimum. This means you need to buy foods that are highly concentrated and only require hot water to prepare.

There are many drink mixes and dehydrated food packs that are inexpensive and can be found in any large grocery store, although they are not actually advertised or sold as emergency or camping supplies. Be sure to check all expiration dates and purchase only the newest stock. Most of these recommended products can provide good nutrition and taste variety over many days. The packaged meals I am recommending are sold in individual moisture proof foil pouches and require only a cup of very hot water to reconstitute into a tasty hot meal that will serve two people.

As you start shopping for the food items I have listed, you may find different items you would like to add or change. Just make sure they only require hot water to prepare and still provide a good variety.

You may also want a few things to eat that do not require any hot water or cooking. Several small sealed packages of beef jerky and trail mix or candy bars are a good choice. However, avoid any foods or snacks that contain ingredients like chocolate, which can melt when stored in a heated car trunk.

Heating foods and drinks

No matter what brands and types of "instant" meals and drink mixes you purchase, you will need an easy way to heat water. The water can come from gallon jugs of bottled water you hopefully remembered to bring along in your trunk, or from creek water or snow you heated or chemically treated with the purification tablets. Since most of these meal packets are sized for one to two servings, each will require only one or two cups of hot water. It would be nice if you could find enough dry twigs and sticks lying around to actually build a campfire each night, but this will be impossible in a blizzard or heavy rainstorm.

Since you would be living out of your car or truck cab during this emergency, you will need a simple way to boil water inside or outside the vehicle. Your emergency food supply should include a large handful of "strike-anywhere" kitchen matches, but these are becoming very hard to find due to endless government safety regulations, so you will probably only be able to buy "safety" matches that must be struck on the side of the matchbox. Camping stores offer all kinds of low-cost fire starting and cooking products, but again, I am assuming you are only able to buy supplies from a nearby grocery store. Place your matches in a discarded prescription drug bottle or empty baby food jar to keep them dry. Those lucky enough to find "strike-anywhere" matches can dip the heads in melted candle wax, which makes them virtually waterproof.

For heating water inside your vehicle or on a car hood, you will need a metal container of "canned" heat, typically sold at grocery stores to keep food serving trays hot. If you have the space, keep several handy, but one should last several days and is reusable, thanks to an air-tight cap. Please use good common sense when burning canned heat inside any vehicle, small tent, or storm shelter, and make sure it is placed on a solid, non-flammable surface. You must leave a window open enough to prevent asphyxiation, and keep clear of any other fuel containers or gasoline leaks.

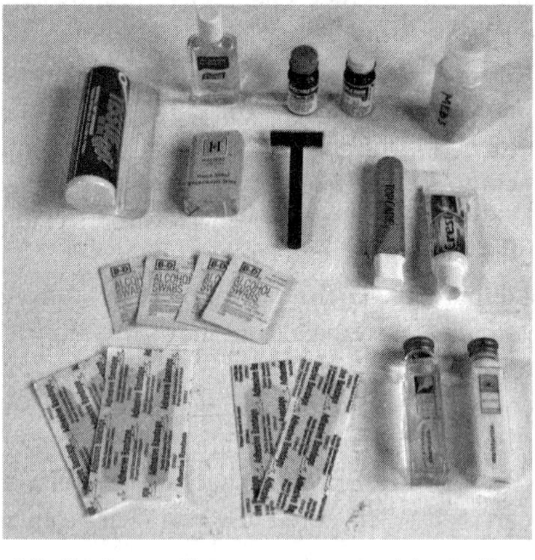

Medical supplies you may need including water purification tablets, toilet tissue, band aids, and travel-size hygiene supplies.

I found a small, lightweight saucepan that cost $5 and an enameled-metal coffee cup for $4 at a Wal-Mart, and either will serve our purpose. Make sure any water-heating container you buy has a sturdy handle that will allow holding over an open flame without burning your hand, as you will not have a

Canned heat and an enameled-steel cup is all you need to boil water.

stove-type surface or fire grate. I was able to heat a large cup of cold water to more than 180° F in just six minutes using the inexpensive enameled-metal coffee cup and canned heat as shown in the photo. It was not that hard to hold the cup for this length of time, and the handle remained fairly cool.

Camping stores sell fold-up metal supports for this canned heat, but these supports are not usually stocked in grocery stores. And I really like the stainless steel cups with long sturdy fold-up handles that will keep your fingers away from the flame, but again, these are sold only in camping supply stores.

You need only one or two cups of water at a time, so you will not want to hold a large pan full of water over a fire for very long. Your saucepan or metal cup will most likely also serve as your "plate" to eat from after preparing a dehydrated food packet. However, if you have extra trunk space, it's really nice to have some paper plates and paper towels along, which store forever if kept dry. Most dehydrated food packaging uses strong Mylar or plastic coated aluminum-foil construction, and some brands may even allow adding the hot water right into the pouch. You must carefully cut off the top and support the pouch on a solid surface to prevent tipping over. Do not try to hold a food pouch in your hand while pouring in boiling hot water or you may scald yourself.

Most pre-packaged meals require the water to be extremely hot, so you may need to stir the mixture and let slightly cool for a few minutes before eating. Since you can heat only one cup of water at a time, you may want to prepare your meal first. You can then refill the cup with water after eating to make hot water for coffee, tea, or hot cocoa to sip as you try to relax while waiting for the storm to end or rescuers to arrive.

Non-food items needed

Your emergency food pack will need a few items you should already have around the house or farm that you can re-use. These include some eating utensils and a really good locking-blade pocket knife or small kitchen knife. I also suggest taking a discarded prescription medicine bottle and filling it with a mixture of aspirin, Tylenol, Unisom, Benadryl, and Advil caplets, which should get you through most minor medical emergencies. If you really want comfort, for another $5 you can purchase travel-size packages of toothpaste, shampoo, hand lotion, toilet tissue, bar soap, hand sanitizer, some first-aid supplies, and a disposable razor.

While you are putting your emergency pack together, save up all those free packets of salt, pepper, and condiments they toss into the bag at every drive-through restaurant, as these will also come in handy for emergencies. If you don't have a spare flashlight, purchase one of the new small LED-type flashlights that use three AAA-size batteries. These flashlights are small and very bright, and will operate weeks on these tiny batteries.

A 50-foot roll of 1/8 inch nylon rope and a 10x10 ft. plastic sheet are very handy for many emergencies. And finally, don't forget that roll of duct tape.

You will need a container to keep your emergency food supply clean and protected from all those field mice that manage to get into any car or truck that contains food. You want a container that is fairly inexpensive and sturdy, includes a carry-handle, and could have other emergency uses like something to carry water. I recommend buying a small "6-pack" style plastic insulated cooler. Their small size and durable construction are perfect for keeping foods safe in a car trunk or behind a truck seat. Be sure to duct tape the lid shut, as most do not include a latch.

Finally, toss in a few self-tie kitchen-size plastic trash bags. They take up almost no room, and are a great way to store your discarded food and trash, which will reduce problems with waste smells and insects. Δ

Chapter 15
My peppermint tin survival kit

By Kim Robertson

Years ago, I came across a tin of mints imported from England. They had all-natural ingredients and did not melt under extreme temperatures (or when stored in a pack or glove compartment in a car). I was hooked!

But I especially loved the funky, hinged tins in which the mints were packaged. Every time I emptied one, I tried to think of another use for it. I have used them to store tea bags, sewing pins and needles, and loose change. I hate to do it, but when my supply of tins gets too big, I recycle them.

The plan

I have become a big fan of survival books and magazines over the past couple years. One day, I thought, "Why can't I make a peppermint tin survival kit?" Within days, I had a new obsession.

I gleaned advice from several sources, my favorite being the *SAS Survival Handbook 2E* by John "Lofty" Wiseman (published 2009 by Collins, NY, NY). I rummaged through my fishing tackle, workshop, studio, and kitchen in search of useful items to pack into the tin. I then scoured hardware stores, dollar stores, craft stores, drugstores, and sporting goods stores, looking for gear for my kit.

Contents

The kit has had several incarnations to date. The earliest were just small tools and gear placed in the tin, which I then sealed with duct tape around the lip. The current version is wrapped with Day-Glo orange duct tape, topped and bottomed with more duct tape.

The tea bag is for comfort and morale. The cotton swabs are for first aid, tinder, and cleaning. The glass signal mirror is attached to the lid with double-sided tape. You can also polish the inside of the lid for a more reflective signaling surface. The craft blade can be used as a scalpel and the salt and sugar are to help balance electrolytes.

Labeling

On the top of the tin, I write a list of all the contents with permanent marker. I then take the extra precaution of sealing the writing with clear

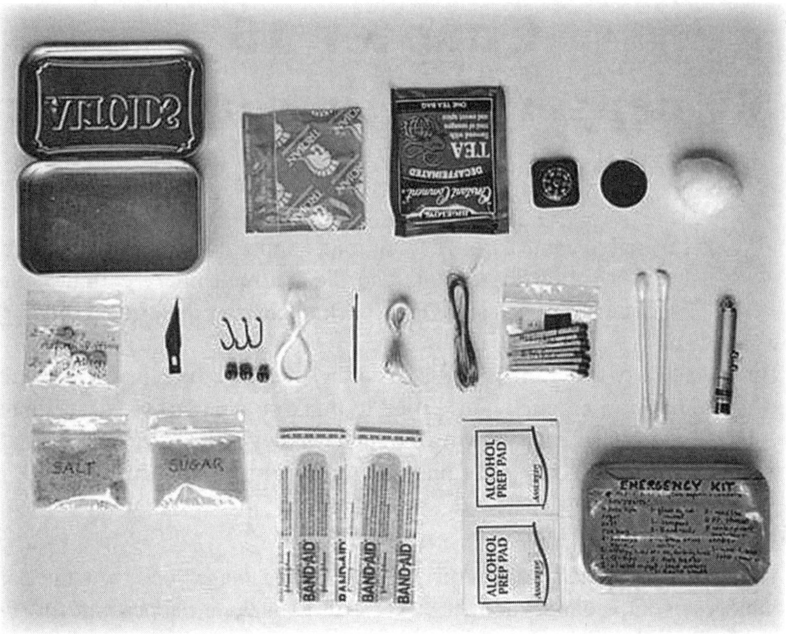

***Top row** (left to right): empty peppermint tin, non-lubricated condom, tea bag, compass, signal mirror, cotton ball.*
***Middle row**: 2 allergy tabs and two 325 mg aspirin (in bag), hobby knife blade, 3 fish hooks, 3 lead sinkers, 10 feet #4 fishing line, 2 sewing needles, 8 feet sewing thread, 10 feet 28-gauge brass snare wire, 8 waterproof matches with striker pad (in bag), 2 cotton swabs, 1 micro LED light with laser pointer.*
***Bottom row**: 1 bag real salt, 1 bag organic sugar, 2 band-aids, 2 alcohol wipes, and a finished kit, covered with duct tape.*

packing tape. I also write an expiration date so the owner can open it and replace the aspirin, allergy tabs, and condom with new ones.

On the bottom of the tin, I write hints for use. They are:

1) Use the cotton ball for tinder.
2) Condom holds up to 1 quart water.
3) Needle and thread make good temporary sutures.
4) Duct tape is flammable. It makes great fire starter tinder. Also use it to close wounds, mark trails, or as a bobber for fishing.

The entire survival tin measures 2½ inches high by 3¾ inches wide by 7/8 inches deep. It weighs only 3⅛ ounces filled and fits just about anywhere. I have made eight of these kits to date. My husband and I always have one with

Here is a photo of the finished kit filled with all its contents.

us and we have extras in our bug-out bags. I have given three away to friends, one of whom is a Vietnam War Marine Corps veteran. He liked it enough to add it to his pack, which is a great endorsement because he knows survival tactics for real.

I always keep a lookout for more small-scale tools and goods to improve my kit. I found my mini-LED flashlight, including the batteries, for $1. I purchased packs of 100 miniature, plastic, ziplock bags at a local "superstore." The mirrors were 25 for $2.99 at a craft store, and I only spent $2.59 for six liquid-filled compasses at the same location.

While price is a consideration, I never sacrifice safety and quality. Why include items that will fail to work when I need them most? I always test my gear before it goes in my kit.

Cost

I estimate that the total cost of my peppermint tin survival kit is about $4 (exclusive of the original mints purchase). Now that is what I call a sweet survival bargain! Δ

Chapter 16
Power your bug-out bag

By Jeffrey R. Yago, P. E., CEM

More and more people are starting to see the advantage of having a bug-out bag for each member of their family. Normally these bags are kept in a closet near the front door with everyone instructed to grab theirs if forced to evacuate due to an approaching forest fire, tornado, chemical spill, or other disaster. Most preppers will also keep an additional bug-out bag in each car or truck in case disaster strikes while they are away at work or school.

There are numerous articles and books describing what each bug-out bag should contain so I will not repeat that advice here. I will point out, however, that a bug-out bag is not a camping backpack designed to hold a tent and a week's supply of food. The main purpose of any bug-out bag is to contain just enough emergency supplies and equipment to evacuate from where you are to a safer location when disaster hits. A bug-out bag for someone living or working in a city might include a fold-up dust mask, loud whistle, Bic lighter, thermal rain sheet, and universal tool; while a camping backpack may not include any of these emergency items.

For example, a city street map, state highway map, compass, and GPS device would be indispensable when trying to escape a disaster area, but not if you were heading out to a favorite campground. As for food, a bug-out bag will typically have a few high-energy bars, some beef jerky, and bottled water to hold you over if you have to walk 20 miles when all normal vehicle travel has stopped. However, a camping backpack would have a multiple-day supply of freeze-dried foods, fold-up cooking equipment, and eating utensils.

Most weekend campers enjoy getting away from the noise of city life and do not want radios, cell phones, and electronic devices. However, these electronic devices could save your life by receiving weather alerts, providing travel directions, and communicating with relatives during an emergency evacuation. In other words, traditional campers do not normally require power to charge electronic devices, but this ability is mandatory for a bug-out bag. In addition, while most of us rely on our cell phones for calls, text messaging, surfing the Internet, and even streaming live radio and Internet news programs, a cell phone can fail or be out of range. Don't rely on a single device for all your emergency evacuation and communication needs.

In addition to your cell phone, you will want a compact AM/FM radio, preferably having an earpiece instead of a larger speaker. Without a speaker

New rechargeable 130-lumen Black Diamond LED headlamp

Most portable radio devices are available with optional car chargers.

7800 mAh capacity Goal Zero battery pack with multiple USB charging outlets

these radios can be made very small, lightweight, and will operate far longer on a small set of rechargeable "AAA" or "AA" batteries. While it's doubtful you will normally keep your iPad in your bug-out bag, grabbing your battery-powered computer along with your bug-out bag as you head for the door will be extremely useful, especially if it includes both wireless Bluetooth and cellular Internet access.

Most campers typically pack a large flashlight and lantern to illuminate a tent, but a small LED light with headband would be far more practical in a bug-out bag, especially if you need your hands free while hiking. Finally, most car GPS devices have a "walking mode" which provides block-by-block city and mountain trail hiking directions when not in a vehicle. While all of these electronic devices are perfect additions to any bug-out bag, they still have limited run time on their internal batteries. This means having a way to keep them charged is mandatory, especially if your evacuation requires multiple days of travel.

The first way to keep these portable devices charged can be the 12-volt DC dashboard outlet in every car and truck, if available (and you are not on foot). You will want a charger for each of these devices that fits this 12-volt DC vehicle outlet. Since small LED flashlights, digital cameras, and AM/FM radios are normally powered by multiple AAA or AA batteries, you will need a multi-battery charger that can charge four batteries at the same time. Of course, you will need to replace any disposable batteries in each device with new rechargeable batteries, and you should also have a spare

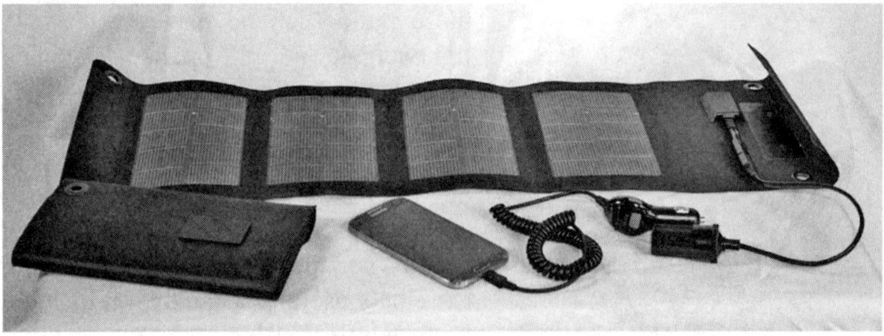

Most fold-up solar chargers come with multiple charging adapters.

set of batteries that can be charging at the same time the other set is being used.

Another must-have item, thanks to recent advances in battery technology, is the rechargeable battery pack. The smallest models are typically used to give a cell phone several additional hours of run time. However, there are now larger models available that can actually start a car, yet are not much larger than a paperback novel. These typically have a USB charging port which will fit almost any cell phone or iPad charging cable and will provide many hours of additional run time.

Last, but not least, is a fold-up solar charger. These are typically sold in 5, 7, 10, 12, and 25-watt sizes, with the smallest ideal to recharge a cell phone. The large fold-up solar modules can power a laptop computer or emergency radio transmitter.

Most fold-out solar modules designed to charge a cell phone, laptop, or other electronic device are normally stationary and need to face the sun during the charging process. When you are stopped for any length of time, the modules can be removed from the bug-out bag, unfolded, and placed on any surface facing the sun.

However, in addition to a smaller solar charger, I recommend adding one of the fold-out solar modules designed to clip to the outside of a backpack or bug-out bag. Most models include a lightweight, but high-capacity, battery pack allowing this

This 7-watt Goal Zero solar module comes with multi-battery charger.

"Hide-in-plain-sight" book bags and gym bags make excellent bug-out bags.

battery to be charged the entire time you are on foot, assuming it's not at night.

Weight is a very important consideration in deciding what to include and what to leave behind for any backpack or bug-out bag. All of the powered devices I have described are lightweight and fold up to very compact sizes and offer enough flexibility to fit into tight spaces.

While less important for a normal camping trip, having communication and mapping devices in a bug-out bag and multiple ways to keep them charged could save your life someday. Since you may need to utilize several different chargers and charging cables, it's a good idea to verify you have the charging cables and adapters to connect each to multiple sources of power. It's also helpful to standardize on the same size battery, with the larger AA being your best choice when selecting flashlights, radios, walkie-talkies, and other devices with removable batteries.

For example, you can find some brands of LED flashlights and portable radios that require the small AAA flashlight batteries, and others using the much longer-life AA size batteries. If all of the devices you purchase use the same size battery, that is one less battery charger and charging cable to pack.

Keeping a cell phone charged is your main priority since it can provide online maps, directions, and communication, but you need a backup in case cell phone service is out or you are out of range. Also remember most mapping and turn-by-turn direction software running on a cell phone or iPad require constant updating by satellite or cell phone service as you travel from one zone to the next, and if this communication is lost, your primary source of travel information may also go down. Do not forget to pack a fold-up city, county, and state map for the areas where you will be traveling in the event of a major "get-out-of-Dodge" event.

Summary

Having a bug-out bag is really important if you live or work in a large city, in which case a book bag or gym bag is a perfect solution. Either of these would appear to be carrying nothing of value and would be far less likely to be stolen or attract unneeded attention in a panicked crowd, while a large camo backpack screams, "Get your emergency supplies here!"

In addition to the small electronic devices and chargers I am recommending, each bug-out bag should be stored along with a really-good pair of walking shoes and absorbent socks. If you do need to evacuate you will be on foot since most forms of public transportation may be blocked. Work boots and tennis shoes are not designed for miles of walking over all types of terrain and should be avoided.

While I hope you never are faced with a situation where you will actually need your emergency bug-out bag, there is great peace of mind knowing it will be there silently waiting if you do. Stay safe.

Jeff Yago is a licensed professional engineer and certified energy manager with more than 35 years of experience in the energy conservation field. He has extensive solar and emergency preparedness experience and has authored many articles and texts. His website is www.offgridprepper.com. Δ

Chapter 17
How to suture skin

By Joe Alton, M.D.
and Amy Alton, A.R.N.P.

In modern society, we have relinquished many important duties to those with special training. If you have a clogged drain, you might call a plumber; if you have an electrical short, you might call an electrician. It stands to reason, therefore, that you should call a surgeon when you need surgery. In the aftermath of a disaster or in a remote setting, however, we may find ourselves without access to modern medical care. In such a situation, we will regret the loss of those forgotten medical skills with which every pioneer was acquainted.

Suturing is best done by someone with experience, but where can one obtain this kind of education outside of medical schools? You won't get that kind of knowledge from your typical first responder course. Aside from classes that a few medical professionals teach to those in the preparedness community (yours truly included), you'll be hard-pressed to find suturing or stapling classes in your area. Yet, you must obtain some know-how to be able to function effectively when closing a wound.

Here's a practice session that will give you an introduction to suturing. Remember the practice of medicine without a license is illegal and punishable by law. If you have access to modern medical care and experienced professionals, seek them out.

In the last issue of *BHM* (Issue #137, Sept/Oct 2012), we went into detail about something even more important than knowing how to close a wound: *when* to close a wound. Please review that article carefully before attempting any suturing on a live patient. Suffice it to say that most wounds in a disaster or wilderness setting will be "dirty;" that is, they will have significant debris and bacterial contamination. It is extremely important to thoroughly flush out fresh wounds with antiseptic solution or, at least, with clean drinkable water.

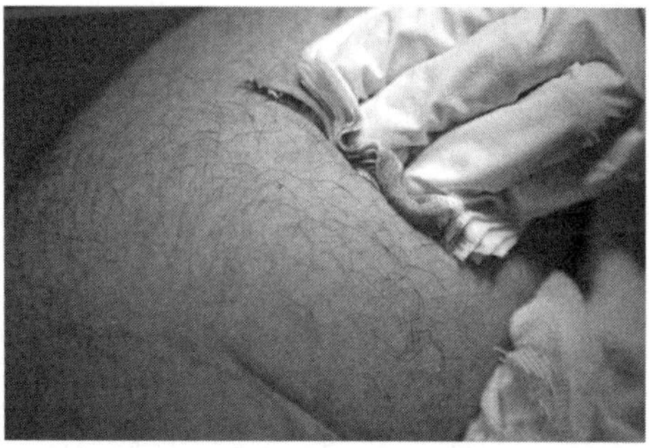

Laceration

Don't close obviously infected wounds; they will appear red,

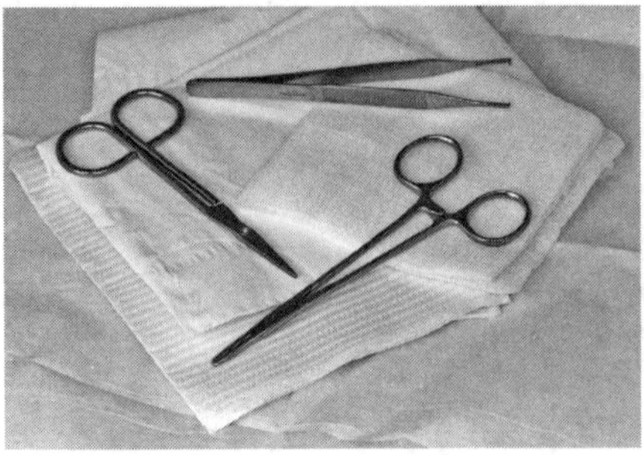

Three-piece suture kit

swollen, and hot to the touch. If these wounds are closed, there is a high risk that they will not only worsen, but that bacteria will find their way into the circulation (sepsis) and become life-threatening.

When you close a wound, you cannot leave pockets of air in deep layers of fat or muscle. These are areas called "dead space" and are highly prone to infection. If you see a deep wound, consider how many layers of closure would be needed to approximate all lacerated layers. You may need to use different types of sutures for each layer. There are various suture materials to choose from. A good choice for suturing skin would be nylon, which is permanent and must be removed later. Other permanent materials include Prolene, nylon, and silk. There are other suture materials that are absorbable, such as chromic "catgut," which disappears after 2-3 weeks, and Vicryl (Polyglycolic acid), which disappears after 6 weeks or so. These are best used on deeper layers.

Suture material comes in various thicknesses: 0, 2-0, 3-0, 4-0, 5-0, and 6-0 are most commonly used on humans. If you own a shotgun, you'll notice the similarity to buckshot: 0-thickness, for example, is sturdiest, while 6-0 is very fine and is used in delicate cosmetic work such as the face. The heavier suture has more strength, but the finer suture leaves less of a scar. For our purposes today, we'll use 2-0 nylon, which is easy to handle and long-lasting.

Let's assume that you have cleaned out a fresh wound and you are certain that it is not currently infected. You have considered closure with lesser methods such as Steri-Strips tape, butterfly closures, and medical glues and find the wound too large to be closed in those ways (too bad — they are a lot less traumatic than suturing or stapling). You will have to break out your precious supply of suture materials or the skin stapler. Let's discuss the ins and outs of suturing skin.

Suture kits are easy to locate and purchase at various online sites, and are usually comprised of the following items: a needle driver, a forceps (looks like tweezers), gauze pads, scissors, and sterile drapes to isolate the area being repaired. Some type of antiseptic solution such as Hibiclens (Chlorhexidine) or Betadine (Povidone-iodine solution) will be needed. Gloves, preferably sterile, will also be needed. Always ask about allergies first, as some people have reactions when exposed to latex. Nitrile gloves might be preferable.

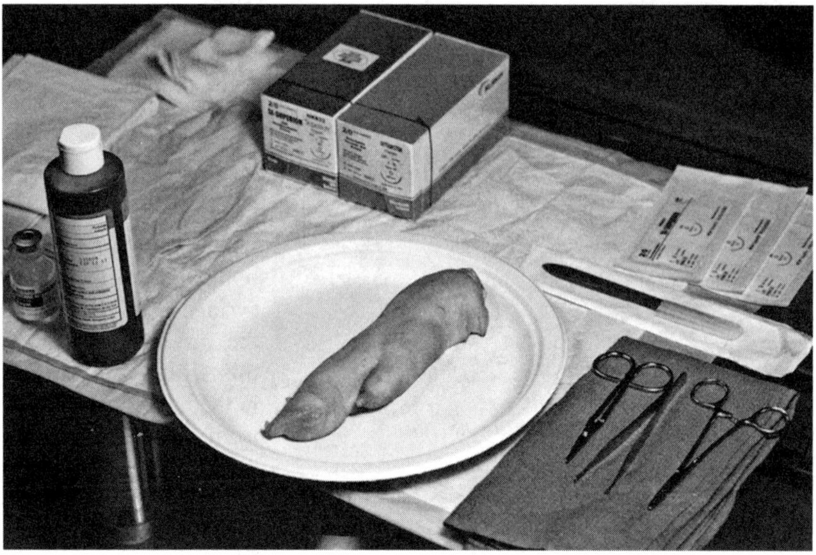

Suturing equipment

Of course, you'll need a patient. While various templates have been used on which to practice suturing, pig skin is probably the closest thing you'll find to human skin, although it is somewhat tougher. Many supermarkets carry pig's feet, which are what I use to teach suturing to my students.

As you follow this article, refer to the images below and/or access our YouTube video called, "How to suture with Dr. Bones." This video goes through the entire process in real time with narration.

Defrost and wash your pig's foot thoroughly. After placing it on a level surface, use an antiseptic solution to wash your hands and forearms. Standard surgical scrubs last from 3-5 minutes: Longer for the first scrub of the day, shorter for subsequent scrubs.

Now, put your gloves on. If you have the luxury of a gloved assistant, they can help you put them on without your having to touch the outside of the glove. You will then perform a "skin prep" (paint the area to be sutured) with a Betadine 2% solution or other antiseptic. Alcohol may be used if no other antiseptic is available. Start cleaning at the laceration edge and then work your way outward in an ever-widening oval all around the wound.

Next, you will isolate the "prepped" area by placing a sterile drape. The drape will usually have an opening or "fenestration" in the middle so that you can expose the area to be sutured or stapled. This is called the "surgical field." Although you are suturing a (deceased) pig's foot, I'll describe the process as if you are working with living tissue.

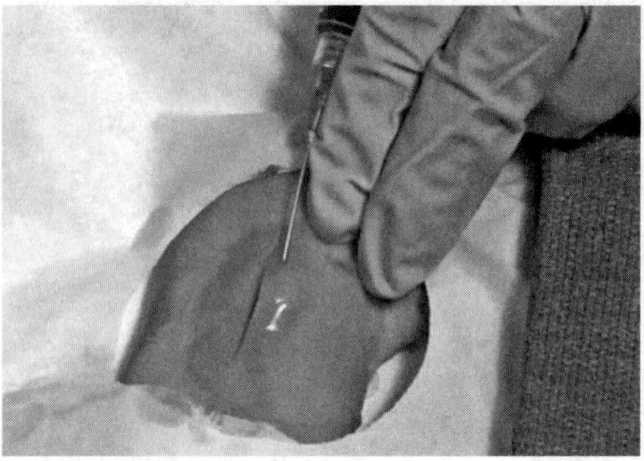

Administering local anesthetic

Assuming your patient is conscious, you would want to numb the area with 1% or 2% Lidocaine solution (available by prescription). Use an alcohol wipe on the end of the bottle, then fill a small syringe with air. Inject the air into the bottle; this will cause pressure in the bottle, causing the local anesthetic to fill the syringe. Place an injection at a 45 degree angle to the skin with the open end of the needle tip (the "bevel") up. Puncture the skin, then angle the needle so it is parallel with the wound and advance the needle as far as possible. Then, inject as you draw out to form a raised area on each side of the laceration (see figure above). This is known as a wheal. Within a few minutes, the area will be numb. Be careful not to inject into a blood vessel, as this could be dangerous.

If you lack Lidocaine, you can apply ice to the area to be sutured until sensation decreases. Most anesthetic creams and ointments are lacking in strength for suturing purposes. Veterinary Lidocaine has been proposed by some, but there are several additional ingredients in veterinary Lidocaine. Although labeled as "inert," I can't recommend veterinary Lidocaine as it is not the exact same solution as the human version. As such, prepare for some discomfort on the part of your patient.

Now, open your suture package and use your needle holder to grasp the curved needle therein. Remove it and the attached "string" from the package. Now adjust the needle on the needle holder so that it is perpendicular to the line of the instrument. If you are holding the needle holder in your right hand, the sharp end of the needle should point to your left (opposite for left-handers). For the best command of the suture, the needle should be held at the midpoint of the curve (see figure below).

Now take your forceps (tweezers) and grasp the edge of the right side of the laceration (left, if left-handed) near where you wish to place the stitch. Insert the suture needle at a 90 degree angle to the skin and drive it through that side of the laceration with a twist of the wrist (see top figure on next page). Your puncture of the skin should be away from the lacerated skin edge by the width of the head of your needle holder.

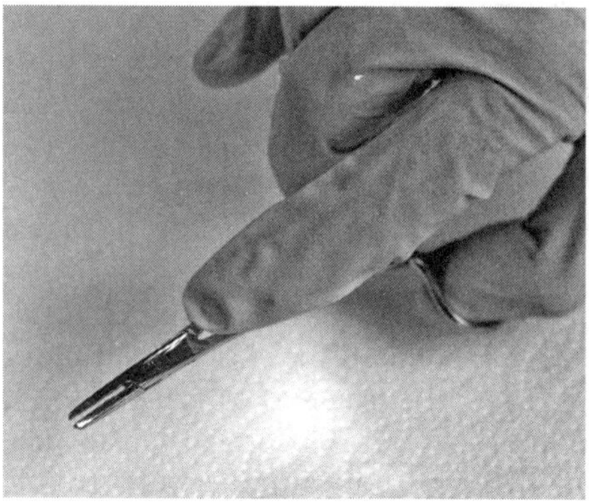

Suturing pronated

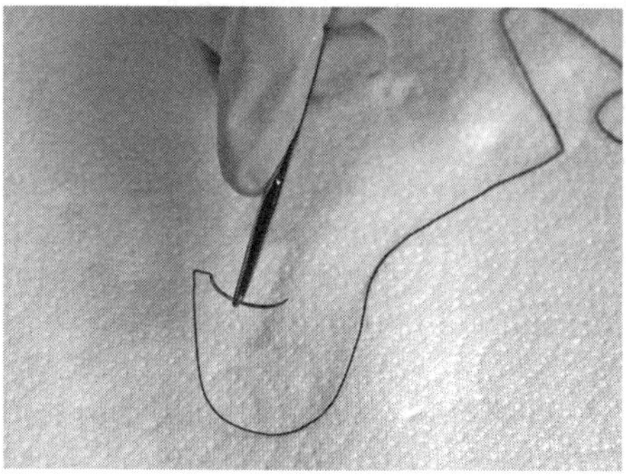

Suture needle in place

Release the needle and reclamp it on the inside of the wound and pull it through. Replace the needle on the needle holder and, going from the inside of the wound, drive the needle with a twist of the wrist through the skin on the other side of the laceration. Pull the string through, leaving a 2-inch length for knot-tying (the shorter, the better). You will end up with a long length of suture with the needle at the end of it and a very short end.

Now, about knots: There are various ways to tie knots in wound closures. The method that saves the most suture material while placing the most knots for closure integrity is the Instrument Tie. Placing the needle holder over the wound, wrap the long end of the string once or twice around the end of the needle holder (see figure above). Many place two loops on the first knot, and then one loop on all subsequent knots.

Open the needle holder end slightly and carefully grab the very end of the 2-inch length (see figure above), then clamp and pull it through the loops tightly to form a knot. Repeat this knot at least four times per stitch.

Finally, grasp the two ends and cut the remaining suture material ¼ inch from the knot with your suture scissors. Place each subsequent suture about ½ inch apart from the previous one, even closer if over a joint.

It's important to tighten your knots only enough to close the wound. The pressure on blood flow from a knot that is too tight can prevent healing in the closure. You can identify sutures that are too tight easily: They will cause an indentation in the skin where the string is. To finish your procedure, paint it once again with Betadine solution and cover with gauze and tape. Monitor the progress of the wound closely. Any dirty wound is a candidate for antibiotic therapy.

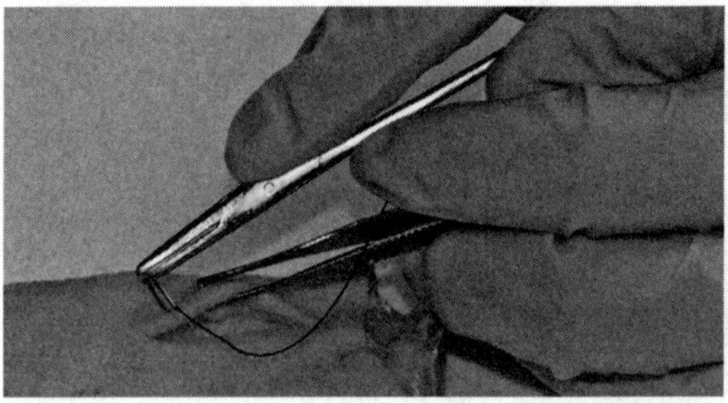

Correct angle to start suturing

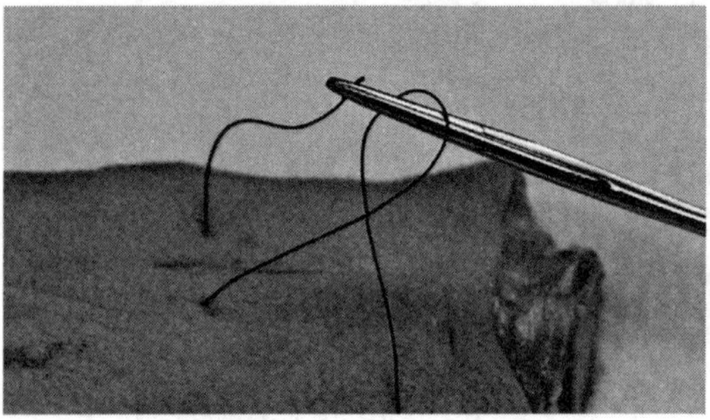

Grasp tip, clamp, and pull it through

To be successful in treating lacerations or other soft tissue injuries, you must be able to:

1) Determine when it is better to close a wound than leave it open.

2) Choose the best method for closure (tape, glue, staplers, or sutures).

3) Correctly place the sutures when they are the best choice.

4) Provide close follow-up of the treated injury to assure complete healing.

If you can absorb this knowledge and implement it, you will have learned an important skill. Don't think it is beyond your reach; as a physician, I didn't learn to change the oil in my car until I was in my 30s. Despite this, I am not a licensed mechanic and you wouldn't want me to work on your car. You are not a licensed doctor, so don't perform any surgical procedures on your fellow human beings in any situation where access to modern medical care is possible.

Joseph Alton retired after more than 25 years as an Obstetrician and Pelvic Surgeon. Amy Alton is an Advanced Registered Nurse Practitioner and a Certified Nurse-Midwife. Dr. and Ms. Alton are both Master Gardeners for their state and grow extensive medicinal herb and vegetable gardens.

As "Dr. Bones and Nurse Amy," they host a radio program called Doom and Bloom™. Their website is www.doomandbloom.net Δ

Chapter 18
Survival infection control

By Joe Alton, M.D

For several months now, news regarding the devastation that the Ebola virus is causing in West Africa has been in the headlines. A disease once found only in the most remote regions of the continent, this time Ebola hit capital cities with large airports that could, theoretically, export the virus rapidly throughout the civilized world.

Ebola is just one of the many infectious diseases for which the family medic must be prepared. Even in West Africa, many more have died of malaria and dysentery than have succumbed to Ebola. A strategy must be formulated that would prevent infectious diseases from ravaging your family.

Medical preparedness

We have become quite dependent on the modern technology that has eliminated infectious diseases in many areas. Antibiotics are in their third and fourth generations and new antiviral drugs are now available. These are used liberally in both humans and livestock; physicians don't hesitate to use them when necessary, leading to consequences both good and bad.

There are very few who realize that a major disaster may eliminate the ability to manufacture these drugs. The average citizen feels a certain invincibility with regards to their health due to the availability of modern medicine. This attitude is not only foolhardy but dangerous when it comes to infectious disease. Medical preparedness is not a goal reserved only for conspiracy theorists; indeed, it is only common sense to be ready to deal with medical issues associated with catastrophic events.

The medic for a family or group has various responsibilities. These include medical officer, counselor, dental care provider, and quartermaster of medical supplies. Perhaps the most important duty, however, is that of sanitation officer. It is their responsibility to make certain that conditions at their home or camp do not allow the invasion of infectious diseases.

Microbes that cause infectious diseases are known as pathogens. Germs may be bacteria, viruses, or protozoa. Bacteria can live and reproduce on their own in many cases, but viruses are only "alive" and reproduce in a host. Parasitic protozoa live in streams and other bodies of water and cause diarrheal disease when improperly sterilized fluids are ingested.

Pathogens are often carried by "vectors." These are microbes, animals, or persons that carry and transmit a disease to others. These vectors may or may

The medic must put together a room to separate the sick from the healthy.

not be ill themselves — a mosquito can carry the organism that causes malaria to humans, while having no signs of the disease. "Typhoid Mary" was a domestic servant who carried typhoid fever to many other people without having signs of it herself.

With Ebola, the vector is probably an African fruit bat. It doesn't get sick, but people who eat plants laden with the bats' droppings do. Some animals, like apes, can get sick from Ebola and are highly contagious if ingested — bats and monkeys are part of the diet in West Africa.

General prevention

It's logical that the healthier you are, the less likely you are to catch an infectious disease. The standard medical recommendations apply here:

- Eat a healthy diet.
- Get plenty of sleep.
- Avoid stress.
- Stay hydrated.
- Eliminate bad habits like smoking.
- Boost your immune system with vitamins, minerals, and natural supplements.

The medic's strategy

The following duties will be useful in preventing the spread of Ebola, but they are useful for any other infectious disease.

Enforce hygiene standards: Your group will be most likely to remain healthy if you enforce strict hand and respiratory hygiene. Proper hand hygiene involves a healthy supply of soap and alcohol-based hand sanitizers.

Hand washing should be performed in the following manner: Lather up, wash the palms first, then the back of the hands, and finally between the fingers and under the nails. This should be done for 20-30 seconds each time.

Hand washing should occur before and after eating, after using the bathroom, after sneezing or coughing, and before and after treating patients.

During epidemics, hand washing should be performed even after shaking hands.

Respiratory hygiene involves covering your mouth and nose with a tissue when coughing or sneezing, rapid disposal of the tissue, and hand washing. If tissues aren't available, don't use your hands to cover your mouth and nose, use your upper arm instead.

Use a mask if coughing. Although others caring for the sick individual may wear masks (N95 masks are affordable and best for healthcare providers), it is most important for the afflicted person to wear one. Sick patients who are coughing and sneezing should stay four feet away from healthy individuals, as infectious droplets can carry that far.

General hygiene and washing of clothes is also very important to prevent issues like body lice. These aren't fatal, but they can be a constant irritant to group members at times when they have to be at 100% efficiency.

Sterilize water: Clean water is important for safe drinking and preparation of food. This can be accomplished in various ways. There are large commercially-manufactured filters available, as well as portable ones. If you don't have these, there are several ways to sterilize water using simple methods.

Chlorine bleach is an effective way to sterilize water. Two drops of bleach per quart of water will suffice, but use 4 drops if the water is cloudy. Wait 30 minutes before using. Of course, bleach doesn't remove particles of debris.

For removal of particulates, you can place washed sand, gravel, and rocks in graduated layers separated by cloth in a two-liter bottle with the bottom cut out. It should be noted that bleach degrades over a short time and should be re-constituted daily for safest use. Solid calcium hypochlorite (68%) may be useful for long-term storage. This can be constituted into bleach by adding ¼ ounce of granules to 2 gallons of water.

Iodine: 12-16 drops of iodine 2% tincture per gallon may also be useful to sterilize water.

Boiling: If you can make a fire, bring questionable water to a vigorous boil for one minute to kill most disease-carrying organisms. Some sources recommend a longer time. This water has a very flat taste, which can be improved with aeration by pouring the water several times from one container to another.

Sunlight: Sunlight's ultraviolet rays will also sterilize water. Fill a 2-liter bottle 80-90% full with water that has been filtered of particles, shake well for 20 seconds, and leave in full sunlight for 6-8 hours.

Prepare food: Oftentimes, disease-causing organisms are present on the outside of fruits and vegetables. Use clean, drinkable water to thoroughly rinse these before cooking. Meats must be fully and evenly cooked at specific temperatures to make them safe. In West Africa, food is often cooked over 55-gallon oil drums. This makes it very difficult to evenly cook food, and may have led to the first Ebola cases.

A meat thermometer is an important item for the survival/homestead kitchen. Cooking temperatures for various meats are:

- Fish and beef: 145° F
- Pork: 150° F
- Ground meats and lamb: 160° F
- Poultry, sauces, gravy, and soups with meat: 165° F

Safely dispose of human waste: Improper disposal of human waste is a major cause of the spread of Ebola and other infectious diseases and a sure way to cause problems for the medic.

If there is available water, even unfit to drink, a toilet in your home that is rendered non-functioning due to grid loss can still work for you. Fill the tank with water before flushing; add a couple of gallons into the toilet bowl after using it. This activates the siphoning mechanism of the plumbing.

Warning: Blocked sewer mains and septic tanks may render this method ineffective. This is due to "backflow." Some homes have backflow prevention valves; find out if yours has them.

If there is no water, you can still use your non-functioning toilet. Empty it and place two layers of sturdy garbage bags inside; lowering the lid will keep them in place. Once you have used it, pour sand and, optionally, a small amount of very dilute bleach over the excrement for deodorization. Don't use pure bleach, which may eat through the plastic. Kitty litter is an acceptable alternative. After a few uses, you can dispose of the waste, which is already bagged.

Your ancestors performed these bodily functions outside, for good reason. You may be well-served by doing the same if the grid is down. Obtain a five-gallon bucket from a hardware store. Line it with two garbage bags and place your toilet seat, two short boards, or even a "luggable loo" on top. The "luggable loo" is a top made specifically for turning a five-gallon bucket into a toilet. Use sand, kitty litter, dirt, or quicklime to cover. Dispose of the bag when it is half full.

If you are in charge of a community in an off-grid setting, consider constructing a communal latrine. Dig a trench three feet deep, one foot wide, and 12-15 feet long. Place two planks on either side for support during use, and have a shovel and dirt from the trench available to cover the excrement. Fill in once the dirt has reached the one foot level. For privacy, some type of barrier should be constructed. Make sure that the latrine is at least 200 feet from your water source. A raised area may be best if the water table in your area is close to ground level. Sunlight will help speed decomposition.

Prepare a sick room: The medic must put together a room to separate the infected from the healthy. In a sick room, the furnishings should be minimal:

> ## Social distancing
>
> Highly deadly infectious diseases like Ebola or the plague are reasons for vigilance when the epidemic is far away, but what additional precautions may be needed if a community-wide outbreak occurs in your area? In extreme circumstances like this, the concept of "social distancing" may be appropriate.
>
> Social distancing is the act of avoiding areas with gatherings of groups of people. Municipalities have a social distancing policy, in which schools, workplaces, and events may be canceled or closed until the outbreak is under control. Personal social distancing includes wearing masks; sequestering in your home; avoiding shaking hands, hugging, or other social niceties; and the storage of food and supplies for an extended time. I recommend staying away from hospitals or emergency rooms. During epidemics, these will be full of infected individuals.

A work surface, a cot (or cots), and a chair may be all that's necessary. Flooring and work surfaces should not be fabric, as you'll need areas that can be easily decontaminated with dilute bleach solution.

The room or tent should be well-ventilated and lit. It should be as far away from common areas, such as kitchens, as possible. Outside the entrance should be a work station with a basin, soap, water, and alcohol-based hand sanitizer. A door or other barrier is useful.

If a highly contagious disease is of concern, plastic sheeting may be appropriate to cover bedding and other areas where blood, vomit, or feces may land. Bedding, towels, and eating utensils should be designated for the sick individual, and washed separately from materials used by others. A separate bathroom is a plus.

Only the medic should be involved for caring for the sick and the maintenance of the hospital room. This will serve to decrease the chance of contagion. Those with injuries should be cared for separately from those who are sick with infectious illnesses.

Disinfection of sick room surfaces can be easily accomplished by daily cleanings with bleach solution. A 1:100 bleach solution will be effective in routine washing of floors, work surfaces, and other items used by the sick. A stronger 1:10 solution is appropriate for spills of blood, vomit, feces, urine, and other bodily fluids, especially in cases of Ebola.

Some prefer to use ammonia, but *don't* mix ammonia and bleach, which is a toxic combination which releases dangerous fumes (chloramine) and liquids (hydrazine) which, in pure form, could even be explosive. The vapors are especially damaging to eyes and lungs. Leave the area immediately and, later, hose down the area thoroughly with water if possible.

Stock medical supplies: In the case of infectious disease, equipment for the medic should include:

- coveralls (with head and shoe covers)
- masks (N95 or N100)
- goggles/face shields
- nitrile gloves (many are allergic to latex)
- duct tape
- aprons
- hand sanitizer (lots of it)
- alcohol, BZK wipes
- hazardous waste bags
- tissues
- soap and water
- chlorine bleach
- thermometer
- noisemaker (for your patients to summon you)

Some of the above may, in your opinion, be more than you need. Rest assured that they will be useful in full-out epidemic outbreaks, especially of deadly diseases like Ebola.

Your infectious disease medicine cabinet should contain:

- fever reducers (acetaminophen)
- pain relief (acetaminophen)
- decongestants
- anti-diarrheals (loperamide)
- vitamins and natural immune boosters
- oral rehydration solutions
- antibiotics/antivirals

(Learn how to recognize the various infectious diseases on our website at *www.doomandbloom.net* or our books, *The Survival Medicine Handbook* and *The Ebola Survival Handbook.*)

The effective medic will have a plan of action in place for the next epidemic, whether it is influenza or Ebola. Consider what you can do now to be ready to keep infectious diseases from affecting your family. Δ

Section 3

Long-term Preparation

"By failing to prepare, you are preparing to fail."

— Benjamin Franklin

Chapter 19
How to power your house from your car

By Steven Harris

The power fails, and you are left in the dark. The electricity is out, and you do not own a generator. What you might not realize is that there are one or two generators sitting in the driveway: your car or truck. You can power many of the items in your house using only your vehicle and an inverter.

What is an inverter?

An inverter is a device that plugs into your power outlet inside your car or clamps onto the battery. It will convert 12 volts DC into 120 volts modified sine wave AC, which is the same voltage of the electricity in your house outlets. The short story is that you take an inverter, plug it into your car's power outlet, plug in an extension cord and run it inside, and then you have power inside the house.

Let there be light

Let's solve your first problem during a power outage: you need light. Take a lamp that has a compact fluorescent (CF) bulb or an LED bulb in it and plug it into the extension cord, and you now have light. Do not use a traditional incandescent light bulb with the inverter; those draw way too much power. The idea is to sip your electricity off the car's battery, so use the lowest wattage light bulb you have.

For a blackout situation, most of the light bulbs you have in your house give off more light than you really need. Use 3- or 5-watt LED or CF bulbs instead. These lights give off about 200 lumens and are about as bright as a single-mantle Coleman lantern. Remember, the idea is to sip energy off the car battery with the car off.

Your first inverter

My favorite inverter, which I have used the most for the simple things we are talking about, is a Bestek® 300-watt inverter. It has two 120-volt outlets (sometimes called 110 volts) and two USB high current outlets on it. It only

Pictured are RoadPro battery clamps with inverter plugged in under the hood.

costs about $27 and is sturdy and reliable. Inverters for less than $30 can also be found at Walmart.

The Bestek® is a 300-watt inverter, but keep in mind you can only draw about 150 watts from a cigarette lighter socket or power socket in a vehicle, no matter what the size of the inverter is. If you need the full 300 watts, plug the inverter into a power socket that is attached to two battery clamps that attach to your battery under the hood of the vehicle.

Power your cell phone, radio, and tv

What a small inverter is best used for is for lights, small personal fans, and charging your cell phone, tablets, and other small electronics. New rules for cell phone networks that went into effect after 9/11 now have the cell antenna locations with significant back up power and more reliability. A United States Government report on Hurricane Sandy showed that 97.5% of the cell towers were operational. So your cell phone could be a huge resource in a disaster. I should also mention you can power an AM/FM radio or police scanner all day long off the inverter. These draw very little power, a few watts or less each. The inverter can also be used to power the smallest TV in your house. This should be a portable 7-inch or 9-inch TV (27 inches at the largest). You don't want to power up your 80-inch TV with the inverter. If you had to, it would do it, but you'd have to let the car idle the whole time the TV was on. Don't forget to buy a set of $8 rabbit ear antennas for your digital TV.

How long will the battery last?

So how long does the battery last? A good illustration is a five-gallon bucket filled with water. It will last for a while if you just drink from it one cup at a time, but it will last five seconds if you dump it all on your head. It is the same principle with the battery and gasoline in your vehicle. That is why I want you to sip energy off the battery with low-power electronic devices.

When to idle your car

If you are drawing 30 watts or less from your car with an inverter, you can leave the car off all night long while you sleep, and then idle it for an hour in the morning. One 3-watt light bulb and a few small personal fans would work great for overnight. If you are drawing 30 to 100 watts, you want to idle your car for 30 minutes in each three-hour window. If you are drawing 100 to 200 watts, you want to idle the car for an hour, run off the battery for an hour and then repeat. If you are drawing 200 or more watts per hour, then the car should be idling all of the time.

How do you know how many watts you are drawing? Well, the easy way to tell is to just look at the wattage of each item, and then add it up. If you are using five 3-watt LED bulbs, that's 15 watts. If you have two personal fans going at 8 watts each, that's 16 more watts, and if your 27-inch LCD TV is on, that's another 55 watts. The wattage is on the back of the TV and probably on the back of the fans. So 8 + 16 + 55 = 79 watts, so you'll idle your car for 30 minutes during each three-hour window of usage. You can also use a Kill-A-Watt® meter to measure how much power you are using.

Supplies

- 3- and 5-watt light bulbs
- Bestek® 300-watt inverter
- power socket & battery clamps
- rabbit ear antennas
- Kill-A-Watt® meter
- 800-watt inverter
- thermometer
- NiMH AA AAA batteries

(all supplies are listed for sale at www.battery1234.com)

How long can my car idle on one tank of gas?

So how long can you idle your car on a single tank of gasoline if it's full? The answer is about 24 hours. Smaller cars with smaller engines are more fuel efficient at idle, but they have smaller fuel tanks. Bigger SUVs and trucks use more fuel at idle, but can have up to 30-gallon fuel tanks in them. So they can both idle for about 24 hours. If you idled your vehicle for one hour in the morning, one in the afternoon and one before you went to bed at night, then that's three hours of idle, which would give you eight days of power. Eight days of electricity from your car will get you through most natural disasters in the USA.

Power for the refrigerator and freezer

If you want to power your refrigerator and freezer from the car and inverter, I'd recommend taking the ice cream out of the freezer and giving it to the kids, the dog, or a neighbor. Then, take the milk and meat from the refrigerator, put it in the freezer, and start to eat everything else in the refrigerator.

However, if you're in Arizona in the summer, with half a cow in your freezer, it is possible to power it off your inverter. If you have a brand new ENERGY STAR refrigerator or freezer, it might only draw about 120 watts, with a surge of 300 watts when you first turn it on. It might run off the 300-watt inverter, but it's likely it won't. So you'll need an 800-watt or larger inverter.

The inverter will need to be clamped onto the battery, and the car will have to idle the entire time you are powering the refrigerator or freezer. Make sure the battery terminals are clean. A wire brush or steel wool will clean them up nicely. Also, make sure the clamps are on tight. Loose clamps or dirty posts will not deliver enough power to the inverter. Inverters have buzzers in them that sound like a squeal when low power flows through them. Your clamps might have been on good enough for 300 watts of power, but not for 800 watts.

You do not need to power the freezer all of the time. It's perfectly fine to power the freezer for one hour at a time with the car idling and to do this two, three, or four times in a 24-hour period. You don't need to keep the normal freezer temperature of -5° F, you just need to keep it below freezing, 32° F. With the help of a thermometer, you can idle the car more or less based on the temperature of the freezer.

Hooking up inverters to the car battery

Inverters 800 watts and less will have jaw-like battery clamps that go on to the posts of the battery. Inverters 1000 watts or more usually have cables that are screwed down to the battery post for the best possible high current con-

Make sure the clamp attaches securely to the battery.

nection. You'll need a socket wrench to attach them to most batteries. You unscrew the nut that clamps the terminal to the post, put on the eyelet of the inverter cable, and then put the nut back on and crank it down nice and snug. This only works on top post batteries. If you have a side post battery, you are out of luck and will probably only be able to get 300 watts or less from the clamps going on to it. Side post batteries have very small terminals.

The sump pump

If there is one thing that will drive a person crazy quickly, it's the thought of a basement sump pump overflowing and flooding the basement. Sump pumps can draw about 800 watts. That is a lot of power. The great news is that they only do this for about 30 seconds. Depending on how much it's raining, it will run for 30 seconds about every 10 to 60 minutes. For a sump pump, you will need a 1200-watt or larger inverter, but the good news is that you don't need to idle the car all of the time because you are only running your pump for 30 seconds. Follow my rules of thumb for the idle times for your car. If your sump pump is running like crazy, then idle more often.

Modified sine wave versus pure sine wave

Your inexpensive inverter generates what is called a modified sine wave. What comes from your wall outlet is a pure sine wave. There are all sorts of

Heavy-duty triple outlet adapter

stories (most false, a few true) on the Internet about modified sine wave inverters not powering some electronics or motors. The vast majority of these stories are untrue. I have had zero problems running anything with a modified sine wave inverter. Pure sine wave inverters are two and a half to five times more expensive. As a prepared person, you have a lot of things to spend money on. If you can't afford it, then you won't have it when you need it. Get the affordable inverter.

Unlimited AA and AAA batteries from your car

The best rechargeable AA batteries on the market are pre-charged, low self-discharge, nickel-metal hydride (NiMH) batteries. The best NiMH batteries are the Panasonic Eneloops (formally Sanyo Eneloops). You can recharge them up to 2,400 times. One of my favorite AA and AAA battery chargers is the Powerex MH-C800S Eight Cell Smart Charger. It will charge eight AA or AAA batteries from dead to full in two hours. Two hours for eight batteries is fast enough.

Recharging AA and AAA batteries takes very little power compared to many other items. You can recharge these batteries off the inverter all day long and never worry about having to idle the car. These batteries will run headlamps, flashlights, lanterns, and radios, and you can use them all with abandon. For AA and AAA batteries, you have all the power in the world from your car or truck with an inverter.

Conclusion

I have had all the items used in this system for years, some even a decade or more. This system will help keep you safe, comfortable, and even help you survive a disaster. If you want more information on how to power your house from your car, I have a one-hour long audio podcast at www.Solar1234.com.

Steven Harris has been focused on preparedness since 1993, and has been working with electricity, electronics, batteries, and power for 31 years. You can contact him with questions at his website, www.steven1234.com. He is also founder of a publishing company that focuses on energy (www.KnowledgePublications.com). Δ

Chapter 20 Bugging out in place

By Jackie Clay-Atkinson

Some emergency situations require quick evacuation. You barely have time to grab your bug-out bag, gather the family, and run out the door. Most of us are ready for that situation, with a fully-stocked backpack equipped with such things as lightweight food, shelter, survival gear, clothes, and possibly a weapon and ammunition for both self-defense and food procurement.

But some other bad situations (economic collapse, EMP, widespread terrorist attack, etc.) will last longer than a few days or weeks. For these situations, you might find yourself traveling to a survival retreat in a very rural area or bugging out in place on your own homestead.

I believe in being reasonably prepared for not only short-term emergencies, but also long-term ones. My late husband, Bob, with our son, David, and I did just that while living in the remote mountains in Montana. We were snowed in for six or seven months of the year, so I can give you a few hints on real-life survival skills needed to bug out long-term.

Location & shelter

Hopefully, your survival homestead is in a relatively isolated location far from any major highways or large cities. You'll need room for a garden, a natural source of water, and the ability to harvest firewood.

In Montana, our homestead was located seven miles up an extremely rocky, eroded Forest Service trail, accessible by only a four-wheel drive in the summer, an ATV in the spring, and snowmobile in the winter. Once up the mountain, you still had to actually *find* our homestead, located through a dense patch of pines.

Here in Minnesota, our homestead is a mile and a half up a logging road from an infrequently-used highway. I use the term "highway" loosely; a dog could sleep on it undisturbed for most of the day. We are two hours away from a city or freeway.

For long-term hunkering down, you really need four solid walls and a room. A travel trailer or tent gets way too cramped for long-term living, and there's not a lot of room for food storage.

Be sure your home is well insulated and has plenty of windows. In warm climates, you probably won't have the capability to run air conditioning or even fans (which is when opening a window can come in handy). In cold climates, insulation added while times are good will reduce the amount of fuel you'll need to keep you warm in the winter.

Windows will also let in natural light, reducing the fuel you'll need to see during the days. We have south-facing floor-to-ceiling patio door windows to let in warm sunlight in the winter months.

Water

Most folks have a well with an electric pump or a community water system. Neither is going to work without electricity if the power is down.

Three of my homesteads have had gravity-fed springs piped into the house. These required no electricity in order to have water and water pressure (albeit minimal) to the house. Since then, I've discovered I could have had a driving shower by simply installing a 12-volt pump with battery and charger in the bathroom vanity base to increase the water pressure on demand. A 12-volt pump costs under $100.

On our current homestead, our well is 375 feet deep and water is supplied to our home by a 220-volt submersible pump. Unfortunately, to get water we have to run our generator. This fills up our 600 gallons of water storage tanks in the basement. Water pressure to our fixtures is provided by a 12-volt water pump and batteries, charged by our solar panels and wind charger. But this system still needed gas to run the generator.

So, my husband, Will, developed a shallow well with a homemade point, installing a 110-volt submersible pump which will run off our solar and wind capabilities. It provides water to the barn, but it can be switched to supply both the barn and house, if need be.

Having any source of water nearby is a bonus. Even a river, creek, lake, or pond is a huge asset. From these sources, you can get water to bathe, wash clothes, and water your livestock. And with treatment via a good water filter (such as a Berkey), you can use it for emergency drinking water. Even straining this water through a clean cloth, then boiling it will render it fit to drink if you must. One year, our water

A good garden will refill your pantry and supply most of your food during the summer. Prepare it well in advance of when you need it.

line froze, so we had to get through three months of winter using just melted snow and about 400 gallons of stored water in our basement tanks. This was not ideal, but it worked.

Washing clothes & bathing

A conventional washer and dryer will no longer be an option for most folks in a long-term survival situation. These appliances use way too much electricity and water.

I've used a wringer washer for the last 40 years. (Before that, I used a washboard.) A wringer washer will not only get your clothes cleaner than a conventional washer but will use about 40 gallons less water, too.

With a start-up from the generator, it will continue running on our inverter, powered by a battery bank charged by our wind charger and solar panels.

Although I currently have a propane dryer, I still have clotheslines.

Bathing or taking a shower is something folks don't think about while considering a survival situation. When we lived in Montana, we alternated between using a solar shower hung on a tree in the summer to that same shower hung above our clawfoot bathtub in the winter. I'd heat the water in a canning kettle then we'd pour the deliciously hot water into the solar shower bag and hang it up. By working quickly, both of us could take a shower and wash our hair. My son, David, took his bath in a washtub in front of the wood cook stove.

When we first moved to Minnesota and were living in a travel trailer, we upgraded to a battery-operated shower. I heated the water in a canning kettle, but it only took one kettle to give a long, hot shower.

Now we have water pressure and a propane water heater. But, if need be, we could go back to "the old days." Or, Will could install a homemade, wood-fired water heater (see page 61).

Storing up food

In Montana, we added a lean-to addition on the cabin, just for a homestead-type kitchen and a large, walk-in pantry. In this pantry, we built shelves from waist high to the ceiling for canned and dry food and used the lower area for bins of potatoes, rutabagas, carrots, and onions.

Unless you've ever been in the position where you can only eat what you have stored or are growing in the garden, your perspective on what you'll eat in a long-term bug-out situation is likely unrealistic.

I've had many people tell me they're all set with 100 pounds of flour, a bucket full of rice, and a bucket full of dry beans, along with some MREs (Meals Ready To Eat).

Canned venison ready to stock up the pantry shelves.

I found that in six months, three of us went through 300 pounds of flour, 20 pounds of cornmeal, 200 pounds of potatoes, 50 pounds of rice, 50 pounds of sugar, 40 pounds of dry beans, 20 pounds of dried milk, 10 pounds of popcorn, 20 pounds of rolled oats, not to mention hundreds of jars of home-canned foods, and an elk. This is not including spices, salt, dehydrated foods, nuts, eggs, cheese, baking powder, and yeast.

Remember, you'll be baking a whole lot more than you usually do. I quickly discovered that when you're shut in by weather or circumstances, you crave goodies. Meals of plain beans and rice quickly wear out.

I have several cans of dehydrated eggs, but I found that by gathering our chickens' last fall eggs into cartons and storing them on the cold floor of our pantry, I could keep relatively fresh eggs for six months. In Montana, our hens did not lay in the winter, as we were off grid and could not keep a light on in their coop. We're planning on building a new coop on our current Minnesota homestead, complete with a battery bank charged by additional solar panels which used to power our house. Then we'll have fresh eggs all winter.

The first winter in Montana, I didn't store enough butter and we ran out before the deep snow melted. Luckily, I did have dehydrated butter. I learned to add peanut oil to rehydrate it instead of water, as the taste was much better. Then I learned I could can butter, which works much better.

When you're hunkered down, you'll be baking a whole lot more.

Margarine will keep longer without going rancid than will butter, when just kept cool. However, don't use tub margarine as the first ingredient is water. This margarine will get moldy when you try to store it. Solid, stick margarine will

Good hay will last indefinitely when stored indoors. We work every summer to stock up extra hay in our hay loft and storage barn.

store much longer in good condition.

Be sure to store up on cooking oil and fat. I can up plenty of lard from the pigs we butcher and also keep plenty of peanut, olive, and sunflower oil on hand in the pantry. When we lived out of our pantry for six or seven months, it was amazing how fast our cooking oils and shortening went down.

Nearly all of our meat and poultry was canned: chicken, turkey, venison, beef, and elk. We did have a frozen quarter of elk out in the woodshed, covered to keep chickadees and weasels from munching on it. When I wanted some for dinner, Bob would go out and saw off a roast or steak with a meat saw the morning before I planned on cooking it for dinner.

Now, we have an electric freezer powered by our wind charger and solar panels.

Remember that although plain unbleached flour will last for several years when stored in a dry, rodent/insect-proof container, whole wheat flour will only last for a few months at best before going rancid. So in addition to bags of unbleached flour, I always store up a couple hundred pounds of wheat. Not only can I grind this, using my hand-powered grain mill, but I can also plant it to increase our stored wheat in the future. And the beauty is, wheat will store for decades and still remain good.

The same goes for dry corn. Store-bought cornmeal has the germ removed, just like plain unbleached flour does. Thus, it will store for a long time. But whole, dry corn will store longer and you can grind your own cornmeal as you need it or you can plant the corn to increase your bounty and replace what you've already used. I keep 25 pounds of popcorn and 25 pounds of a heirloom corn, Seneca Round Nose, in the pantry for this reason. I also keep 10 pounds of masa harina (corn flour) on hand at all times.

I always have about 20 pounds of different cheeses in the freezer along with about 10 pounds in the refrigerator. I rotate the cheese to keep it fresh.

I also can up many pounds of cheese (see my book *Growing and Canning Your Own Food* for directions) and I keep a few #10 cans of dehydrated cheese blend powder on hand in both my kitchen and pantry.

I buy my baking powder in large, restaurant-sized cans. I remove about a cup to store in the kitchen, then freeze the rest. Frozen, it retains its leavening powers much longer than if left out at room temperature.

Likewise, I buy yeast in one-pound bags, taking about a cup out to keep in the fridge, then freezing the rest. Should things start looking dicey, I'd recommend buying another pound as I go through a pound in six months. You can always make sourdough starter and bake sourdough breads, but yeast is nice to have around, too.

I keep a pound of baking soda and several pounds of iodized salt in the pantry all the time. Baking soda keeps its leavening power when stored at room temperature. I also keep several pounds of pickling salt around for pickling, as regular salt can darken pickled foods.

When storing dry foods in your pantry, remember to protect against mice. I lost some of my dry foods when mice decided to come into the cabin for the winter. They chewed through the bottoms of a few of my gallon plastic jars. That's why glass or tin storage jars are much better.

Gardening

No matter where your survival retreat is, you need to keep your garden ready at all times. This means keeping the weeds down, tilling in rotted manure every spring, and keeping the garden fenced with 6-foot-high fence to keep out the deer. If you have a lot of rabbits and other small, hungry critters, line the bottom two feet with 1-inch chicken wire. I've seen cottontails run right through 2x4-inch or larger fencing.

Keep your garden either in use or tilled up twice a year, spring and fall. You don't know when you may need to plant it, and gasoline for your tiller will most likely be scarce. If your garden has been plowed/tilled in the fall, with rotted manure worked in, it'll require little work in the spring to get it ready to plant. About a gallon of gas will till our one-acre main garden, if it has been worked up in the fall. If not, it will most likely take three times that amount of gas.

You'll need to grow potatoes, carrots, corn, rutabagas, turnips, tomatoes, squash, beans (both snap beans and dry beans), cabbage, peppers, greens, and herbs, at the minimum.

Once the garden has been tilled and planted, it is an easy matter to mulch it deeply as the plants grow in size, so you'll have to do no further tilling and very little weeding. Hand-weed the rows, then mulch them deeply with leaves, pine straw, straw, or non-seedy hay which has never been sprayed with chemicals.

Watering can be a problem if you need electricity to draw water from a well. Instead, think about using a 12-volt pump, powered by a deep-cycle battery, charged via a solar panel, to pull water from a nearby creek, river, or pond; building a simple hydraulic ram pump to bring water from a spring, creek, or river; or even carrying water in five gallon buckets, then watering row by row with a tin can with holes punched in the bottom. Been there, done that, but I wouldn't recommend it.

On our Montana homestead, we were lucky and had a good, strong spring above our garden. We had running water right to the garden, although not enough pressure to use a sprinkler; we watered by hand-held hose.

Here in Minnesota, we water using a gasoline pump in our spring basin. During tough times, we can switch to using our new shallow well with its 110-volt pump and several garden hoses. Again, the pump will run off of our battery bank, charged with our solar array and wind charger.

As well as gardening, consider planting an orchard and other permanent crops while you can. Our little one-acre orchard is now six years old and is really starting to produce lots of fruit. In tough times, you'll be so very glad you have your own fruit as well as berries, rhubarb, and asparagus.

Livestock and pet food

Don't forget your critters when preparing for long-term emergencies. Our Labradors have gone through 250 pounds of dry food in six months, along with table scraps and elk bones/innards which were frozen. Forget canned food; it's too expensive for the nutrition provided, unless you plan on home-canning food for your pet. I knew of an old woman who, during the Great Depression, shot woodchucks out of her garden then canned them up for her beloved Fox Terrier to eat during the winter.

For your livestock, remember that good-quality hay kept in a dry place, such as a barn loft or hay shed, will keep for decades. It's a good idea to keep a year's worth of extra hay on hand, just in case. This is the reason Will and I try to make hay on all available hayfields, even if we have plenty.

Grain may be hard or impossible to get during an extended emergency. When building our new barn, Will planned for a cement-lined grain bin on the north end of our barn. Holding several tons, it'll keep our critters in grain for quite some time, if fed sparingly. If necessary, we'll reduce our livestock to a few goats, a team of horses, a milk cow, and bull.

When we lived in Montana, we kept two tons of "Packer Pellets" — a grain/hay pellet made for outfitters who packed hunters into remote mountains — right in our cabin, stacked along the north wall (insulation!). We also hauled hay in and stacked it in a covered pile on pallets to last the horses all year.

We also kept a small flock of chickens for eggs and some meat. We would have had more chickens, but we could only store ten 100-pound bags of feed over the winter in a tiny room on the end of the chicken coop.

A small flock of chickens is inexpensive to feed and will provide both eggs and meat from extra roosters raised from setting hens.

Firewood & fuels

As you know, firewood may be the only means of heating a home, should things go south. We try to keep two years' worth of firewood in the wood shed every year. Dry, split firewood, kept inside, protected from dampness, will last indefinitely.

However, all that wood will eventually get burned up faster than usual because in an emergency you'll be cooking with wood as well as heating. We have hand saws for cutting firewood and have used them a lot, but now that we're getting older, cutting 10-15 cords of firewood every year by hand doesn't sound pleasant. Recently, we found an answer that was pretty unusual. Our friend mentioned that her husband bought a cordless chainsaw and an electric chainsaw. We could use a cordless chainsaw to cut down dead trees in the woods and drag them home with the horses. Then, we could cut the trees into pieces with an electric chainsaw, powered by our battery bank while the cordless chainsaw's battery recharged using the same battery bank … charged by our solar panels and wind charger. It's one of our next priorities to buy both a cordless and an electric chainsaw.

We use our tractor-mounted hydraulic splitter for firewood, but we realize that at some point fuel might not be available. So it'd be back to using a splitting maul and wedges — a little tougher, but definitely doable.

It's also good to have a supply of fuels on hand. When we lived in Montana, we bought 55 gallons of gasoline. We used this gas over winter to supply our minimally-used generator, the Coleman multi-fuel lantern, and occasionally the snowmobile. By being frugal, this gas also powered our tiller, come May, when the snow was still deep on the side-hills going down to "civilization." While using a gasoline life-extender, such as Stabil, would have been best, we didn't have any trouble using this stored gas.

We had a propane light in the kitchen/living room, a propane refrigerator, and a propane kitchen range that we only used in the summer. Fortunately, we had an excellent propane company with a four-wheel-drive delivery truck. In the summer, he'd come up and deliver 500 gallons of propane, which would last all year long.

Our four-panel solar array and battery bank allows us to function without the use of gas for the generator most of the time. In an emergency, it would handle everything with more moderate usage.

Now, we have a 1000-gallon tank which gives us hot water, a propane kitchen range for use in the summer, a propane dryer, and two propane refrigerators. We use less than 500 gallons of propane a year.

It's a really good idea to keep your fuel tanks full. Keep your gasoline as fresh as possible by rotating it through your vehicles to avoid gummed-up carburetors.

In an emergency, I'd get rid of the propane stove, water heater, and dryer in order to keep one refrigerator going as long as possible. After that, we'd have to use a spring box and have a whole lot less refrigerated food.

Lighting

You don't think much about lighting in the summer. But in the fall and winter, when the days are shorter and the nights longer, you'll need some light to keep from losing your sanity.

When we lived in Montana, we had several kerosene lamps and two Coleman lanterns. One was fueled by white gas or Coleman fuel and the other used both that and regular gasoline from the pumps. (Now, there's a multi-fuel lantern available called BriteLyt, which shines brighter and burns more fuel types than Coleman lanterns.) We bought a 55-gallon drum of kerosene and dozens of gallon cans of Coleman fuel each fall to see us through the winter. But when both kerosene and Coleman fuel prices shot up, we switched to propane lanterns and fixed propane wall lights.

If you use any of these lamps, you will need to have some replacement parts on hand, such as globes and mantles. I have had moths fly into fragile mantles and shatter them. Once, a single drop of water dripping from a frosted nail in the ceiling cracked a glass Coleman globe.

For instances needing minimal lighting, we have used candles protected in a holder with a kerosene lamp chimney, set in the center of the table. This included bath time, story time, and times we just sat and listened to the radio. The candles helped save our fuel for better uses. I saved the leftover wax and remade the candles using new wicks. You can also make dipped candles from venison and beef fat. Be extremely careful when using candles, especially around young children and pets; many fires have been started by candles.

Now, with so many easy-to-use solar options, lighting with solar lights is very doable and will cut down on dependency on fuels. One easy option is to use outdoor solar yard lights. They can be charged outside during the day and brought indoors and set into stands in the evening. (See "Use solar landscape lights for emergencies" in *Backwoods Home Magazine* Issue #141, May/June 2013.)

Or you can use a smaller solar panel to charge a deep-cycle battery during the day and use that battery to power one or two LED lights at night.

Guns and ammunition

While not wanting to get into "the great gun debate," I will say it is extremely important for a family to have at least a couple of guns available along with the proper ammunition. Family protection aside, guns will keep your family eating meat when you are hunkered down. Whether your game is rabbits taken with a .410, grouse with a 12-gauge, or an elk with a .30.06, a gun can keep your family in meat when there's no store to buy it.

Our guns furnished us with deer, moose, and elk on a variety of our homesteads, all taken in season, with licenses. That meat filled our bellies and our pantries. To us, a gun is as much of a tool as a shovel or rake. All of our children were raised around guns with respect for them and for us. They never touched a gun without permission and an adult present. Those who wished to learn to use a gun soon were hunting and bringing in their own contributions to the family pantry.

Keep in mind that when times get tough, *everyone* will be out there hunting, which will quickly make game wary and scarce. Back in the homestead days, elk and deer were nearly exterminated in many areas, as families hunted these animals out of existence. It could happen again. So don't depend solely on hunting to feed your family.

Entertainment

While many folks worry about getting "cabin fever," which is severe depression due to being in one place over many weeks, we never found that the slightest problem. In the daytime, we were often outdoors, shoveling trails to the outhouse and around the wood pile, hauling more firewood, hiking on snowmobile tracks, feeding the birds, doing chores, and playing in the snow. During the day, I also did my baking, cooking, house cleaning, and washing.

In the evening, we'd sit around and tell stories, read books and magazines, and work on jigsaw puzzles. We also played a lot of UNO and board games. It pays to have some entertainment available at all times. Do you enjoy art or other creative hobbies? You might get a chance to oil paint, sketch, or do that beading you've always wanted to get at.

We have always had battery/solar/hand-cranked radios about the place, not only to provide quiet music, but to listen to impending weather reports and any news we feel is important.

Don't forget about kids — put away some toys, coloring books, crayons, paints, and sketch pads. Although most kids today are tech savvy, if the grid goes down, they'll still enjoy old-fashioned fun.

A lot more preparation is needed and I hope you are putting a lot of thought into that before it's too late. Stage a couple of trial runs, shutting off the power for at least a weekend, to see how your family handles it. Δ

Chapter 21
Self-reliance for women

By Kelly McCarthy

Three and a half years ago, on the morning of September 11th to be exact, I was just ending a White House tour with my husband, children, and four friends from overseas. We were evacuated, along with all White House staff, into Lafayette Square in central DC. The security guards who had been clad in suits on our arrival were now wearing Kevlar, and there were men with SAMs on the roof. We were being shouted at, "This is not a drill. Clear the area." We drove home past the smoking Pentagon.

We all changed that day. Suddenly we began to look at things differently. I know I did. Is that a briefcase or a bomb? Would the kids know where to go if I couldn't get to them? What would I do if a biochem cloud were coming my way? What is a hemorrhagic fever? How do I purify ground water? Does powdered milk go bad?

At home I started to prepare for whatever life could throw at me, whether it's a terrorist attack, freak weather incident, fire, mugging, or an outbreak of disease. I don't live in the backwoods. I'm guessing that people out in the countryside are better prepared than we suburbanites. After all, if you're following Jackie Clay you must have canned fruit and veggies out the wazoo! You're probably all tooled up with big guns, solar power, artesian wells, and more wood than you can shake a stick at. Well, where I live, in Northern Virginia, the neighborhood would pretty much grind to a halt if *Trader Joe's* shut down.

So I set out to make alternative arrangements in case the world gets complicated, or just goes to hell. And why *Self-Reliance for Women*? Because women think differently, that's why. We're big on "what if?" questions. We like to be prepared. We like to have back-up plans. And we're more than likely to be the ones that have to organize food, sanitation, and morale during an emergency. I want to know I'll have enough calories stored away to cope with a super volcano erupting, enough fuel options to cook food in a power outage, alternative solutions for water purification, many ways to light and warm my home—whatever happens.

As I write this, a review of the government's first response plans have just been judged woefully inadequate. Well, duh! Did we really think they'd get it right? Just look at the flu vaccine fandango. If they can't get enough shots out into the community to protect our old and young folk against a predictable annual problem, how good will they be when there's a real emergency?

So, since 2001 I have been collecting all sorts of information that might help me to protect my family and friends in an emergency. As I live 12 miles downwind of the Capitol, one of my big concerns is a biological terrorist attack.

A bioterrorist attack

Bioterrorism is the intentional use of biological agents, or germs, to cause illness. Biological agents include viruses, bacteria, fungi, and toxins from living organisms that have illness-producing effects on people, plants, or livestock. Toxins are poisons produced by living organisms and their synthetic equivalents. The effects of a biological agent disseminated in a public place may not be known immediately because of the delay between exposure and onset of illness. Those most likely to identify the symptoms of such attacks are the primary care physicians. School nurses or teachers may be the first to detect an illness from a biological attack in children. Among the biological agents of greatest concern are: anthrax, smallpox, plague, and botulism. A biological agent may be introduced to the system through the skin, or by ingestion or inhalation.

It makes no sense to me that we aren't all offered an inoculation against smallpox. I for one would opt to have it. It is a terrible disease, with a 20-30% fatality rate, that scars and blinds its victims. It is highly contagious and we all know that vials of a lethal strain went missing with the break-up of the Soviet Union. How long before it ends up in terrorist hands—if it isn't there already? Vaccination takes a couple of seconds to perform (I know, I've had two). It's a slightly uncomfortable scratch, and its effects last ten years. A 1968 study conducted in the United States involving over 14 million vaccinated people resulted in just nine deaths from all age groups and levels of immunity. Yet family doctors are not allowed near the government's stockpile of vaccine. Surely, if most of the nation were vaccinated, the potential threat from releasing smallpox into our population would become irrelevant?

And remember, all the powers of Homeland Security couldn't track down the Capitol Hill anthrax mailer. Three years later and we're still waiting for an arrest. And this was finely milled, highly distinctive pharmaceutical grade anthrax produced in a place where people require high-level clearance—not some naturally occurring anthrax that came in from a field.

My advice: Stay home. Don't touch your mail or newspapers. Wait it out. Avoid contact with other people and things they may have touched. During any type of bio attack, everyone should wash their hands frequently; avoid close proximity to an infected (or potentially infected) person. Isolate potentially exposed family members. If one member absolutely has to come and go, they should live separately from the others. Make sure you are thorough with cleansing; bleach surfaces, sinks, taps, toilets, etc. Boil-wash clothing that an infected person may have touched in disinfectant/bleach and soap. Avoid touching your eyes. These basic hygiene practices will greatly increase your chances of avoiding infection. Make sure you have weeks of supplies—not days, as FEMA suggests. I recommend having at least a month's supply of essentials. I always aim for at least two months. I'll share my list of supplies and how to calculate the basic requirements that your family would need to survive in a later column.

Some biochem weapons are spread through human contact. Remember to drain standing water as it attracts mosquitoes, which can be disease carriers. Keep your house clean so that it doesn't attract disease-infested flies, rats, and other creatures. You may even have to bury your dead. This isn't as straightforward as you'd imagine, so I hope to cover this some other time.

Consider your own psychological state. Do not underestimate this. To endure a major biological attack you may have to cope with:

- The death of family members and close family friends.
- The disappearance of reassuring and familiar rituals and people. No store visits, maybe no TV or radio, certainly very different TV and radio. No sport to play or watch, no daily papers, customers or deliveries, or group worship.

In crisis situations, interestingly enough, it often seems that those who survive are those who don't give in to despair. In order to prepare yourself psychologically for any type of disaster, there are several steps you can take:

- Fear and despair are contagious; discuss the impact of a possible attack (calmly) with your family. Do not panic them, just present the situation as realistically as possible and get them involved with possible solutions. Advance planning solidarity and mutual aims will help you to work as a unit.
- Put together two comprehensive emergency packs. One in case of evacuation, the other for "sheltering in place."
- In your emergency pack include something diverting such as a game (a set of cards, a board game). No matter how dire the situation, human beings need to be able to switch off occasionally.

Fitness

It might seem obvious, but the people most likely to survive a bio attack are those who are fit and healthy in the first place. If you have no health regime, ignore exercise, smoke and drink excessively and are either significantly over or under weight, then you are more likely to become a victim of a deliberately induced contagion. Even if you suffer from a medical condition such as diabetes, or asthma, the fitter you are the more likely you are to survive.

Communications

Keeping in touch with the outside world will be important. We are used to 24/7 news. However, most modern forms of communication rely on a regular power supply, which cannot be guaranteed in an emergency. An exception is the clockwork radio, now used widely all over the world where power supplies are erratic or absent.

For cell phones, there is a device that makes it possible for you to recharge your cell battery without main power. Called the SideWinder, you attach it to your phone via a cord that comes with it, and turn the crank, much like you would on an old-fashioned pencil sharpener. Two minutes of cranking creates about six minutes of talk time and significantly more time in standby minutes. If the SideWinder is cranked without being attached to a phone, it produces a small, white light, bright enough to read by. Turn the crank for 30 seconds and you will get five minutes of light. It costs around $25 and it's guaranteed for life.

As for TV viewing, if the TV networks are broadcasting you might not get to see them if your signal comes in via satellite or cable. Consider a portable battery TV such as fans use at football games, or an AC/DC TV with a "rabbit ears" aerial that plugs into the cigarette lighter in your car. Relatively cheap and easy to run, these devices have proved their worth and it might be an idea to invest in one.

Backwoods bioterror

Maybe you didn't know it but deer mice, cotton and rice rats and white-footed mice carry the potentially deadly Hantavirus. This causes a disease known as Hantavirus Pulmonary Syndrome (HPS), a very dangerous hemorrhagic fever. Although it is on the list of potential biochemical weapons, it is also becoming a reality in barns across America. Victims become infected by inhaling infected mice droppings, urine, or saliva in dust/aerosol form, often when sweeping or moving hay around. It is not spread through humans. Symptoms can take up to five weeks to appear and include a fever, muscle aches, nausea, and vomiting.

After these initial flu-like symptoms, victims experience shortness of breath and have coughing fits. The final stages of HPS disease include internal bleeding and breathing failure. Over 50% of reported cases of HPS have resulted in death. Although there aren't many cases, it's wise to keep your homestead rodent-free, as this disease appears to be on the increase in the US. Hantavirus can be killed by bleach, household disinfectant and UV rays, but you must be careful not to stir up the dust. The virus can live for two to three days at normal room temperature. If you have been exposed to rodent infestations and display any symptoms described above, see your doctor immediately.

Of course the big problem with biological threats, whether naturally occurring or from terrorists, is that either you are unaware a substance is being dispersed or you have very little time to react to it. However, there is a practical aid now available. It is a mask, small enough to fit easily inside a purse or briefcase and can be put on in six seconds. It filters out smoke and its related gases, tear gas as well as biological and chemical agents including anthrax, smallpox, sarin and cyanide. It's called the Potomac Emergency Escape Mask. At around $125 it's the perfect accessory for alert commuters in at-risk cities—and people with mice in the barn.

I hope in future columns I'm able to bring you some new ideas and solutions for dealing with emergencies. I also hope to share some of the things I do to teach myself how to deal with day-to-day threats such as personal assault and general stupidity. And I hope I can explain some of the self-reliant—and often contrarian—thinking that goes with it. Δ

Chapter 22 Gardening as a hedge against hard times

By Jackie Clay-Atkinson

Have you considered the fact that your garden might actually save your life?

Oh come on now, you may say, really? Hey, have you ever been hungry? I mean truly hungry, with very little or no food in the house, no way to get more and your kids looking at you with sad, hungry eyes? Yes, it can happen. And yes, it can happen in this country. (Any of you ever hear of the Great Depression?)

Today with all our technology, hunger can be just an EMP, terrorist attack, natural disaster, cyber attack or sunken economy away. And it can happen overnight, without warning. How's your garden?

Being a person who believes in being as self-reliant as possible, I've always had a garden and have canned food nearly forever, it seems. I started "helping" my grandma and mother can peaches in the basement of our house in Detroit, 67 years ago. Like most folks, I've had a few rough patches in my life where money was extremely tight and it made me rethink my own take on "stocking up," as Mom and Grandma called it. Some preppers only store up prepared "emergency" foods, bought from preparedness companies. This is fine. I buy some, myself. These include things I can't easily put up myself, like powdered butter, sour cream, etc. But please realize this food will not last forever, if an emergency lasts for an extended length of time. Nor will it last for the year it's supposed to, if you eat more than the minimum, or you suddenly find you have more people than you planned on having to help you eat that food. (Your older kids may have to come home, due to unforeseen circumstances.) Regardless, that stored food *will* eventually be eaten. Then what?

Gardening as a hedge against hard times

I've heard over and over, "I've got my seed bank; I'll just dig up the backyard and grow my food there."

Oh boy.

That's where really being prepared comes into play. (Not just mouthing the words.) As growing a first year's garden nearly always is a near-disaster, a person needs to "get into the swing of things" way before an emergency

A big garden is your best hedge against tough times.

situation hits. (For instance, I know a family, living in a very nice house, on a huge lot. They buy what they are going to have for supper at lunchtime. There's no garden. They don't can. No backup food. He just, suddenly, got laid off. Big house, new cars; big payments ... one income.) It doesn't have to be the "end of the world"... it can just feel like it!

Nearly everyone who reads this magazine can garden. Somewhere. If you live in town, there is container and square foot raised bed gardening. Like Grandma, you can plant fruit trees and shrubs along your fences and buildings. Permanent crops such as asparagus and rhubarb are easily planted and will be able to be harvested for years to come with minimal work to keep them going.

But please realize that you cannot grow enough food in the city to feed yourself or a family indefinitely. Sure, a well-tended city garden can and does provide a lot of good food, but it's just not enough to live on. Period.

Do you have a friend or relative who lives in the country, yet fairly close to you? How about suggesting the two of you go together and develop a nice big garden? Be honest and share in the work, the cost of seeds and plants as well as other expenses.

This doesn't happen overnight. The ground must be tilled, and rotted manure hauled in and worked in. As wild critters love helping themselves to your garden, it's best, and in some areas, such as ours, essential to fence that garden with six-foot-high 2 x 4 inch welded wire fencing. Deer can jump anything lower. (They hop right over five-foot fence, which is why we went to six-foot. And I've never had a deer jump into the garden over that fence.

By using this gardening space, you and your gardening partner can not only improve the soil and get it ready for possible tight times, but you can, and should, begin to can and otherwise put up the food you're growing, and begin to stock up.

How big a garden?

A whole lot of folks feel safe, with their handful of raised beds in the backyard. They're nice, but not nearly as productive as necessary. (Hey we have seven raised beds in our side yard for a house garden, so I don't have to walk down the hill to our main garden if I want an onion, pepper, tomato or salad greens.)

But to be perfectly honest with you, a garden of ¾ of an acre is a whole lot more realistic when it comes to truly feeding a family when there is nothing else available. Consider you will be raising wheat to grind for flour (40 x 150 feet as you'll need not only flour but seed for next year's crop.), corn for both fresh eating and for grinding into cornmeal (20x150'). There will be a large potato patch, as potatoes are one crop that is used nearly every day, especially when things get tough. (You can eat them three meals a day; hash browns for breakfast, potato salad for lunch and baked potatoes for supper.)

Root crops you might not grow, or just grow minimally, such as rutabagas, parsnips, carrots and turnips, should be grown both for their nutrition and filling qualities but also for variety.

From living very remote in three homesteads, I quickly learned the value of producing enough crops to be able to create and can a huge variety of recipes many folks just buy day-to-day, such as several flavors of spaghetti sauce, barbecue sauce, salsas, pizza sauce, etc. To do this, you certainly need to have room to not only grow many more tomato plants than the "normal" garden does but also the other ingredients of each, such as onions, peppers, garlic, mushrooms, and herbs. I like to have at least 50 tomato plants for all my recipes and for fresh eating.

Likewise with beans. Sure, you'll love your green and yellow beans, eaten and put up fresh. But you'll need additional room to grow dry beans to store and use. It takes about four 100-foot rows of dry beans to make a 50# bag.

You'll also need more onions than you probably grow right now as not only will you use them for flavoring and as a condiment, but also as an ingredient for hearty meals such as scalloped potatoes and onions, onions, potatoes, and carrots with a canned beef roast, and creamed onions or fried onions. Two 30-foot rows of onions will last over winter, into spring.

How about peas? Not only will you want fresh peas to eat, can, and dehydrate, but also dry peas for pea soup. That little ten foot row of peas won't last very long. You're going to want something more like five 100-foot rows, or better yet, three four-foot beds of peas as they support and shade each other nicely … and it saves garden space.

Squash? You say you only eat a couple of meals of squash a year. But when an emergency situation comes up, you'll quickly see you will eat more of this tasty and nutritious fruit. And a good, vining squash takes up room. You'll want at least a 100-foot row with ten feet or more on each side to allow for vigorous vining. What the heck will you do with all that squash? Fry, bake, stuff, and simmer it as soup. Use it in baking. My husband, Will, and I would rather have a "pumpkin" pie made of Hopi Pale Grey squash than any pump-

It takes a whole lot more food if there is nothing else available. Here's part of our fall harvest.

kin! Then there are pumpkin muffins, quick breads, cookies, etc. And squash fills you up, too. Any extra can be fed to chickens or livestock.

Other permanent crops such as asparagus, rhubarb, berries, etc. can be grown along the sides of the garden.

Have I convinced you that you need a large garden yet? I hope so.

Getting ready ahead of time

Let's say you have a relatively flat area about 150 by 150 feet available. First you'll need to have it cleared enough to till up. When we first moved to our current homestead in Northern Minnesota, it was logged off Potlatch timber company land. There was a south-facing gentle slope below where we planned on building our house. So we started clearing it — by hand — digging and pulling up smaller stumps and roots, hauling off trailer loads of rocks and old logs, until we finally had an area cleared about 10 by 50 feet. It takes time by hand.

Then my oldest son, Bill, came up with his crawler-loader. With that, in one afternoon, he cleared three spots, one next to our little garden, making it a whopping 100x 100, an area next to the old mobile home we were using as a camping shelter and a bit of what is now our orchard. Some equipment is a huge help.

So if I had massive clearing to do so I could have a big enough garden, I'd definitely bring in the "big guns", even if you have to pay an operator to do it. Around here, you can hire a track hoe or small dozer for about $100 an hour, with an operator. It sure doesn't take long to get that garden cleared.

You will find you eat a lot more squash and other garden produce if you can't run to the store. Will is bringing in part of our squash harvest.

Once it is pretty much cleared, you'll have to go over it by hand and remove rocks, tree roots, and other debris. You may also have to kind of level it off. I did that with our four wheeler, dragging a weighted down bed spring. It leveled off the humps and bumps quite well so I could till.

Once level, I began to till the spot with our Troy-Bilt Horse rototiller. (I very much endorse the Troy-Bilt Horse; I've had three since the early '70's, tilling acres with them. Very good machine.)

I set the depth to only a couple of inches to start so the tiller would continue to level out the rough spots and not dig too deeply, causing it to lurch and jump. I made one pass over the whole thing. The next day, I did it again, setting it only a little deeper. Over a week's time, I continued picking out rocks, with the help of my youngest son, David, and tilled deeper and deeper.

You can shorten this process if you have access to a tractor-mounted three point rototiller. If you have a friend with one, great. If not, and you can afford it, you can hire someone to do this; it's much faster.

If your prospective garden is a piece of a pasture or hayfield, so much the better. It is probably rock and tree-free. But it is a very good idea to use either a brush hog or riding lawn mower to cut down all grass and weeds before you till.

When you have farm equipment handy, a two bottom plow makes quick work of turning over the sod deeply enough that it will quickly rot. And running a disc and harrow over the plowed ground quickly cuts up the soil and smooths it down nicely.

But if you don't, again, back to the rear-tined rototiller or tractor-mounted tiller. Get the ground worked up.

Amending the soil

Get a soil test on your garden-to-be. You can even do it yourself with inexpensive kits available through garden centers and catalogs. A garden won't grow when the soil is either too acidic or alkaline. And if your life is depending on what you grow, you want to make sure that plot will produce abundantly.

Once you have your soil tested, you will also have ideas as what you'll need to add to your soil to get the pH around neutral. If it is too acidic, you will probably be adding limestone or wood ash; if too alkaline, you can add sphagnum moss, sulfur or aluminum sulfate. Work any necessary amendments into the soil.

Once this is done, try to add at least a foot of well rotted manure to the new garden, preferably in the fall. If this is done, let it sit over-winter. If you must add it in the spring, till it in well before you plan on planting.

Now your new garden is ready to plant.

But wait!

Fencing the garden

There's no sense in going to all the trouble to make a new garden that will stand by you in case of hard times if the wildlife is just going to come in and have a banquet. Critters like rabbits, woodchucks, and especially deer will quickly clean out that beautiful garden just as it is starting to look good.

To protect it, you're going to need to fence it well. I mean *fence* it. I've tried everything from predator urine, electric fences, pinwheels and sprays. Nothing keeps wildlife out of your garden reliably except a six foot high 2x4 inch welded wire fence. If your life and your family's life depends on the food you produce there, getting lazy or cheap on the fencing is inexcusable.

We've always struggled financially. But over one winter, we started buying a few 8 foot high steel T fence posts at a time, or a roll of 6 foot high wire … a little at a time, as we could afford it. By spring, we had enough stockpiled and we fenced. The actual fencing goes up very quickly.

In our newest acre-and-a-half garden, we used wooden corner and brace posts along with the steel T posts as we are stretching the wire tighter than in our house garden. The wooden posts, driven four feet into the ground will not pull over from the stretch and weight of the wire on the fence.

If you have raccoons in your neck of the woods, be sure to pound your T posts with the flat side facing out. Once the welded wire is in place, you can add two strings of electric wire, one 18 inches from the ground and another one a couple feet above that, held by stand-off plastic insulators. This keeps climbing varmints from climbing the fence and getting at your crops. Both raccoons and possums will climb a wire fence easily…unless you bar their way. You can use a 12 volt battery operated fencer, as we do, in more remote locations. (It's a good idea even if you do have power, as in an emergency, there may not be any power.) Our battery is charged by a small solar panel.

You'll need lots of mature, open pollinated corn to grind into cornmeal and to save seeds for next year's crop.

Plant the garden

The most sensible thing to do now is to use that garden. If you don't really need all that space, consider raising a cover crop on part of it to cut and use as green manure. Such crops include buckwheat, rye, field peas, and alfalfa. These not only keep the weeds out, but by cutting them when they are only partly grown, you will be adding organic material to the soil, making it richer and easier to till later on. An alternative to just cutting the green manure and letting it rot in place is to cut it a bit longer in length, then letting it dry. This makes the very best mulch you can imagine. Weed free, too. And as it rots, it will improve the soil. Remember, any legume you plant for green manure (peas, alfalfa, clover, etc.) will also add nitrogen to the soil through the plants' roots. What a win-win situation.

Consider at least keeping most of the new garden producing food ; you never know when an emergency will happen. They seldom come with an advance warning! Here, near Minnesota's Iron Range, just recently, over 1,500 mine workers with very good paying jobs got laid off pretty much permanently, with no warning. Not the end of the world as we know it, but it feels like it to these folks whose unemployment benefits are now ending.

While things are still good for you economically, you can gain experience gardening, learn to can and dehydrate your own foods and eat the very tastiest, gourmet-quality food imaginable. Keep that garden working. Not only will it keep you in food but through the years you'll see a dramatic reduction in weeds in the garden as new gardens tend to have more weeds than established ones. Use your rototiller or tractor mounted tiller while you still have gasoline available, adding rotted manure annually. Your garden will just keep getting better and better, putting more and more food in the pantry and on the table.

Emergency gardening checklist

Once the "big ticket" items are out of the way, such as a tiller, fencing and initial seed, it's very provident to keep on hand tools, seeds, and supplies to keep your garden going for quite awhile, if need be.

While a tiller is great, should gas become unavailable, you will need hand tools to keep your garden going. Once well-tilled and pretty weed-free, you should be able to garden without tilling, using heavy mulch. So don't think you'll have to spade up that whole three quarters of an acre.

But such hand tools as a couple of good, pointed shovels, a garden fork, hoes, and cultivators are very necessary.

Think about how you will water your garden during a long-lasting emergency. (If you have a pond, creek, or good spring nearby, consider buying a gasoline water pump and water line to reach your garden.)

Yes, in an emergency, gasoline will be hard to find. But hopefully, you've already bought a fuel tank such as farmers store gas in aboveground and have some gas available. In many years you won't have to water often. Our big pump puts out over 2,000 gallons an hour and that costs us less than ½ a gallon of gas. Some older farms have windmills which still work. Wonderful!

We've also hauled water in a 300-gallon poly tank from a spring and creek to water our gardens via gravity. It "cost" us ¼ gallon of gas to get the water; nothing to water the garden.

Get creative here and you'll figure out something do-able.

Only grow open-pollinated crops as you can not reliably save seed to keep your garden going from hybrids. Yes, seeds from hybrids will produce a crop. But you have no way of knowing just what that crop will look, taste, and produce like. With open-pollinated crops, seeds saved will always produce next year's crop just like the parent crop. (Unless it got crossed with a like species.) Most garden seeds, save onions and parsnips, will remain good in a cold, airtight container for at least 3 years. In a freezer they'll remain good for decades. Be sure you have enough seeds put away each year. Just in case….

Be sure to have some natural insecticide saved up such as Spinosad or Bt (Bacillus thuringiensis) in case you get an insect plague such as potato or cucumber beetles or another bug you can't stop by hand picking. Δ

Chapter 23
Create your own emergency water supply

By Charles A. Sanders

Many of us who are otherwise well prepared for weather related emergencies, power outages, or other disasters are put to scratching our heads when we try to figure out a good method of storing water for emergency use. It's easy to have a couple of five-gallon jugs of water stored away, but the storage of a larger quantity of clean, usable water is a more difficult task. Not all of us have bubbling springs or deep, clear wells on our property. In some instances, without electricity, even those water sources can be inaccessible.

It is commonly known that under extreme emergency circumstances, a person can get by for quite a while without food, but only for a short time without water. Under normal conditions in moderate weather, an adult needs about two to three quarts of water each day. That amount would naturally be increased if the person is engaged in heavy physical labor or any hard physical activity. Therefore, a minimum of about four to five gallons would need to be stored for each person for one week's needs. The problem then is to come up with a plan to supply the needed water for your family for an extended period of time.

One method which I have come up with is quite simple, inexpensive, and effective. It is made up of materials which are obtainable at no cost or at low cost. It can add an additional 125 to 150 gallons of water to your storage supplies.

The system consists of connecting three used water heater tanks in series to your existing water supply to provide a battery of water storage tanks. The number of tanks is arbitrary. Theoretically, you can plumb in a tank for each member of your household. This method will maintain up to 150 gallons of consistently fresh water as a backup to the quantity already contained in the existing water heater. An added benefit of this method is that, until it is needed in an emergency, it allows incoming water to warm to room temperature before entering the household water heater, thereby reducing the amount of electricity or gas required to heat your normal household water supply.

To obtain the parts and materials necessary for your water storage battery, you'll need to hit up a local plumber or appliance dealer. They usually have

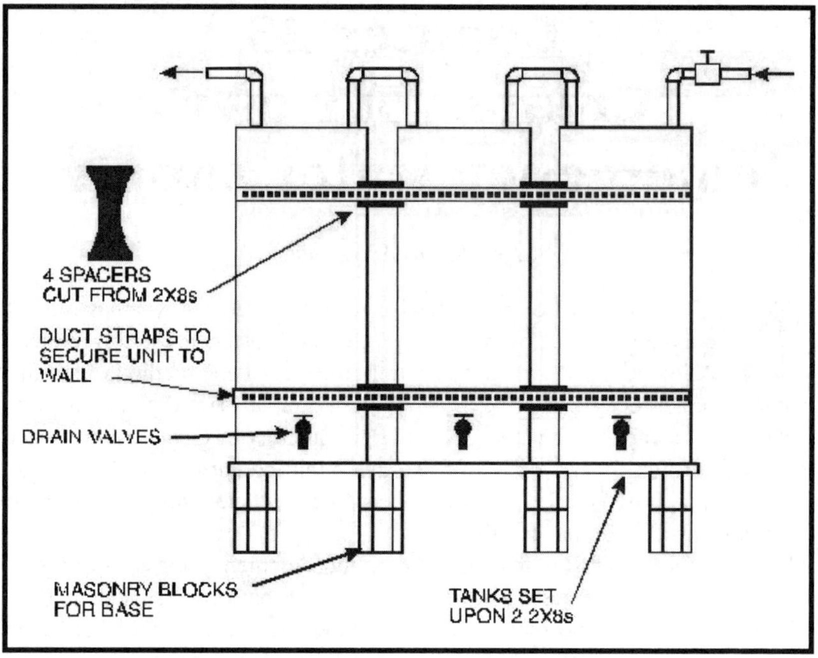

old water heating units waiting to be hauled off and can be easily persuaded to let you have a couple of old water heaters just for hauling them off.

It may require a bit of diligence in searching for the tanks to use in your system. Most water heaters are not discarded unless the tank has developed a leak somewhere. Stay with it, and you should be able to locate the needed tanks.

For purposes of setting up the water storage battery, you'll first need to remove the outer jacket and insulation from each unit. To do this, start by removing any panels or covers attached with screws. With a hacksaw-type blade in your sabre saw, cut down the length of the metal cabinet near the seam. By carefully removing this metal cabinet, you can end up with some good heavy-gauge sheet metal to be used for a variety of projects around the homestead.

Once the tank has been removed from the water heater jacket, it would be a good idea to clean it out a bit. To do this, you can remove the heater elements and flush out the inside. This should remove most of any buildup of limestone or other deposits which may be inside the tank. If you live in an area of heavy mineral deposits, such as limestone, this may take a bit of effort. Once the tank is flushed out, you may wish to go a step further and wash out the inside with a bleach solution. Rinse well and reinstall the elements, tightening them well to make a tight, leakproof seal. Instead of replacing the elements, you may install threaded plugs in their place.

Placement of the tanks will have to be customized to your particular location. Remember that each of the tanks weighs in the neighborhood of 50 pounds and 50 gallons of water weighs an additional 417 pounds or so. This will make the weight of a three-tank battery about 1400 pounds. A good solid floor will be required to support a load of this size. As a base for the units, you can easily place concrete blocks atop each other or on end and place over them a couple of 2x8s. While the raised tanks are not absolutely necessary, they are helpful, if for no other reason than to make withdrawing water from the tanks easier through the drain valves located near the bottom of the tanks. And consider using a metal strap to secure the units to the wall for protection against upsets during an earthquake or other disaster.

Plumbing in the tanks is an easy enough matter. Simply connect the tanks so that the incoming household water supply enters the first tank, leaves it and enters the second tank, exits it and enters the third tank, then reconnects to the existing household supply line. The fittings needed for the required connections are easily obtainable at the local hardware store.

If or when the emergency supply is needed, you must first immediately shut off the main water supply valve to your water line. This would be especially critical in the event that you suspect your main water supply has been contaminated.

Once the water main has been shut off, you can easily draw off needed water from the tank drain valves located near the bottom of each tank. For a good water flow, you may have to open a faucet or two in your household system to allow air to flow into the pipe system.

The beauty of this system is that it is adaptable to nearly any water system and can be sized from a single tank to as many as you need and have room for. It can help you to be better prepared for an unexpected "long dry spell." Δ

Chapter 24
Survival storeroom

By David Eddings

This story begins in the mid-nineties when the Y2K threat was in the news. Several members of my family thought it would be prudent if we started stocking food just in case Y2K turned out to be the major problem that a lot of people predicted it would be.

We contacted a company that specialized in providing long-term foods to the public. Our order was not large enough, so we contacted a Mormon group that lived in a nearby town. They were delighted to have us go in with them on an order because they were just short of enough to place the order.

A few weeks later, we met in the small town and watched as an 18-wheeler rolled in with 73,000 pounds of food. This is how our food storage program began. We left there that day with more food than I had imagined. We had made some provisions for storing the food by buying some shelving, but it was barely enough to hold the two-year supply of food we had brought home.

Each 2x4x6-foot unit has 20 running feet of shelf space and is rated to hold 5,000 pounds.

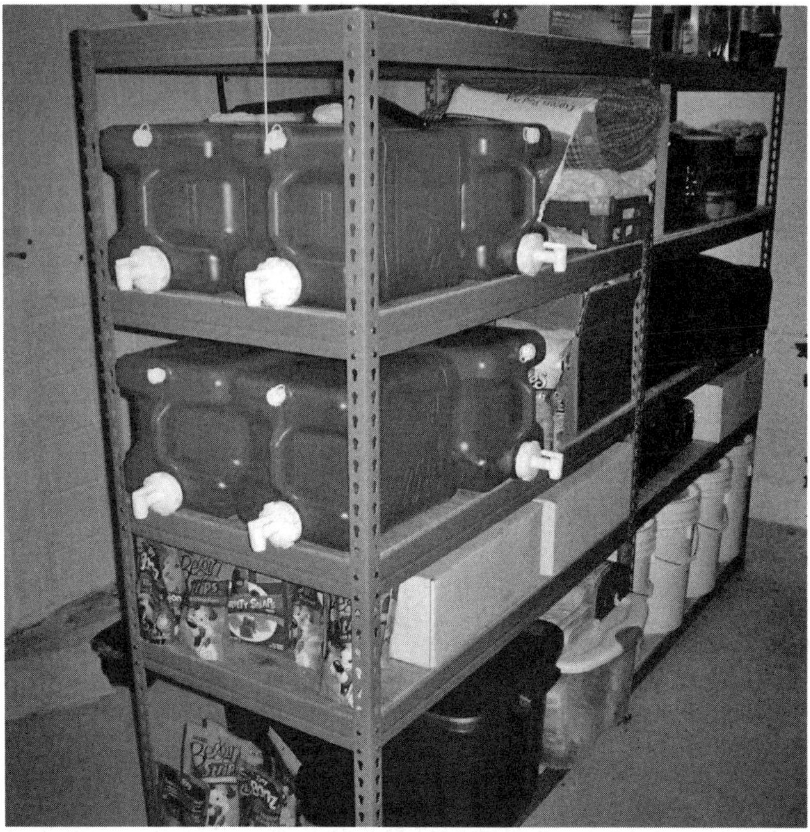

Each "Aqua-Tainer" holds seven gallons of water and has a convenient spigot.

As you all know, Y2K turned out to be a non-event. As time went on, a lot of our friends began doing away with their stored foods, either by giving it away or consuming all of it with no thought that it might come in handy later on. We knew that what we had was long-term foods and they would still be good for years. The problem was that we didn't know very much about planning a storeroom for people that lived in a city. We wanted to keep what we had and make it the core of a storeroom that would provide for us and our extended family.

Backwoods Home was a great help along the way. The information we gained from the magazine and other sources kept us from making a lot of mistakes and gave us ideas that we could put to our use. I recognized the need for a plan for a storeroom for city folks. The key for that storeroom was shelving.

Two shelf units bolted together have 80 square feet of shelf space to house bulky non-food items.

Shelving

Most of the information that I had read dealt with building shelving from scratch using wood. Living in a subdivision and not having the tools or skills to make our own shelving, I ruled out that option. Since we had already bought some shelving to store our long-term foods, we decided to continue with that method. This works out well because the shelves can be taken down and moved, if necessary. In our case, that was a plus because we did buy a place in the country and had to move all of our food at that time.

I like to call a set of shelving a module because my plan is expandable by adding modules as they are needed. That is also why I wanted to write about this project, in hopes that it might help others get started with a storage program of their own, by starting with one module and doing it one step at a time.

The shelving kits we used are the Muscle Rack 5500 series. They cost around $70 at Lowe's. The shelving is rated at 5,000-pound capacity. They are 48 inches long, 24 inches wide and 72 inches tall and have five shelves. The shelves are adjustable in 1.5-inch increments.

The box states that the unit can be assembled in 30 minutes. Once you get the hang of it, you can do it in less time. The only tool needed is a hammer. I have gotten good results with a rubber mallet. One person can do the job, but it is much easier and safer if two people do it. I strongly recommend that the shelf boards that come with the kit not be used. The shelf boards are heavy-duty particle board but they will not support the weight of canned goods for very long without sagging. Lowe's carries plywood sub-flooring that works fine for shelf boards. I wouldn't use anything less than 5/8-inch thick. One 4x8 sheet will make four shelves and they charge a nominal fee to cut it for you. Buy the cheap grade of plywood. It doesn't have to be pretty, just strong. Once completed, you will have 20 running feet of shelf space and the start of a storage program. Since this shelving is free standing, it is important to always load the heaviest items on the lowest shelves to reduce the chance that the shelves will tip over. Never use the lower shelf as a step up to reach something from a high shelf.

Warning: The shelving used in the construction of this storeroom is industrial-strength steel. Using any shelving not rated such should not be used for obvious reasons.

One big advantage of a shelf module is that it can be loaded from either side. We date every perishable item that is placed on the shelf. You can load from one side and remove from the other if you want to. The rule is "first in, first out." This will help you with a rotation plan and keep your stored foods fresh. We prepare our grocery list by walking through the storeroom and listing each empty space and buying a replacement item with a trip to the grocery.

Water storage

We all know that food storage is important, but you should make arrangements to store as much water as you can, also. A person can live for a long time without food. Water is critical for survival. We have two methods for storing our water that will provide several days' worth of water for our needs. We purchased Aqua-Tainer brand water containers. These can be purchased from several places, but we bought ours from the sporting goods section at Walmart. We got two prices even at the Walmart stores. One Walmart had them for $10.80 and the other was a dollar more for some reason. I have seen them online for $16.95 plus shipping, so it pays to shop around.

I have found the Aqua-Tainer to be a quality product. The box shape makes them very easy to store on your shelves. Each one holds seven gallons of water. It comes complete with a spigot and an air vent. You must open the vent before opening the spigot or the water won't flow. When the container is full, the water will come out almost as fast as from a kitchen faucet.

The second method we use to store water is saving plastic soda bottles and large juice jugs. Even 32-ounce Gatorade bottles make excellent water containers. We keep around 70 gallons in those alone. We keep our water for about six months before replacing it with fresh water. It is important when filling the plastic containers to fill them to the brim and to splash some of the chlorinated water into the lid. We try to avoid having any air space between the water and the lid.

Water filtration kit

We have a water filtration system that is made from a kit we purchased from Cheaper Than Dirt! (800-421-8047, www.cheaperthandirt.com). The kit is a Camp-352 by Monolithic and will filter to .5 microns and meets NSF standards. We plan to treat the filtered water, just to be on the safe side. The kit consists of a ceramic filter, a filter sock, and a spigot. The kit sells for $29.97 and does not include the buckets needed to assemble the filter. We purchased the two five-gallon buckets from Emergency Essentials for $7.95 each.

For less than $50, you can have a filter system that rivals one that costs around $200 and filters 14 gallons of water per day. The filter can be cleaned with a soft brush and by back flushing. By adding a Gamma Seal lid, you have the convenience of a screw-on lid. This system should last a pretty good while.

Food savers

I feel that one of the best investments a person can make for a storage program is a vacuum sealer for foods. It will pay for itself in being able to buy foods in bulk and re-packaging in smaller quantities. It can be used to seal dry foods also. We buy rice in large bags and freeze it for several days, then divide it into smaller bags and vacuum seal it. It is as hard as a rock and stacks very well on the shelves. Foods that are vacuum-sealed stay fresh for months without freezer burn. A good unit can be purchased at Walmart for around $70 dollars. I can't say enough about this product.

Combining modules

By placing two modules side by side and bolting them together you can create space to store bulkier items. Each shelf is 4x4 feet and gives you 16 square feet of space. We use this space to store paper towels, toilet tissue, cleaning products, paper plates, and any other non-food item that doesn't have a use-by date. We also stock items for ladies' special needs. We store paper plates and cups to help conserve our water. Because water is critical, you don't want to be wasting it to wash dishes.

Alternative cooking

We had all the food stored, but we didn't have a viable method for cooking it. A two-burner Coleman camp stove didn't provide the cooking time needed to cook a lot of the foods we had on hand, plus it is labor intensive because it requires constant attention by pumping the fuel tank and also the small tank. Gasoline is dangerous and breaks down over time, so we ruled that out and decided to go with kerosene. Kerosene will also be useful in space heaters and emergency lighting. It will store for long periods without breaking down. It will turn yellow, but that doesn't seem to affect its quality. We live in an area where ice storms can happen anytime during the winter and we

Butterfly oven, Alpaca kerosene stove, and Butterfly two-burner kerosene stove.

have been left without power for days at a time, so fuel reliability over the long term is critical.

I contacted a fuel oil company in our area and they gave us a 55-gallon drum and came out and filled it for us. I went to Northern Tool and bought a hand crank pump that screws into the top of the drum. This setup has kept us warm, snug, and fed when the power goes out.

I went online and located a two-burner kerosene stove that looked promising. It's called the Butterfly Stove, and I got mine from St. Paul Mercantile (888-395-1164, www.stpaulmercantile.com). The stove sold for $120 with a small shipping charge. My brother wanted one also and the company gives a 10% discount for two. If you purchase four you get a 15% discount, so if several people want to go together you get a pretty good discount. The stove is 30 inches wide and 30 inches tall — a nice height for cooking. The instructions for assembly left much to be desired, but with a little patience, one person can do it. The company also has a three-burner model.

The stove has a center reservoir which supplies both burners by gravity feed. The glass tank holds 1.8 quarts of fuel and can be refilled while the stove is in operation. While testing the stove I found fuel wasn't going all the way around the wick. The burners are adjustable, so that wasn't a problem. I had to loosen the adjustment screws and tilt the burners back and that solved the fuel flow problem. It is important that the stove be set up on a level surface. The height of the flame depends on the rate of fuel flow, so there is a lag between the time you turn the valve until you get the desired result. When first lit, the burners do smoke a little. Once the combustion chambers get hot, the smoke stops. In my opinion, this a dandy little lightweight stove that can cook a lot of food.

The Butterfly oven is a companion for the Butterfly stove. The oven was designed to fit on top of one of the burners. St. Paul Mercantile sells it for

$55. The instructions are pitiful; you almost have to look at the picture to assemble it. It is a two-person job to put together. It warns that the sharp metal parts can cut and I will attest to that. After it was assembled I added some sheet metal screws to the corners at the top and a few other places. Even with all the problems I had putting it together, I have to say it's a darn good little oven. The oven has inner baffles that make it very efficient for its size. It has a temperature gauge on the door. The temperatures are shown in centigrade, but you can find a conversion chart online to convert it to Fahrenheit. I decided to test the little oven by cooking two frozen biscuits. That is a pretty tough test and it passed with flying colors. The Butterfly oven works well on the side burner of an outdoor gas grill.

The Alpaca kerosene heater/cooker is a heavy-duty single burner stove with a tank capacity of .9 gallons. The top of the stove is configured like a gas range burner. We got it from Nitro-Pak Preparedness Center (800-866-4876, www.nitro-pak.com). We have used ours several times and it does a great job as a cooker as well as a room heater. As a heater, it works best with a pan of water over the burner because you can turn the burner up high without it smoking. The Butterfly oven will work on this stove. When we bought ours, the price was $65. Now the price is approaching $100. You can sometimes find them on eBay for much less. These two stoves and the oven should take care of all your cooking needs.

Should you decide to go with kerosene as your energy source, you should contact your local codes department to see if there are any restrictions on bulk storage.

Grain mill

Our long-term food supplies include around 300 pounds of wheat. Our problem was we had no means of milling the wheat. We ordered the best mill that Lehman's Hardware had for less than $200 dollars (877-438-5346, www.lehmans.com). This mill came with both stone and iron burrs, and does a fine job of milling wheat almost as fine as store-bought flour. Lehman's still carries the mill, but it only comes with iron burrs now. If you want good flour from your wheat you really need the stone burrs. Another mill that will fill the requirement having both types of burrs is the Wondermill Junior Deluxe from Homegrown Harvest (866-900-3321, www.homegrownharvest.com). I'm not going to list the features of this mill, but the company claims it is "the world's best," so it must be pretty good.

An electric grain mill is nice to have, if your budget will allow it. There are several good ones out there, but remember you won't always have electricity available, so the hand-powered mill should be your first priority. I suggest that you mill some wheat and practice making bread. It is a good feeling to know that you can make bread from your storeroom if you ever have to.

SuperPails

Emergency Essentials carries most any dry food you would want in your storeroom in 6-gallon "SuperPails" which are equal to eight #10 cans. They have wheat (both hard and soft), corn, and all types of dried beans. We added popcorn and soybeans to our long-term storage. We use popcorn for corn meal and soybeans have many food uses.

When ordering SuperPails from Emergency Essentials (800-999-1863, www.emergencyessentials.com), your order must weigh at least 200 pounds. A few SuperPails will add up pretty quick. They charge $12 dollars shipping for any order over $120 and you can't beat that.

Vitamins

One of my reference books advises that your storeroom should contain a large quantity of vitamin C. This is one vitamin your body doesn't store and it is possible a survival diet won't provide enough of this vital vitamin. Store it where light can't get to it. It has a shelf-life of about five years.

For quite some time I have wanted to write about our storeroom and how it came about. Is this the best possible storeroom? Probably not. Is it flexible? Yes. Can anyone do it without any special skills? Yes. Is it expensive? No. Anyone can do it without busting the budget if it is done in baby steps like we did, one module at a time. I would caution that if this type of storage room is built in an above-ground room on a wood floor that some consideration be given to reinforcing the floor from underneath. Stored foods are extremely heavy.

Other books we found helpful when stocking our storeroom were *Gateway to Survival is Storage* by Walter D. Batchelor and *Passport to Survival* by Esther Dickey. Δ

Chapter 25
Keep your vittles cool with a modern spring box

By Kai Moessle

Keeping food cool without electricity isn't a huge challenge anymore. These days, propane and kerosene-powered refrigerators and freezers are readily available. However, if you're not willing (or able) to spend the rather large amount of money they cost, it seems you are doomed to an ice trip to the nearest convenience store every few days, which will cost you more over time than the refrigerator itself. That was the situation I found myself in when I started to plan for more than just the three-day-weekend stays on my property. I had planned on getting a kerosene fridge (I don't like propane), but I would need something to keep milk, butter, cheese, etc. cool until then.

Fortunately, my property has a good spring that feeds a little pond with really cold water about 10x15 feet and one foot deep. Bottles are easily kept

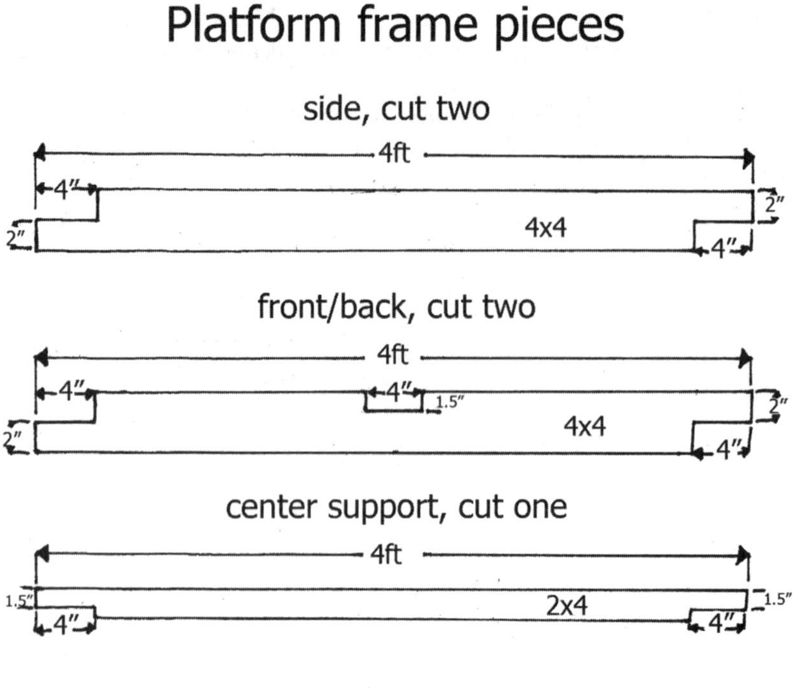

Frame parts for the platform with tools used

cold by putting them right in the water along the edge, but a Tupperware with cold cuts or a zip-lock bag with bread tends to float away and end up right in the middle of the pond. Starting your day trying to prod breakfast to shore with a stick or wading into 35 degree water to get it tends to put a damper on the best of moods; although your doctor will probably tell you that the latter is excellent for improving circulation in your legs.

So, after a few weeks of thinking and planning, I decided to upgrade the old spring box design to a "water jacket cooler." I figured that by finding two plastic boxes that fit inside each other with about a one-inch gap in between, I could let the spring water flow through this gap and cool the air in the inner box where I could keep my vittles.

The whole cooler would have to be located far enough below the spring pond to let gravity do the work of pumping the water. To make sure the water circulates all around, it needed to have the intake on the bottom and the outlet near the top of the outer box.

All the parts and tools needed are readily available at any hardware store or home improvement center. The dimensions of the wooden shell are based on the outer plastic box, so I would recommend buying this first and then figuring out the size and lumber necessary for the shell.

Tools used:

25-foot tape measure
hammer
24-inch hand saw
2-inch wood chisel
wooden mallet (homemade)
framing square
utility knife

Container parts:

14-gallon storage tote (inner box)
16.5-gallon storage tote (outer box)
(2) ¾-inch galvanized couplings
¾-inch galvanized close nipple
1 foot (or longer) of 1-inch PVC pipe
1-inch slip to 1-inch threaded PVC bushing
1 inch-threaded PVC coupling
5 pounds of 8d nails

Lumber list

Platform:
2 pieces 4x4x8 feet
1 piece 2x4x8 feet
4 pieces 1x6x8 feet
Wooden shell:
1 piece 2x4x8 feet
6 pieces 1x6x8 feet

Altogether, I didn't quite spend $100.

First on the "to-do" list is the inlet and outlet on the outer box. The inlet goes on the bottom on one side; the outlet near the top on the opposite side. To be able to use a regular garden hose as the supply pipe, I decided to use a hose bib in the intake; it's also easy to disconnect the line without any tools that way. Thread on ¾-inch coupling onto the rear end of the hose bib and the ¾-inch close nipple into the coupling (use Teflon tape on both joints for a tight seal). Next, cut a hole into the outer box along the bottom edge of one sidewall just big enough for the close nipple to fit through. Also cut the same size hole in a 2x4-inch piece of 3/8-inch-thick wood. This piece of wood reinforces the box wall somewhat on the outside and acts as a backer

Platform frame assembled and leveled on concrete blocks

Outer box (front) and inner box (back) on the finished platform. Note the water outlets on the outer box.

Wooden shell completed with both boxes inside. Note the two 1x3s that keep inner box from floating.

After a few hours, the inner box started to bulge inward from the water pressure, so I built a brace out of some 1x6 and 2x4 scraps.

for the coupling to insure a watertight seal. To finish the intake, thread the wood piece on the nipple, push the nipple through the box wall, add an O-ring (or homemade rubber gasket from a piece of inner tube) and screw on the second coupling. Make it good and tight, but don't overdo it or the box wall might crack.

For the outlet, take the piece of 1-inch PVC pipe and glue on the slip-to-threaded bushing. Cut a hole into the box wall on the opposite side of the intake and near the top just big enough for the threaded part of the bushing to fit through. I didn't use a backer piece here because it doesn't have to be watertight (the water flows out here anyway). Push the bushing through, screw on the 1-inch threaded coupling and — *presto!* — the outer box is done.

To set up the whole affair, you need to find a spot along your stream where you can build a small platform. The spot also needs to be low enough to keep the water outlet below the start of the intake pipe (the far end of my garden hose). If there are a lot of leaves or other debris that could get sucked into the hose in your stream, it might be necessary to add an intake filter or tie a piece of screen across the opening.

I was lucky, since my little pond is dammed up and the stream has enough drop, I only had to go about 50 feet down from the dam. To keep the platform off the ground I used four old concrete blocks I had lying around, but some flat rocks will work too. The frame of the platform consists of four 4x4 pieces, 48 inches long with a half lap joint on each end and one 2x4 piece, 48 inches long with a half lap joint at each end. The 2x4 helps to keep the 1x6 boards from sagging when you step on the platform. Nail the frame together, set it on the blocks (or rocks), and level it in all directions. Next, cut the 1x6 to length (48 inches again) and nail on for the decking.

The wooden shell for the two boxes will vary in size, depending on the dimensions of the outer box. My shell is 26 inches wide, 21 inches deep, and 19 inches high. It's nothing more than a box without a bottom, fastened to the platform. This not only makes it look pretty but keeps the inner box from floating up by way of two 1x3 crosspieces that slide into slits cut in the front and back walls of the shell. Of course, the inlet and outlet need openings cut as well. A lid to cover everything and to keep critters out completes the cooler shell, again built from 1x6 with 2x4 crosspieces. I also added a piece of metal roofing on top of the lid to keep rain out — you could just throw a tarp over it.

The last piece I had to build was a brace for the inner box, which had started to bulge inward after a couple hours. It only took some of the 1x6 and 2x4 cutoffs. I also cut some leftover two-inch foam insulation to size and laid it on top of the inner box (it fits perfectly under the lid) to keep more cold air in. All that's left to do now is to hook up the intake line (garden hose) to the bib, fill it with water to start the flow, drop the other end into the water upstream, and wait a while for the inner box to cool off.

And just how cold does it get? Well, it doesn't work as well as your kitchen refrigerator, but on a 75 degree day the inner box stays between 45 and 50 degrees, cold enough to keep my butter and cheese from melting. It might be possible to get it even colder by putting insulation between the outer box and the shell, but I haven't tried that yet. One minor problem seems to be some condensation on the inside, which is probably due to the lid not sealing airtight like on a regular fridge. As long as all the food is in plastic bags or lidded bowls, it's not that big of a deal.

Finally, as long as your water supply doesn't freeze up, you don't have to drain the cooler for winter. The lowest temperature this past winter was -24° F and the water ran steadily without even so much as a ring of ice around the outside. Δ

Chapter 26
Build this sturdy large-capacity food dehydrator

By Charles Sanders

Drying of food as a means of preservation has been around for a long time. Populations in suitably dry climates all around the globe have dried meat, fish, fruit, and vegetables in times of plenty as a way to provide for the leaner months of the year. My grandmother used to tell us of when she was a child, helping to spread apple slices on the top of a tin-shed roof for drying. An aunt once described stringing fresh young bean pods on a long heavy thread and hanging them to dry, coming up with what they called leather-britches beans. Obviously, these were simple and imperfect food drying systems, but they do show ways in which food can be dried at home.

Essentially, dehydration of food removes the moisture that provides the environment conducive to the growth of bacteria. Removal of the moisture results in a product that can be stored for months or even years. Fortunately, for those of us in the less arid climates, methods exist which enable us to dry suitable quantities of foods at home without having to spread the food out on our rooftops. In fact, a really good food dehydrator can be made easily.

For the past few years, some round plastic food dehydrators have been available at retail outlets, by mail order, and from "infomercials" on TV. These units introduced many people to food drying. The ones I examined, however, were too lightly constructed to stand up to many years of regular and heavy use. They also lacked the capacity to do much in the way of drying a large quantity of food.

Other commercially available dehydrators that I have seen used were large, high quality units. These models were mounted on rollers and resembled a portable dishwasher in size. These units could dry a considerable quantity of food at a time and were being put to heavy use by the family who owned the two of them. They were also way too expensive for me.

When I decided to begin food drying, I did so after visiting with the folks using the floor model dehydrators described above. These friends showed me containers of dried, diced carrots, onion slices, apples, and other fruits and vegetables. What impressed me the most about this method of preservation was the amount of space that was saved by drying the foods. For example, a five-gallon bucketful of carrots could be sliced, steamed, and dried and made to take up the space of a shoebox. Half of a five-gallon bucket of apples, when sliced and dried, fit nicely in a gallon-sized freezer bag.

Since building our own dehydrator, we have dried jerky, apples, strawberries, carrots, onions, green beans, bananas, fruit leathers, and several other fruits and vegetables. Some of these were experiments, but we use the dryer each year to put up several bushels of sliced apples. These treats make a healthful and tasty

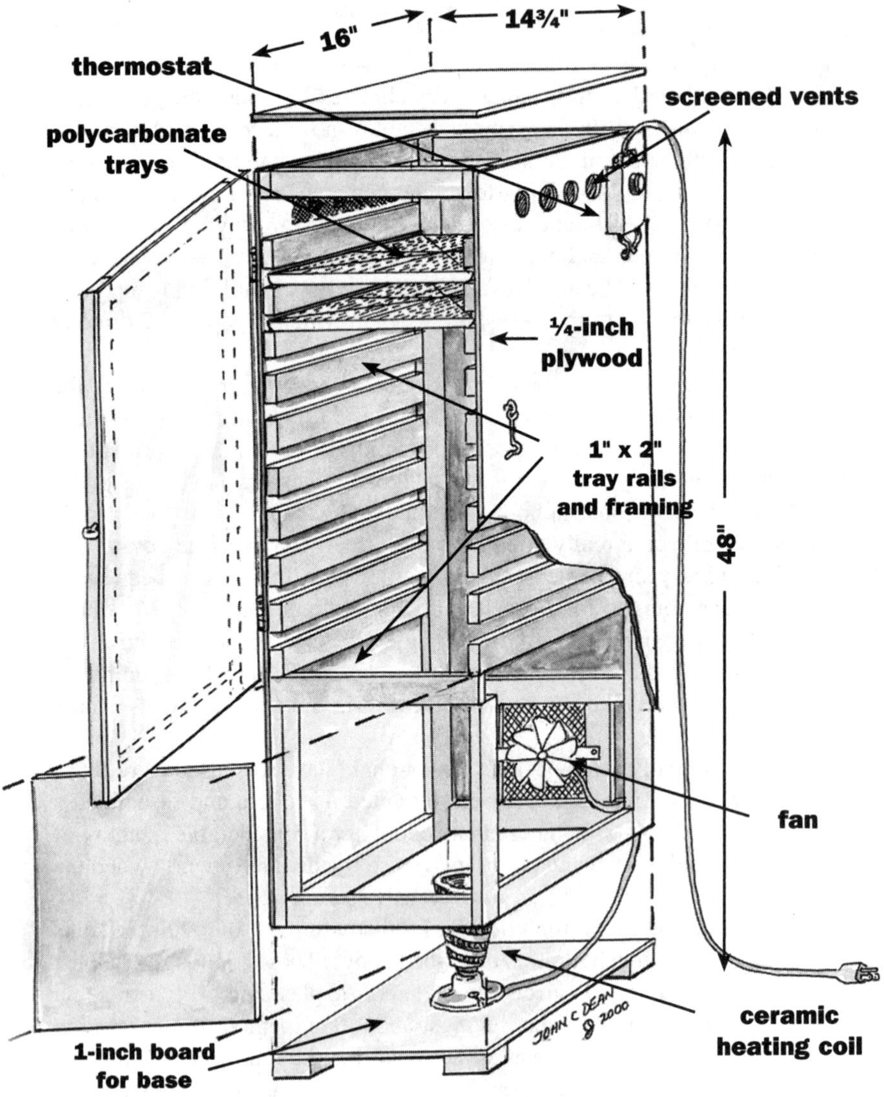

alternative to junk snack food for the whole family, much better to munch on than potato chips.

Below are instructions for building a food dryer similar to ours. Use your imagination, intuition, and abilities when building your own. Use what you have or what you can obtain easily and cheaply in the way of materials. Make your food dryer to suit your own circumstances. It might be nearly identical to the one described or a vastly improved version.

For our dehydrator, I began by purchasing the light polycarbonate trays. I then designed and built the dryer cabinet around them. After considering various materials for constructing the trays from scratch, and after studying the effects of these materials on some foods, I decided the trays were what were needed. The acids in some foods may react unfavorably with certain metals such as aluminum screen. Wood, as used in dowel rod-type trays may absorb food tastes and odors. Fiberglass screen can leave minute fiberglass splinters sticking to the dried food. Galvanized screen is out, due to its zinc-based coating reacting with foods. One material which I have not tried, and which may warrant experimentation, is nylon screening. If stretched tightly on light wooden frames, this material might be durable enough to withstand repeated use. I do not know of any health problems posed by the use of the material on dryer trays. The trays that we used were simply better than any alternative that I could come up with at the time.

Whatever the size or material of your trays, design the cabinet size around them allowing for sufficient room below for the heat element and room to easily fit the trays within. I am providing the measurements below to serve only as a guide for your own construction process, because the type and size of trays that you come up with may vary from that which I devised. Our dryer measures 48" tall by 14¾" wide by 16" deep. The trays themselves measure 13¾" square. A slightly different size tray is available from Excalibur Dehydrators, listed at the end of this article.

In the accompanying photographs and drawing you can see some of the construction details of our dryer. I made the base of heavy one-inch particle board because that is what I had. Quarter-inch plywood made up the sides and top of the cabinet. I ripped 1 x 2s for the framing in the cabinet and for the rails which support the drying trays.

Ordinary screen wire covers the six x six-inch fan opening. Holes cut near the top of each side are covered on the inside with strips of screen and allow moisture and air to escape.

If you do not have one, a wide variety of suitable fan and motor assemblies are available from: W.W. Grainger Distribution Group, 1901 Plantside Drive, Louisville, KY 40299. Request one of their catalogs. This is an electrical supply wholesaler. You may have to have a retailer order this unit for you. Order fan-motor assembly #7C7-27. The cost was under $20. Just remember to use a relatively small fan (about four inches in diameter) to move the air rather slowly through the dryer. You want the fan to ventilate the box and move the heated air throughout, but not to cool the food on the trays.

The heat source is a ceramic heat coil screwed into a regular porcelain lamp base. The lamp fixture is secured to the base and either wired directly to a three-prong plug or through a thermostat. The coil was purchased from a local hardware store and is rated at 600 watts. The cost was less than $5. The lamp base cost about a dollar.

Although it isn't absolutely necessary, I added a thermostat assembly that I had scrounged up. This addition helped to cut down on tending and tray rotation. The thermostat easily handles the appropriate 100°-150°F temperature range. If you purchase a thermostat, specify a fairly narrow temperature spread for the on-off cycle.

Old unmatched hinges for the door and hooks and eyes for the closures were scrounged from the workshop.

Dried apples

Since dried apples are so popular at our house, I will give you the simple directions for drying them as an example of how simple it is to dry foods. First, I use one of the clamp-on slicers that core, slice, and peel the apples in one operation. It takes about three to five seconds to do one apple with one of these peelers. I have looked over several models and prefer the one I purchased from Back To Basics Products, listed at the end of the article. With this peeler, a simple knife cut is all that is needed to produce a handful of neatly prepared apple rings. By the way, you can save the peelings and cores and make a nice batch of apple jelly from them later.

As I peel the fruit, I place the rings in a bowl containing a solution made from about a half-cup or so of lemon juice and about two to four cups water. This acid bath prevents the apples from turning brown as they dry. I have also heard of some folks dipping the apple rings in plain 7-Up or Sprite for the same purpose.

After dipping the apples, I drain them in a plastic colander and arrange them on the dryer trays. Let them dry to a chewy leathery consistency and they are ready to store. We have found that the 10 trays full of freshly dried apples fills up a one-gallon zip-top plastic bag. After bagging, they are stored in the freezer. They make great snacks for work, camping, hiking, or TV-munching. They make a really good apple pie as well.

Vegetables are similarly easy to dry, usually requiring a simple steaming prior to going into the dryer. My wife has also used the dryer to dry sprays of flowers such as baby's breath, statice, and globe amaranth for use in dried bouquets and wreaths. It worked quite well for that, too, as she prepared those items for sale. Herbs can also be dried in the dehydrator. Δ

Chapter 27 Alternative food preservation

By Jackie Clay

When one is striving for a self-reliant lifestyle, food is one of the most important things to consider. "Grow your own!" is our battle cry. Our garden is bountiful and we spend a blissful summer, eating chiefly from it: fresh beans, squash, corn, cukes, lettuce, chard, broccoli, and more. And of course, we butcher our home-raised chickens and pig, harvest our deer in the fall, and enjoy fresh rolls from our homegrown wheat.

We certainly can up tons and tons of great food to serve not only during the winter, but during the coming years, as well. But have you considered the other methods of food preservation? Like canning, there are several other tried and true ways to put up your bounty. (If you've read any pioneering books, like Laura Ingalls Wilder's series of *Little House* books, you'll remember some of them.)

Not only do the other methods of preserving food give you an alternate way of keeping food from spoiling, but more importantly, I think, they provide variety and interest to your everyday meals.

There are a few alternative food preservation methods I'm not going into detail about. These include salting and larding. Both of these methods *do* keep food, but due to health concerns, they probably aren't a great idea today. We are all trying valiantly to cut down on our salt intake to improve our blood pressure and also to reduce our fat consumption so our heart lasts as long as our plans and dreams do. I'll also skip over freezing. Yes, you can freeze most foods, but if you lose power, there goes your food. Or the freezer quietly dies and you lose your food without even knowing you've got a problem. Or the food stays in the freezer too long and develops freezer burn. Instead, here are some other methods you might want to try.

Dehydration

Dehydrating food at home is a great idea. The food remains very fresh-tasting on rehydration, it takes very little room to store, the food is extremely light so it can be carried, and best of all, dehydrating is very easy and fun to do. Like canning, once you start, you will be on a mission.

A bowl of fresh strawberries waiting to be dehydrated

What foods can you dehydrate? Here is just a sample: raisins, cherries, pineapple, peaches, apples, plums, watermelon, peas, corn, hominy, beans, tomatoes, onions, potatoes, peppers, squash, pumpkin, apricots, mushrooms, asparagus, turnips, rutabagas, raspberries, blueberries, citrus peel, bananas, mangos, fruit leathers of all types and mixtures, and jerky. Gee, I get hungry just making this list.

Is it hard? Expensive to get into? No to both questions. If you can cut up food, you can dehydrate it. There are no "sulfuring" or lengthy pre-treatments necessary. And you can pick up a new electric dehydrator for less than $50 at most stores that carry canning equipment. I got mine several years back from Wal-Mart. My second one came from our local thrift store, complete with fruit leather trays and a manual for $3.

I've also dehydrated on nylon window screens in the back of our sun-heated Suburban with the window up, on flat roof tops, the hot, dry attic, and in the oven of my gas range with only the pilot on. Dehydrating is an ancient art, requiring no special equipment. But I will say that using an electric dehydrator sure makes things easier, quicker, and more reliable.

Here are instructions for dehydrating several foods so you'll get the idea. Then pick up a good book—even at the library if you can't afford to buy one—and read it thoroughly, making notes for the future. Like I said, dehydrating is really easy for anyone to do. The main things are to lay the food out in a single layer so the pieces don't overlap, and to check the trays periodically to make sure one area isn't drying faster than the others. You may need to switch trays around to ensure that the food dries evenly throughout the entire dehydrator. Make *sure* the food is dried to the dryness recommended for each food. If there is too much moisture in the food, it will mold. You will be storing your dehydrated food in airtight containers, probably jars. Pay special attention right after you store the newly dehydrated pieces. If there is any condensation on the inside of the jars, *immediately* put the pieces back in the dehydrator and dry a little longer.

Apples:

Peel, core, and slice solid apples into ½-inch thick slices or rings. To keep from turning brown, soak the slices in 1 cup lemon juice to 1 quart of water for 10 minutes or in 1 Tbsp. ascorbic acid (Vitamin C tablets, crushed) in 1 quart of water. Neither will affect the taste of the apples and they will keep white. Lay on a single layer on your dehydrator trays and dry until they are leathery. In the old days, apple rings were strung on stout string and hung from the rafters of the hot attic to dry. While this works well today, you do risk having dust and insects on the drying apples. Use as a snack or in pies, crisps, and other baked goods. You can also make sweet spiced apple pieces by rolling the pieces in cinnamon sugar before dehydrating. They are very good.

Strawberries laying on dehydrator tray so they don't touch

Cherries:

Wash, cut in half, and pit. Lay in a single layer on your dehydrator trays and dehydrate until leathery and slightly sticky like raisins.

Seedless grapes and blueberries:

Wash and stem fruit. Dip into boiling water for 30 seconds to crack skin. This lets them dry "wrinkled" instead of "fat" looking, which isn't too appealing. Dry until leathery as raisins. Use as a snack or in baked goods.

Raspberries or blackberries:

Simply pick through the berries, removing any stems or leaves. Lay in a single layer and dry until leathery. Quick and tasty.

Pineapple:

Peel, core, and slice fully ripe pineapple. Cut into ½-inch slices. You may roll the pieces in sugar to dehydrate "sugared" pineapple, like you get in trail mixes, or simply dehydrate for a natural fruit. Use as a snack or in baked goods.

Strawberries:

Remove the leaves and core of fully ripe strawberries. Cut smaller berries into halves or larger ones into ½-inch slices. Dry until more crisp than leathery. You can also grind the dehydrated slices for ease of using in yogurt, desserts, and baked goods. They don't rehydrate well; the color is darkened and they look unappetizing.

Peaches:

Peel by immersing in boiling water for a minute, then remove pit. Cut into ½-inch slices and dip into either lemon water or ascorbic acid water to keep from darkening. Dry until leathery. Use as a snack or in baked goods and desserts.

Carrots:

Wash, scrub, and peel if desired. Slice or dice. Blanch for three minutes, drain. Dry until more brittle than leathery. Use in soups, stews, and casseroles.

Mushrooms:

Wash gently to remove dirt, but don't soak in water. Cut into ¼-inch slices. Dry until brittle. Use in stews, soups, on pizzas, or in casseroles.

Onions:

Trim ends, peel, and cut into ¼-inch slices (complete rounds). Dry until brittle. If onion flakes are desired, whir in blender to make the size pieces you like. If powder is what you want, whir longer, then dump powder onto dehydrator sheet tray and dry further to ensure that the powder is dry enough to prevent clumping in storage. Use in soups, stews, casseroles, or for general seasoning.

Hot peppers:

Rinse, cut into pieces about ½ inch thick or halve small chiles. You may also roast the peppers on a grill or in your oven until the skins are charred, place in a paper bag for an hour or so, then dip in ice water to remove skins. Then dehydrate. Peppers should be crisp when dehydrated. You may also whir in a blender to make your own hot seasoning powder.

Sweet peppers:

Wash, remove stems and seeds. Slice or dice in ½-inch pieces. Dry until leathery/brittle. Use in stews, on pizzas, in casseroles, Spanish rice, or for general seasoning.

Tomatoes:

Use a meaty type tomato that isn't too juicy. Wash, dip in boiling water for 30 seconds, then hold in cold water. Remove skins. Core if necessary. Cut into ¼ to ½-inch slices. Dry until crisp. You can also sprinkle moist tomato slices with Italian seasonings such as basil or oregano. We like dehydrated Sungold cherry tomatoes as a snack. They are very fruity and sweet, almost like apricots. You can use dehydrated tomatoes

Asparagus is great dehydrated.

I store a lot of my dehydrated food in jars and tins.

in soups, stews, on pizzas, or in general cooking. You can also powder in a blender for an even more versatile product. Like the onion powder, return the tomato powder to the dehydrator trays, lined with fruit leather plastic trays, and dehydrate more to be sure no moisture remains that would cause clumping during storage.

Potatoes:

Wash, peel, and cut into ¼-inch slices. Blanch for 5-6 minutes. Rinse well in cold water, which removes starch that would make them less palatable. Dry until brittle. Use in potatoes au gratin, scalloped potatoes, stews, and other combined dishes. You can also grate the potatoes with a coarse grater, blanch, rinse and pat dry, and use these as dehydrated hash browns.

String beans:

Use any variety with small seeds, yellow or green. Wash, string if necessary, cut off ends, and cut into 1-inch pieces. Blanch for 4-6 minutes, drain. Dry until brittle. Rehydrate before use. In the old days, folks used to use a needle and strong thread and string whole green beans and hang them from the rafters until dry. These are called leather britches and are very good. Like the apples, you do run a risk of having them pick up a little dust, but you can rinse before rehydrating in boiling water. They have a flavor of their own that many older people fondly remember from their childhood.

Pumpkin:

Pumpkin and winter squash are dehydrated the same way. Peel and remove seeds and goop. Cut into ¼-inch strips. Blanch for 2 minutes, then drain and dry until brittle. Use in baking, soups, and stews. Like the leather britches above, homesteaders and Native Americans in days past used to string up or hang rings of pumpkin and squash on small poles to dry in hot autumn days. I often toss a handful of dried pumpkin or squash into the blender and grind it—then add it to my multigrain bread. You never know it's there, but there *is* a decidedly good sweetness and taste you can't put your finger on. (Of course you don't tell anyone you put squash in the bread!)

Fruit leathers:

You can make fruit leather out of just about any fruit or combination that appeals to you. I often do apple/raspberry or strawberry. It makes the berries go further, as we are often short of wild berries. To make the fruit leather, rinse the fruit, remove the pits/seeds. Puree in a blender until smooth or run through a food mill. Add any sweetener or spices you want. Mix well. Cover dehydrator trays with a heavy food grade plastic wrap or use the special fruit leather sheets that come with your dehydrator. Spread puree evenly 1/8 inch thick on trays. Dry until it is pliable, yet leathery. Peel up and check for moisture. Roll up like a jelly roll and cut into convenient pieces.

Jerky:

Besides dehydrating fruits and vegetables, you can dehydrate meat of all kinds. Do *not* try to dehydrate meat with fat on it, because it will get rancid during storage. Use only lean meat. If you want to make jerky out of hamburger, choose only the extra lean or else be sure to freeze or refrigerate while you wait to use it.

To dehydrate meat and poultry, debone it and cut off all fat and gristle. Slice into pieces ¼ inch thick, across the grain to get the most tender cuts. You may marinate it overnight in the refrigerator in your favorite recipe. This does not affect the keeping quality of the product, only the taste. Typical marinades include vinegar, brown sugar, soy sauce, Italian dressing, etc.

Drain your meat/poultry pieces, then lay out on your dehydrator trays. I always use a fruit leather tray on the bottom to catch the inevitable drips and make cleanup easier. Meat that is dehydrated must be brought up to a temperature of 160° F if it is going to be stored on the shelf. You can do this by boiling it in the marinade for five minutes before dehydrating or by putting the dehydrated meat in the oven and baking at 275° F for 10 minutes.

Meat should be dehydrated until it is very leathery. The drier the better. If it has any moisture, it will cause condensation on the inside of storage jars and will mold. Check it very closely the first few days. If you see *any* condensation, redo it for a few hours more.

In the old days, jerky and dried meat was dried to a stick-like consistency. It had to be held in the mouth several minutes before you could even begin to chew it. Today's jerky is usually softer for ease of eating, but commercial jerky also has preservatives in it to keep it from spoiling; your homemade dry meat either needs to be refrigerated if you want it a bit softer or dried *very dry* to keep on the shelf.

Rehydrating dried foods

Some of your dehydrated food can be used as is, when used in soups, stews, or other moist dishes. Vegetables, especially, can just be tossed in boiling water like you would do to cook fresh ones. They'll rehydrate quickly and plump up nicely. I rehydrate my string beans and potato slices before use; they are more tender and will cook more dependably that way. Simply pour boiling water over them and wait until they are plump. So simple!

You can also rehydrate fruit to use as a dessert or in baked recipes. Simply pour boiling water over the dry fruit and let set until it is plumped up. It will take about 10 minutes. Drain and add sugar or honey, if desired.

Smoking meat

Smoking meat is an ancient food preservation method. While it does make meat last a long while, it is only safely effective during the cold months. High temperatures are hard on smoked meat and even properly cured meat will spoil after awhile. Smoked meat has a sweet, unique flavor and a smokehouse full of home-cured bacon, ham, shoulder, venison, and fish makes winter a wonderful time of the year. Absolutely nothing smells better than entering a cold smokehouse or other meat storage pantry and savoring the aroma about you.

Is smoking meat difficult? No, but it does take a little trial and error to get it perfect. You *can* get edible, good-flavored meat on your very first attempt. But like all homestead skills, practice makes perfect. My first smoking experience was with fish. They are easy to start with because they are smaller and easier to quickly smoke. A neighbor brought me a pan of home-smoked suckers. Not wanting to be impolite, I gingerly nibbled on a bit of one offered to me. *Wow*! I really, really liked it. Suckers are "trash" fish and ugly to boot, but they instantly took on a whole different aura.

With the neighbor's help, I turned an old junk clothes dryer into a sucker smoker. Basically, we just took out the drum, turning the dryer into a "closet" of sorts. I mounted two old broomsticks across the top of it and I was in business. To make the smoke needed, I simply used a small electric hotplate

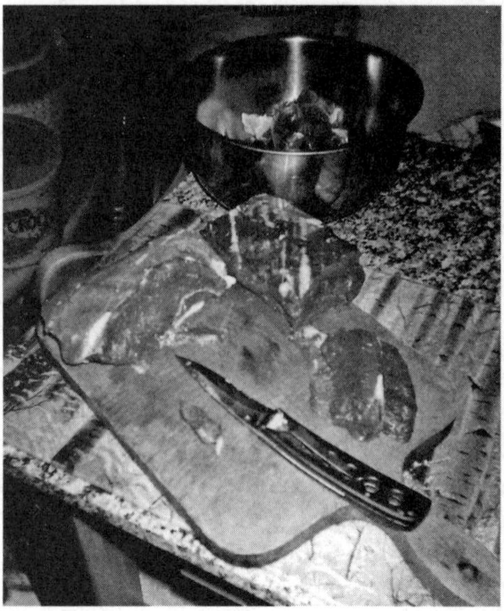

Venison being cut up to make jerky

scavenged from the dump and an old cast iron frying pan full of apple wood chips. Turned on low, the hotplate burned the wood chips, creating a nice cool, dense smoke. I only had to add chips a few times during the day and night, and I had the perfect smoking fire.

Soon after, we caught our own bunch of suckers out of the nearby creek where they were going to spawn. After gutting them, I cut off the heads and soaked them overnight in a mild brine made of 1 cup non-iodized salt to 1 gallon of cold water, with ½ cup brown sugar added. Then I held the fish open with small sharpened branches and hung them from the broomsticks by heavy strings run through the meat just below the bone behind the gill area. No fish were close enough to touch. The spring days were cool and the nights cooler—the perfect weather for cold smoking. I turned on my hot plate and shut the door. The smoker should not get hotter than 70° F during the smoking process for fish.

Smoke medium-large fish all day and night if you plan on eating the fish soon or freezing or canning them after smoking. If you plan on keeping them longer, they must be held in the operating smoker for up to a week. This turns the fish leathery, driving out all moisture. During the long smoking period, you have to man the fire 24/7 or the smoking is ineffective. I smoke my fish for 24 hours, then can it. This works very well for me.

Peppers of all kinds are great dried or pickled for variety.

When you say "smoked meat," bacon and ham instantly come to mind. Of course, venison and beef may be smoked in the same way. In smoking meat, as with smoking fish, there are actually two steps, the cure and the actual smoking. The cure serves to help tenderize the meat and protect it from spoilage during the smoking.

There are two basic types of cures, the brine cure that I used for my fish and the dry cure. While I like the brine cure for fish, as it kind of draws out any "fishy" taste, the dry cure generally works best for meat. It is also easier for the beginner to use.

You can buy prepackaged mixtures for your dry cure from many local stores that sell hunting supplies, or from your meat market. There are also many mail order supply houses that sell cures. Many cures contain saltpeter. This controversial ingredient is believed by some to be a carcinogen, but it has been used—and is still used commercially—for generations in meat cures. It keeps the attractive reddish color of the finished smoked meat. Personally, I prefer not to use it. My meat is darker in color and maybe not as beautiful, but I feel better having left it out. Saltpeter does nothing to keep the meat from spoiling.

One homemade cure formula for 100 pounds of meat is 8 pounds pickling salt and 2 pounds of brown sugar, mixed well. If you choose to add the saltpeter, you would add 2 ounces also. Keep your meat between 38 and 40° F before curing, then try to hold it around that temperature during curing.

You will use about 1 ounce of the dry cure per pound of ham and a bit less per pound of bacon. Rub it well into the meat to be cured. For larger pieces of meat, ham for instance, you will rub 1/3 of the amount, three times, then again a week after the last treatment. Hang the meat so it can drip into a pan below, not onto meat held on lower shelves. You'll cure a side of bacon in 14 days or a ham in a little over a month. Remember to keep the meat around 40° F for safest curing. When the cure is complete, it's time to smoke.

You can build a smokehouse if you are really serious about smoking quantities of meat each year. A smokehouse is simply a small building the size of a small outhouse, usually built of block, that is varmint-proof and convenient to work in. You can find plans in many books. You can even make a "smokehouse" out of a barrel with a fire pit located in the ground a few feet away and a buried stovepipe leading from it, upward to the bottom of the barrel that contains your meat. The main thing is to contain much of the smoke, yet not raise the temperature of the smokehouse higher than 90 ° F. This is a "cool" smoke and does more to preserve the meat than a hot smoke does.

Run a strong cord through your meat so it can hang from poles at the top of your smokehouse. There should be enough room so that the meat pieces do not touch. This lets the smoke completely surround and penetrate the meat. To keep the meat from becoming too salty, you can scrub the outside of the cured meat with fresh water and a brush, then dry it overnight before you smoke it.

The type of wood you choose for smoking greatly affects the taste of your finished product. Some good woods are maple, apple, cherry, mesquite, and alder. Do *not* use pine or any other evergreen. The meat will end up nearly inedible.

The larger the meat pieces are, the longer they need to smoke. In general, bacon will usually be adequately smoked in a 24 hour period or a little longer. You want the outside golden brown, not dark saddle brown. Hams and shoulders usually will be adequately smoked in about 48 hours or a little longer. In the old days, folks smoked their meat longer, resulting in a more jerky-like end product. It held well for long periods but was not as tender as most people like today. Cured, smoked meat will keep all winter and into the spring. But as the days get hot, the meat can become bug infested and spoil.

For this reason, I usually use up most of my smoked meat during the winter and can up the rest for later use. Once in the jar, it is good for many, many years.

Pickling

When you say "pickling," most people think dill or sweet pickles or other cucumber products. But pickling has a much broader scope. You can also pickle onions, carrots, beans, cauliflower, peppers, cabbage, mushrooms, eggs, fish, and meat. While you probably wouldn't sit down to a meal of pickled this or that, pickling definitely has a place on the homestead, as it is a reliable way not only to preserve more food, but to preserve it in a way that gives it a unique flavor. This does a lot to relieve boredom, especially when times are less than wonderful. Often when you eat well, you feel well too.

Here is a sampling of great pickling recipes. If you want more, check your interlibrary loan or Amazon.com for the wonderful pickling book, *The Complete Book of Pickles and Relishes* by Leonard Lewis Levinson. It's out of print, but it's one of my very favorites.

Mustard beans:

(Tastes like honey mustard sauce, not "mustardy" at all.)

8 quarts green or wax beans
salt
6 cups sugar
1 cup flour
5 Tbsp. dry mustard powder
1 Tbsp. turmeric
6 cups vinegar

Simmer beans, cut into 1-inch pieces if desired, in salted water until barely tender. You do not want to "cook" them; they are pickles. Drain. Mix dry ingredients in large saucepan. Add vinegar and bring to a boil. Stir well. Add drained beans and bring to a boil. Simmer 5 minutes. Pack into hot sterilized jars. Process in a water bath canner for 10 minutes.

Pickled onions:

1 gallon small onions
1 cup salt
2 cups sugar
6 cups white vinegar

Scald onions for 2 minutes in boiling water. Dip out and hold in cold water. Peel. Sprinkle with salt. Add ice water and let stand overnight. Drain. Rinse. Drain again.

Add sugar to vinegar. Simmer 10 minutes. Pack onions into hot sterilized jars. Heat pickling liquid to boiling. Ladle over onions to within ½ inch of the top of the jar. Process in water bath canner for 10 minutes.

Pickled peppers:

1 gallon peppers
1½ cups pickling salt
1 gallon ice water
5 cups vinegar
1 cup sugar

Wash and drain long Hungarian or other peppers. Cut 2 small slits in each pepper or cut in half, removing the seeds. Dissolve salt in 1 gallon ice water and pour over peppers in a large roasting pan. Let stand overnight. Drain, rinse, and drain again.

Add sugar to vinegar. Simmer 15 minutes. Pack peppers into hot, sterilized jars. Heat pickling liquid to boiling and pour over peppers to ½ inch of top of jar. Process for 15 minutes in boiling water bath.

I use these peppers, sliced, on my pizzas. Very good.

Pickled eggs:

20 eggs
2 cups white vinegar
1½ quarts water
2 tsp. salt
1 small dry hot pepper
1 Tbsp. mixed pickling spices

Simmer eggs for 30 minutes to make hardboiled eggs. Cool in cold water and peel.

Make a pickling solution of the remaining ingredients, adding spices in a spice bag. Bring to a boil. Add peeled eggs and bring to a boil again. Pack into hot, sterilized jars. Ladle hot pickling solution over the eggs, completely covering them, to within 1 inch of the top of the jar. Process for 10 minutes in a boiling water bath.

Corned beef:

8 qts. cold water
3 lbs. pickling salt
2 Tbsp. brown sugar
1 oz. sodium nitrate (optional; saves red color in meat)
1 Tbsp. mixed pickling spices
20 bay leaves
10 lbs. lean beef brisket
8 cloves of garlic

Combine all ingredients except meat and simmer for 10 minutes. Place meat in a crock with a tight fitting cover. Add garlic, pour cold pickling solution over meat. Weight meat down with a heavy plate and sterilized rock (boiled). Put on crock cover and cover that with 2 layers of clean cloth, tied tightly around crock. Store in a cool (38-40° F) place for 2 weeks. Use after that time or can chunks up.

Pickled mixed vegetables:

2 heads cauliflower
1 quart peeled carrots
1½ cups small whole peeled onions
¼ cup salt
2½ cups sugar
2 Tbsp. mustard seed
1 Tbsp. celery seed
1 tsp. turmeric
2 qt. white vinegar
1 hot dry red pepper (optional)

Cut cauliflower into smaller pieces. Cut carrots into slices or smaller chunks. Add onions and sprinkle salt over them and cover with ice water. Let stand for 3 hours. Drain, rinse, and drain again. In a large saucepan, combine sugar, spices, and vinegar. If you want hot pickled veggies, add hot pepper to vinegar mix. Bring to a boil. Add flowerets, onions, and carrots and bring to a boil again. Boil until vegetables are just barely tender. Pack hot vegetables into hot jar and ladle pickling solution to cover them to within ½ inch of the top of the jar. Process in a hot water bath for 10 minutes.

As you can readily see, you can sure pickle a wide assortment of foods that give variety to your pantry. This is one good reason to use all these alternative methods of putting up food; you get a great variety of tongue tingling tastes at every meal. Boring meals are not acceptable. We can do much better when we combine our traditional home canning with dehydrated, smoked, and pickled foods too. Toss in a few jams, jellies, and preserves along with breads and rolls from our homegrown grains and every single meal is a celebration of self-reliant living. You can't get that satisfied feeling by dumping something out of a box. Δ

Chapter 28
An economical battery of guns for the backwoods home

By Massad Ayoob

Everything's getting more expensive. Food. Gasoline. Guns and ammunition. Not everyone who appreciates the rural lifestyle was "born with a gun in their hand" the way some of us feel as if we've been. Many are urban-dwellers who've figured out for themselves that living closer to nature is a better way, and nothing from their previous metropolitan lifestyle has prepared them for their sudden realization that firearms are important, routinely-used tools for those who live "in the country."

Reading is good, but training is better. My advice to the people new to guns would be to take a firearms safety course before buying their first firearm. It'll give them a better idea of what they want, what they need, and what will suit them in terms of the size, the power, and the mechanics of the many, many firearms they have the option of buying. Your local office of the state Fish and Wildlife Department will be able to steer you toward hunter safety and firearms safety courses. As adult education goes, these courses are extremely affordable. If self-defense is your primary concern, your local gun shop or police department can direct you to armed citizen training programs. Most of these are geared toward folks about to apply for concealed carry permits, but the advice encompassed in their curricula are essential even for those only concerned with defending the home against violent intrusion.

Building a battery

A "battery" of firearms is a selection of guns that will cover multiple needs. The collector has "a collection," but the person who uses guns as tools has a working "battery," like a carpenter having multiple saws for different cutting purposes, and different screwdrivers for dealing with different sizes of screws.

At an absolute minimum, I would suggest four guns for the backwoods home. These would be a .22, a shotgun, a defensive-type handgun, and a high-powered rifle.

Just for the sake of argument, let's assume some frugality at work. I know trapshooters whose custom shotguns cost more than my SUV did new off the showroom floor, and gun collectors who might buy a single rare firearm that's worth more than my home and the real estate it sits on. Common sense economy is one of the values this publication celebrates, after all.

The .22

The .22 Long Rifle cartridge is the most popular in the United States. It has mild blast and mild recoil. Above all, it is cheap. With careful shopping, at this writing you can buy 500 cartridges for $12 to $15. Because it is a low-pressure cartridge, the manufacturers don't have to wrap a lot of super-strong metallurgy around it, and .22s tend to be cheaper than more powerful guns of similar quality.

Let me say it here and now: because it is so mild and inexpensive to shoot, the .22's single biggest advantage for the new shooter is that it lets them shoot enough to grow accustomed to shooting, and to become good at it!

As to shooting needs on a rural property, the .22 Long Rifle is a small game cartridge. It's suitable for rabbits, squirrels, raccoons, groundhogs, and the like. It's good for crows. It's a good choice for feral cats. It can certainly kill feral dogs, or foxes and coyotes, but frankly it's a little on the light side for animals that size. Remember, even if the animal must die so your livestock may live, you owe it a quick and humane death.

The .22 is a traditional gun for slaughtering livestock. In that situation, however, the animal must be penned under control, and the person performing the slaughter must take their time to put the bullet exactly through the skull in the right spot to reach the brain for an instant, painless death. That won't be possible when shooting a wild animal. When a steer goes wild and tries to trample you, or Ol' Yeller turns rabid and is coming at you, trust me: you'll want something a lot more powerful than a .22.

Steve Sager is a Master competitive shooter who has learned to appreciate the inexpensive Mossberg Plinker .22 rifle as a "best buy." Here, he checks out a used specimen at Daddy's Gun Shop in Mayo, Florida.

In most cases, the .22 is a rifle. Whether it has traditional "iron sights" or a telescopic sight, the two-hand grasp and the brace of the butt against your shoulder maximizes accuracy. If you get

This Mossberg Plinkster with vari-X scope, only slightly used and in excellent condition, is a bargain at under $140.

really good with it, a target grade handgun will get the job done at a typical "house to barn distance" of, say, 25 to 50 yards.

The .22 is available in many formats. There is the single-shot, the traditional "young hunter's starter gun" of yester-year. Today, the scaled down Chipmunk or Henry bolt action single shot is the right size for grade-school age kids, and a great choice for getting the young 'uns off to a good start in firearms safety. There are Western style lever actions, and pump-action .22s like the ones we geezers can remember from the live-fire shooting arcades on the boardwalks of our youth. The bolt-action repeating rifle makes a lot of sense for the user who won't be able to keep the working gun as clean and pristine as they'd like. In the humid, rust-inducing atmosphere of the slaughterhouse, the "killing gun" I'm most likely to see is a bolt-action .22. Its mechanism operates like a turnbolt lock, and allows main physical force to operate it should it stick due to rust or crud in its neglected mechanism.

The semiautomatic .22 rifle would be my personal choice. If the fisher cat is about to devour your prize pet Persian, or the rabid skunk is about to lunge at your beloved family dog, one shot may not be enough. You'll want a follow-up shot, and maybe another and another and another. The semiautomatic will fire as fast as you can hold on target and you don't have to think about anything but holding your aim and pressing the trigger. You will, however, have to keep it cleaned and lubricated.

Cost-effective choices: Mossberg now imports a little semiautomatic .22 rifle from Brazil that they market as The Plinkster. It's great for "plinking" tin cans off the back fence, as its name implies, but Master competitive shooter Steve Sager tells me his will put five shots in one hole at 25 paces… and never seems to jam. The price? Steve just bought his for $107 plus tax, brand new, from a big box store. The Ruger 10/22 and the Marlin Model 60 will cost somewhat more, but are longer-established, time-proven choices as splendidly reliable and surprisingly accurate semiautomatic .22 "utility rifles." In an accurate .22 pistol, I've seen the polymer-framed Ruger 22/45 and the Smith & Wesson Model 22A both selling new for $250, and the Browning Buckmark is another cost-effective choice. The shooter more comfortable with the simple mechanism of a revolver can get a Taurus .22 for an MSRP (manufacturers' suggested retail price) of $389 new.

The shotgun

Some bargains pass the point of diminishing returns. Author is checking out an old Stevens single-shot 12 gauge shotgun. With fore-end missing, barrel will come off frame when action is "broken" to load or reload...but, that said, it will still shoot, and price is only 30 bucks.

Designed primarily to put a large spray of multiple pellets called "shot" in the air with each pull of the trigger, the shotgun is the logical choice for flying birds and is a top choice of small game hunters for shooting running rabbits and squirrels for the same reason. Loaded with the small pellets of birdshot for the feathered stuff and the small furred stuff, and with buckshot for close-range deer, bad dogs, and worse humans, the shotgun can also fire a single slug. Slug loads are fine for deer out to plus/minus 100 yards (assuming good rifle-type sights and a steady hand on the trigger), and many Alaskan guides think a short, fast-handling shotgun loaded with slugs is just the ticket for huge, angry wounded bears in the thickets. Because its "shells" can carry so many different types of projectiles, the shotgun is the most versatile of backwoods home utility firearms.

The giant 10-gauge shotgun is a long-range duck and turkey hunter's weapon, and the tiny .410 shotgun is strictly for close range on small targets. Your all-around shotgun should be somewhere between 12- and 20-gauge. The less powerful 20 tends to have lighter recoil but, at close range, will probably do all you need done. The 12 is more versatile because it can carry more of its leaden payload, but you pay the price in notoriously hard recoil, or "kick."

Shotguns can be had in economy bolt-action formats, but they tend to be cheaply made and I never saw one that didn't kick mercilessly for a gun of its size with the shells it was chambered for. The single-shot break-open design has been a staple of American farms since the 19th century because it's relatively cheap to manufacture, but it's light for its power, kicks like hell, and doesn't offer a follow-up shot if the first one hasn't solved the problem. The double barrel is better, but a magazine-type shotgun such as the slide-action or the semiautomatic tends to be more practical for workaday rural needs. The semiautomatic is faster to shoot, nothing to do but pull the trigger, and in a gas-operated model will kick less since much of the recoil is absorbed in operating its cycling mechanism. However, as with .22 rifles, the "auto" demands more maintenance than it often gets. The rugged, manually operated slide-action, or "pump gun," may be the better choice, and will certainly be cheaper.

Cost effective choices: In either 12- or 20-gauge, the Mossberg 500 and the Remington 870 Express models are quality pump shotguns commonly available at affordable prices. I'd give the Mossberg the point for ergonomics (ambidextrous safety right under the thumb, easy loading without pushing shells past a spring-loaded magazine gate), and the Remington the point for smoothness of action and trigger pull. The Mossberg will start at around $350 MSRP, and the Remington, at $359.

The high powered rifle

Jackie Clay, probably our most popular featured writer at *Backwoods Home Magazine*, considers venison a staple of her larder and shoots her annual supply with a lever-action Winchester Model 94 .30-30, the classic "deer rifle." Marlin makes the comparable Model 336, currently in production and in the low $500 range MSRP. Both are suitable for deer and black bear-size game.

If you're located where the meat-bearing critters are bigger (northern moose, western mule deer), or farther (plains antelope, let's say), you want a higher velocity, more accurate rifle, and you'll definitely want a telescopic sight. We're talking a bolt action in the .270, .308, .30-06 etc. caliber range. Bolt action is the overwhelming choice here: its more rigid receiver, or frame, enhances precision. As with other firearm types, the bolt action high power rifle gives the shooter manual leverage that helps when the mechanism is gunked up by mud, bad weather, or owner neglect.

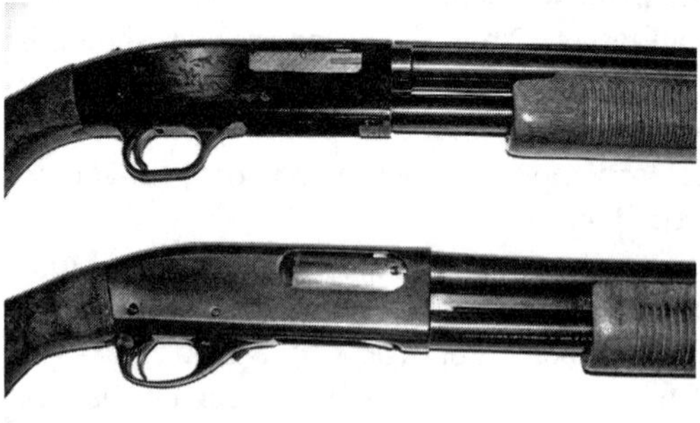

Mossberg 500 (top) and Remington 870 (below) are both good quality, affordable slide action shotguns available in various gauges.

If you're in big, bad bear country, you might want to ratchet the power level up a notch. A .338 Winchester Magnum or 7mm Remington Magnum is more in line here. If I needed to ruin a really big bruin, I'd pony up $1,122 suggested retail for the semiautomatic BAR

(Browning Automatic Rifle) in caliber .338 Winchester Magnum and consider every penny well spent. The bear attacks I've studied have happened very, very fast, and the big guys have soaked up a lot of firepower and kept fanging and clawing. Follow-up rounds of the hefty .338 persuasion as fast as you can pull the trigger would make huge sense here.

The "high power rifle" title also encompasses smaller bullets going faster: rounds like the ubiquitous .223 Remington or the super-fast .22/250. Great for long-range shots on the woodchucks that are tearing up your crops and are WAY out there, but not quite generating the smack and penetration you need for deer size game.

If you're not planning on hunting and don't have problems with either very large, mean animals or very distant ones, the high powered rifle—the "deer rifle," if you will—is probably the one gun in the battery you can most easily do without.

Cost effective choice: You're looking at MSRP in the $600-700 range for a plain-Jane bolt action Remington Model 700, Ruger Model 77, etc.; the Savage bolt action is often found new at "best buy" prices. I'm comfortable with any of them. A lower price is featured on Remington's fairly new, economy-grade Model 770. I've heard good things about this rifle, but haven't had a chance to check one out yet myself.

The defensive handgun

Folks move to the boonies to get away from the sort of lifestyle that makes you feel more comfortable carrying a gun 24/7. Hate to be the one to break it to you, but wherever you are, the need to defend yourself from man or beast tends to arise suddenly, without time to run to the gun cabinet.

A .22 pistol is handy for pot meat from ptarmigan to tree rat ("squirrels," for the city folk), and while it can certainly kill a large, aggressive creature, it won't necessarily stop it in its tracks. A .44 Magnum double action revolver would be my choice if I had big brown bears in my backyard. Most of us south of Alaska don't have to deal with that, though, and a more moderately powerful sidearm that you can wear whenever you're dressed makes a lot of sense. If being visibly armed is not part of your vision of ambient rural living, I understand; however, compact .38 Special or .357 Magnum revolvers are available in a discreet pocket size, and can be with you constantly.

Each of us lives in a different place with different situations that will guide our choices in everything from clothing to vehicles to, yes, firearms. I can only say that on the rural property where I have lived for the last four years, I have a battery that encompasses everything from varmint rifles to elephant guns, yet every time I've had to kill something on this particular turf (multiple poisonous snakes, and one really angry hog) I did it with the .357 or .45

pistol that was on my hip because nothing more suitable was within immediate reach in time.

Cost effective choice: For a small .38 Special or .357 Magnum revolver with a short barrel that lives in your pants pocket, a Ruger, Taurus, or Smith & Wesson will do nicely. The MSRP can range from low $400 to around a grand. In a holster-size semiautomatic pistol in a caliber with authority (9mm, .40, .45, or .357 SIG) you're looking at Glock, Ruger, SIG, Smith & Wesson and Taurus in a roughly $400-700 range bought new.

Purchasing used

The mechanic who purchases a pre-owned automobile is unlikely to get burned on the deal. He or she knows what to look for. The person who doesn't know much about cars except how to drive them won't get burned on a used car either...if he takes an auto mechanic he can trust with him to review the vehicle in question before he plunks down his cash.

Just as a spanking new automobile becomes a used car the moment the first buyer wheels it out of the dealer's lot, a brand-new firearm becomes a second-hand gun as soon as it fires its first shot outside the factory testing range. In either case, unless the machine in question is a rare collector's item, that first transfer of ownership drops cash value precipitously.

This means that careful shopping can get you a helluva deal on a gun someone else has broken in for you. It's all about the condition of the individual specimen. I know some purist collectors who act as if a single freckle of rust on the otherwise perfect blue finish of the gun they want is as much a deal-breaker as if they were collecting Picasso paintings and a cat had urinated on the canvas.

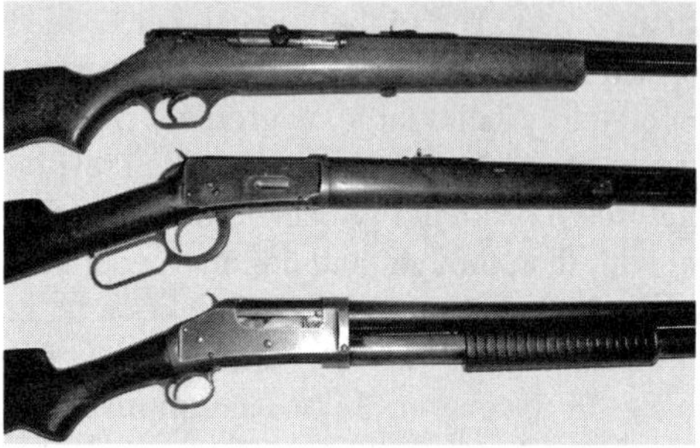

In days of old...When author's dad "moved to the country" in 1945, his household gun battery included a .22 rifle (Stevens Model 87) for his young daughter (top), a Winchester '94 deer rifle (center), and the 12-gauge Winchester '97 pump shotgun (bottom).

With a working gun, external blemishes are going to happen anyway. The stock and even some of the metal is going to get dinged and dented in the natural course of use. Some of the finish is going to get worn anyway. Thus, a rough finish is perfectly acceptable for a backwoods working gun, so long as the arm is mechanically in perfect working order.

Case in point: In 1995, I found myself at Jack First's outstanding gun shop in Rapid

City, South Dakota. Looking up at me from the used gun case was a very well-worn Smith & Wesson Combat Masterpiece Model 15 .38 Special, carrying the even-then unbelievably low price tag of $130. On a whim, I asked to see it.

It was the classic example of what the late, great gun expert Jeff Cooper characterized as a gun that had been "carried much and shot seldom." More of its famously beautiful S&W blued finish had worn off than still remained. The frame was literally pitted, as if it had been worn in an outside holster through the snows and rains of many years of extreme Dakota weather. Someone had probably scoured off the rust with steel wool. Yet the lockup was as tight as a brand new revolver, and the bore—the inside of the barrel—was absolutely pristine.

I reached for my checkbook, and made the arrangements to ship the gun to a licensed dealer for me, in the state where I lived. When I finally got it to the range, I discovered it would put every round of Federal Match grade 148 grain .38 Special ammunition into about an inch at 25 yards. I often used it thereafter to teach classes with, to reinforce the point that shooting is more about the shooter than the gun. This year, that ugly old beast won for me the Stock Service Revolver Champion plaque at the Tri-State Regional Championship (Arkansas, Mississippi, Tennessee) of the International Defensive Pistol Association. We shot that match in a driving rainstorm and, you know, I didn't worry about rusting the gun for a moment. That's as good an example as I can think of for the sort of value you can get in carefully shopping for used firearms.

I'm writing this on a quiet, rainy Saturday afternoon in North Florida. Some friends and I were heading south to Hernando this morning for an IDPA match, but turned back when we met a solid wall of thunderstorms halfway there. We returned home in leisurely fashion, doing a "gun shop tour" on the way. With this article in mind, I paid more attention than usual to the prices on good, used stuff.

At Southern Sportsman in Chiefland, I found a Marlin Model 336 with a generic 3-to-9-power variable telescopic sight. The caliber was .30-30 Winchester, adequate for anything one would be likely to hunt in this part of the country. The scope was the kind we associate with more powerful, longer range hunting rifles, but its magnification is always a one-last-check safety net for making certain that what we're aiming at in the forest at twilight really is a deer, and really does have antlers. This carbine had led a hard life, with a gray patina and some pitting where its blue finish used to be, and lots of dents and dings in the buttstock and fore-end. However, I could find no rust in the bore, and the action still worked smoothly. The price? Thanks to its ugly duckling appearance, a mere $199.95 and certainly a solid value.

An example of an effective four-gun battery today. From top: .22 rifle (Ruger 77/22). .30-06 "Deer rifle" (Ruger 77). All-around 20 gauge shotgun (Mossberg 500). Defensive pistol (9mm Glock 19).

Moving north to Mayo, Daddy's Gun Shop had one of those Brazilian-made Mossberg Plinksters, in virtually new condition, apparently traded in on something fancier. Its owner had installed a 3-9X variable power Tasco telescopic sight, decent optics for ordinary work. This was a full size (one-inch diameter) scope for a deer rifle, not one of those narrow little scopes designed for .22s and BB guns that you can barely find an image in. For sure, neither a .22 nor a BB gun is a toy, but the scopes made for them damn sure are. This new-condition .22 rifle and its good scope were tagged together at $138.

Further up the road, on the southern outskirts of Live Oak, Lundy's Gun Shop had an old Stevens Model 77 12-gauge pump shotgun, tagged at $167. It was an economy gun the day it left the factory, but a sturdy one: the military used a bunch of them for jungle warfare during the Vietnam conflict. It had the same patina and dented wood that spoke of years in the corner of the barn or the back of the pickup truck, but it was in perfect working order.

For $505, plus sales tax and five bucks to each dealer for the NICS computer clearance to purchase a firearm from a licensed dealer, that would have put a .22 rifle, a .30-30 deer rifle, and a shotgun into the backwoods home gun rack, with telescopic sights on the rifles to boot. At manufacturers' suggested retail pricing (MSRP), the Marlin .30-30 alone (without the scope) would have been more than that.

Quality handguns tend to run a bit higher than utilitarian "farm guns." We finished our gun shop tour at Pro Arms in Live Oak, where a gentleman had just purchased a traded-in S&W Model 15 .38 Special Combat Masterpiece like the one I discussed above, but his was in virtually new condition. It appeared to have been fired very little, and was fitted with Uncle Mike's Boot Grips, which allow the gun to conceal in an inside the waistband holster as well as a snub-nosed Detective Special, despite its accuracy-assisting four-inch barrel. The price was $325 before tax. S&W no longer produces the blue steel Model 15 version of the Combat Masterpiece, but its stainless steel Model 67 version has an MSRP of $774 at this writing. Whether for concealed carry or home defense, I could be happy with that.

Counting the revolver, the day's shopping would have yielded a before-tax cost of $830 for enough guns to cover my basic firearms needs if I lived in a cabin in the area where we were shopping. Hell, the light-weight Smith & Wesson Model 340 Military & Police .357 Magnum snub-nose revolver that's in my pocket as I type this would go that at suggested retail, by itself.

Bottom line

Don't go for an A+ in one class at the expense of a grade of Incomplete on the rest of the curriculum. One screwdriver won't do it all for you, nor will one saw, and neither will one firearm. A good, functional, representative example of each type puts a lot more versatility in your toolbox than the most expensive specimen of just one type. That's how it is with tools...and, in a rural home, the working gun IS a tool. No more, no less.

Choose your tools carefully. Learn to use them well. And, above all, demand of yourself and others that they be used responsibly and safely. Δ

Chapter 29
Bury a gun and ammo for 15 years

By Charles Wood

Back in the early 1990s the outlook for the nation in general and gun owners in particular seemed rather grim to many people. A few years earlier in 1986, Congress had banned civilians from owning newly manufactured machine guns. There was ever more strident talk of banning semi-automatic weapons or so called assault weapons. Many of us regarded a semi-automatic rifle as the foundation of a home defense battery. Many of us believed that more laws banning ever more types of guns were imminent. About that time I acquired a Ruger Ranch Rifle through a private sale. I decided to stash it away in a safe place just in case my worst fear was to materialize, another gun ban.

The general location of the pipe after the logging was done. It would have helped if I had had a better method of locating the pipe.

Here is the top of the pipe uncovered with the noose and winch attached.

First order of business was to decide how I would prepare the gun for long-term storage and where I would store it. I decided that for maximum security I needed to bury it. This would keep it safe from all but the most determined government goons. I set about finding an appropriate location. I live in a fairly remote, wooded rural area in the northeast. One day as I was walking in the woods I noticed a hemlock tree had blown down and been uprooted by a recent windstorm. There was a small crater about eight feet across and three feet deep where the root ball had been torn out of the ground. It occurred to me that this would be a good spot for my rifle.

Since I now had the location, I began preparing the rifle for storage. I bought a piece of 6-inch diameter schedule 40 PVC pipe, end caps, and PVC solvent from a hardware store in another town where I had never done business before. Being in a rural area where everyone knows everyone I didn't want to arouse any suspicions about what I was up to. I then disassembled the rifle and completely coated every metal part with a rust preventative oil intended for storing unused machinery in damp locations. This oil dries to form a waxy coating. I was extra careful that the bore was completely coated. I wanted to vacuum-pack the rifle as extra insurance against rust. As it turned out my employer had just taken delivery of a mainframe computer that happened to be wrapped in a large aluminized mylar bag for shipping. This proved to be the perfect material for my purpose. I discovered that with a warm iron I could fuse the edges of this material into a custom-fitted airtight bag for the rifle. I placed each individual component of the partially disassembled rifle in its own custom-made mylar bag with a small bag of silica gel desiccant to absorb any moisture present. Using my shop vac and an iron I managed to produce a professional-looking vacuum-packing job. The barreled action, stock, trigger assembly, hand guard, magazines, scope, and mounts all went into individual bags.

Since the rifle was so heavily preserved I knew I would need something to degrease it with when I finally retrieved it so I included two small cans of 1-1-1 Trichlorethane in the package. Also, since a rifle is of little use without ammunition, several thousand rounds of .223 were included. Because every

The pipe was carefully sawn open to reveal that it remained watertight after 15 years underground.

well-maintained rifle needs to be cleaned and oiled occasionally, I added a cleaning rod, patches, Hoppe's #9 solvent, gun oil, grease, and owner's manual. A set of reloading dies was included as well. If dire circumstances required me to retrieve my rifle I wanted to be sure that I would have everything at hand necessary to put it into service. All of the individually wrapped components were sealed together into a larger mylar bag custom-made for the purpose along with a couple more medium-sized bags of desiccant. A few bags of ammo were taped to the side of this bag and the entire thing was wrapped in duct tape. Additional ammo was packed into zip lock freezer bags.

With everything prepared I was ready to load the pipe. I first put in a large bag of desiccant followed by several bags of ammo, followed by the bag containing the rifle and supplies. Since there was some empty space surrounding the rifle, I dumped in some loose ammo just to fill the voids. More bags of ammo were then added to fill the pipe. Since I had a tank of nitrogen available, I also purged the air from the tube with the nitrogen before sealing it. This was undoubtedly overkill but I had it available so I used it. I took extreme care while using the PVC solvent to insure that the caps were perfectly sealed and watertight. Finally, I painted the pipe black, and at this point, 15 years later, I'm not sure why.

I loaded the sealed pipe in the back of my truck and drove up into the woods to the downed hemlock tree previously selected. With a post hole digger I dug a hole about six feet deep and a foot in diameter in the center of the crater left by the root ball of the tree. After gently placing the pipe in the hole, I carefully pulled the tree upright using a chain attached to my truck. By this time the tree had died and most of the needles had fallen off. Once returned to vertical it was pretty stable and a little dirt and debris shoveled around the edges did the trick. In any healthy, well-managed forest there are always a few standing dead trees, so this one would not arouse the curiosity of anyone who hunted or hiked there.

The contents of the pipe, still in the protective wrapping

All components were individually wrapped and sealed. The contents show no adverse affects after spending 15 years underground.

I never told anyone what I had done and I didn't write down the location anywhere. About five or six years later I had a timber harvest. I had my consulting forester mark the tree as a wildlife tree so it wouldn't be disturbed by the loggers. It was, after all, popular with the Pileated Woodpeckers. It has been 15 years since I buried the rifle and I have recently had another timber harvest. The tree was quite rotted by this time and it didn't survive the harvest. I had been keeping an eye on it, so when it finally fell I marked a nearby tree so I could find it again after the loggers left. Even careful logging causes quite an upheaval in the forest and it can be difficult to locate a specific spot after all the landmarks have been changed. After the logging crew had left it took me several days with a shovel and a rake to locate the rifle. In hindsight, I should have had some additional way of locating it. Since the top of the pipe was about three feet below ground level, my old metal detector wasn't much help. I decided that it would be interesting to retrieve the rifle and see how well my storage plan had worked.

I managed to locate the very rotted stump beneath the logging debris and started digging. Once I located the top of the pipe I excavated around it about a foot on all sides and to a depth of about a foot below the top of the pipe. I attached a noose of polypropylene rope and used the winch on my truck and a convenient log to slowly pull the pipe out of the ground. After all these years the soil was still very loose around the pipe and it was relatively easy to pull it out. I could have accomplished it without the winch had it been necessary. After removing the pipe, I filled the hole with logging debris and covered it up with some loose hemlock boughs to prevent someone from falling into it.

Back at the house I hosed off the mud and prepared to saw the pipe open. Using a handsaw, I very carefully cut completely around one of the caps. I didn't want to damage the contents by being too enthusiastic.

With the cap removed it was immediately obvious that no moisture had gotten into the pipe. I carefully slid the contents out on to a table for examination. After unwrapping the duct tape and removing the outer bag, it was obvious that all was OK. All of the individual packages were unwrapped to reveal the contents were as good as the day they were packaged.

So if you think it is necessary, you can store a rifle safely for long periods in harsh environments. A little attention to detail, some scrounged materials, and a few dollars in supplies are all it takes. Δ

Chapter 30
Stashing junk silver for bad times

By John Silveira

When I was a teenager, a gallon of gasoline was about 25 cents and so was a loaf of bread. Now, each costs around $4. However, there are gas stations today (one is in Medford, Oregon) that will sell you a gallon or more of gas for a mere 25 cents — but *only* if that quarter is a pre-1965 "junk silver" quarter. They call those pre-1965 silver dimes, quarters, and halves "junk silver" because, having been circulated, they are worn and have no real numismatic (coin collecting) value. But they are far from "junk" as each coin is 90% silver, and silver is becoming more and more valuable.

If money becomes worthless, and it's becoming worth less and less every day, possessing junk silver currency in a collapsed economy may bump you to the head of the line for medical services, food, or for a host of other goods and services for your family. There may come a day when $100 face value

This is a pile containing $100 face value of pre-1965 "junk silver" coins, but it could represent 400 gallons of gasoline or 400 loaves of bread.

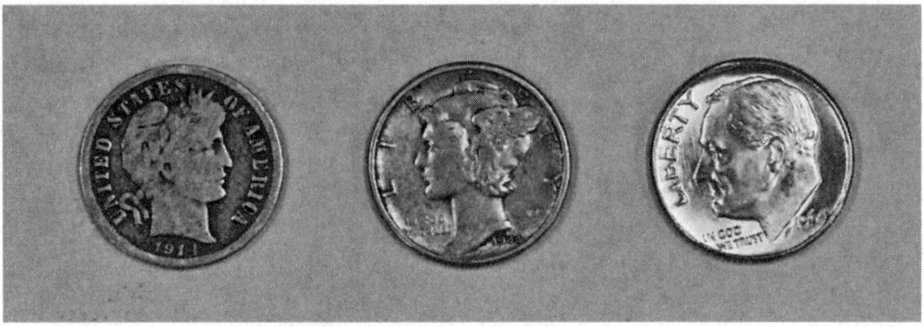

From left to right: the Barber dime, the so-called Mercury dime, and the Roosevelt dime. The figure on the Mercury dime is not the Roman god of that name. It is actually "Lady Liberty" and the wings are part of what's called a Phrygian cap and they represent freedom of thought.

in junk silver coins are worth 400 or more gallons of gas. In a car that gets 25 m.p.g., that can be at least 10,000 miles of travel. On the other hand, it can be more than 400 loaves of bread for your family to eat or maybe 500 to 600 cans of soups and veggies.

Though large corporations, like the electric company, may not be able to take your silver (bureaucracies will have rules and their employees have little latitude to make decisions), the guy who owns the local gas station, the bakery, the grocery store, or even your doctor *can* and, if he or she is any kind of businessman, will value silver over the "legal tender" the Federal Reserve is passing off nowadays.

As I write this, pure silver is worth about $36 a troy ounce (see sidebar on "Weights.") and $1 face value of junk silver has about .715 ounces of silver, the same purchasing power as approximately $25 in Federal Reserve Notes. (That's the funny green stuff that's in your wallet now.)

A hedge against inflation

Junk silver is a good hedge against inflation, which we are now experiencing in almost every area, especially at the supermarket.

One of the few areas in economy where deflation, rather than inflation, is occurring is in the housing market, which is why the U.S. Government is able to claim that the U.S. inflation rate is low. Of course, they neglect to say that for the first time in history, they have included depressed housing costs in the formulae they use to calculate inflation.

Inflation is now hitting us harder than it has in three decades and the price of silver, gold, and practically everything else has taken off. When the latest rise in the price of silver started a few months ago, I discovered I only had about $115 in face value in junk silver stashed away. Today I've got more than double that and I'll buy more as the price drops back.

How much junk silver?

How much junk silver should someone own for bad times? The answer, of course, depends on your circumstances. I'd like at least $300 to $400 worth. However, if you're just beginning, you should only consider buying junk silver *after* you've laid in food, medical supplies, and whatever tools — including guns and ammunition — you feel you may need for the circumstances you and your family are in.

If you haven't bought junk silver before, you're going to encounter several issues.

The first is that you're going to pay a premium of some sort to get it. But given its potential value in bad times, it'll be worth it. Besides, other factors I'll mention later will likely make your silver appreciate more and compensate you for the cost of the premium.

The second problem is the same problem all precious metals have: They are not "productive investments," that is, they don't earn interest, nor do they pay dividends. They are inflation hedges and "real" cash as the dollar declines. If it weren't for those two factors, I wouldn't buy it.

Which junk silver coins?

The junk silver dimes, quarters, and half dollars are an alloy made of 90% silver and 10% copper, as are the new "proof" coins.

When originally made, $1 face value — that is, ten dimes, four quarters, two halves, five dimes and two quarters, or any other combination that adds up to $1 — contained .7234 troy ounces of silver. Today, because of wear and tear, the convention is that $1 face value contains about .715 ounces. In other words, it's assumed that the average silver coin has lost about 1.16% of its mass and, therefore, 1.16% of its silver.

Still, coins of the same denomination do not all weigh the same. Older dimes weigh less than newer dimes, and so on.

To ascertain the weight differences, I decided to buy a scale and weigh my own junk silver coins. I bought an RCBS 505 reloading scale which has a capacity of 511 grains. (One troy ounce is 480 grains.) "But," I asked myself, "how will I know for sure that my scale is accurate even after zeroing it?" So, after spending $112 for the scale and shipping, I spent more than $100 for a set of Class 6 calibration weights and discovered my scale is accurate to about one part in 4800, all the way out to one troy ounce, accurate enough for what I'm doing.

I expected to find quite a bit of variation in coin weights, with the older coins — those which have been circulated longer and have seen the most wear — to weigh less than the newer coins. What I wasn't expecting was the amount of variation in weight within the same year of issue, even when the

From left to right are the Barber, the "Standing Liberty," and two Washington quarters. The second Washington quarter is a silver proof of the 2005 Kansas quarter which the U.S. Mint makes for collectors.

coins showed no wear. Quite a few people didn't believe this could be true. They felt, as I had before I used my scale, that coins fresh from the Mint should all weigh "the same." They don't. Fresh from the Mint, silver quarters should weigh about 96.45 grains. But the 40 uncirculated 2005 Kansas State quarters I have weigh from as little as 95.2 to as much as 99.1 grains. That's as much as 1.3% less to as much as 3% more. That's quite a range of error. I can only attribute it to the fact that the blanks from which the coins are pressed are not uniformly thick. Later, I would discover that the new Silver Eagle bullion coins, uncirculated, average about .5% more than spec and virtually all 40 that I own are overweight.

And this is not a new phenomenon. I've got some old dimes, quarters, and halves which are actually heavier than spec, even though they show more than 20 years of wear.

I'd avoid the older coins like the Barber dimes, quarters, and halves (so named because they were designed by Charles Barber, head engraver for the Mint, and circulated from 1892 to 1916). The Barber coins I have show anywhere from more than 8% wear to almost 14%

Weights

There is a variety of weight measures used in the United States. One involves avoirdupois ounces and pounds which we use to measure everything from our body weight to potato chips. There are 437.5 "grains" of weight in an avoirdupois ounce and as there are 16 ounces in an avoirdupois pound, so that pound is 7,000 grains.

Another weight system, troy ounces and pounds, is used for precious metals such as gold and silver. A troy ounce is 480 grains and there are 12 troy ounces, or 5,560 grains, in a troy pound.

In comparison, a troy ounce is about 9.7% heavier than an avoirdupois ounce.

In the top row, from left to right, are the Barber, "Standing Liberty," and Ben Franklin half dollars. From the left, in the bottom row are a 90% Kennedy half dollar and a 40% Kennedy half.

wear. That's 8 to 14% less silver, but you won't be paying less for them. You may even be paying an added premium because they're "old."

The same goes for the "Standing Liberty" quarters. They show excessive amounts of wear.

Part of the wear on the old coins is because of their age, but part is due to their intricate designs. The so-called "Standing Liberty" quarters are among the prettiest coins the Mint ever produced, but the raised edges and intricate detail wore off fast. The figures blurred and detail wore away. Frequently, the dates were obliterated. With all that wear, silver disappeared.

Personally, I think the old "Walking Liberty" half dollars, designed by Adolph Weinman, are the most beautiful design for any of the silver coins the Mint has ever made. But, with all that detail, wear was inevitable. So I wouldn't get too many of them unless the premium is low or you like them just because they look cool.

I should add that the Walking Liberty design has been returned on the Silver Eagle bullion coins the Mint has made since 1986. However, the beautiful eagle which appeared on the reverse side of the Walking Liberty half was not carried over to the Silver Eagle. The Silver Eagle has a much duller eagle on the reverse side.

Later silver coins, those from the '50s and '60s — these include Roosevelt dimes, Washington quarters, and the Franklin and '64 Kennedy halves — don't show that much wear because soon after the Mint replaced silver coins with the modern (and almost worthless) "clad" coins in 1965, shoppers rapidly gleaned the silver coins from circulation. Thus, many of those coins, though over a half-century old, often look almost like new and even the worn ones have lost less than 1% of their weight. Another reason these coins show less wear is because, unlike earlier coins, they have less intricate detail, so there's that much less to be abraded off.

As a result of my "studies," I try to stick to Roosevelt dimes, Washington quarters (especially those from the mid-50s to 1964), almost any of the Franklin halves, and all the 1964 Kennedy halves.

Where to buy

I won't tell you where to buy your silver because prices, shipping costs, and other costs are constantly in flux.

I've found local stores, both coin stores and some antique stores, with fair prices, but some online stores and some local stores are grossly overpriced. One antique store in Coos Bay, Oregon, is selling junk silver for just over spot (the price of a commodity such as an ounce of gold or silver at that very moment), but another, just a few miles away in North Bend, was asking $4.50 for Mercury dimes — ridiculously overpriced — and buying them from the public for $1.70. Not a bad racket if you can pull it off.

Though they say "one dollar" on them, the two Silver Eagles are actually silver bullion coins made by the Mint for collectors.

I suggest googling "junk silver" online and visiting some of the sites to see who's offering the best deals. Lately, I've been buying mine from www.providentmetals.com, but I keep checking prices at other sites.

To figure out what kind of premium you're paying on junk silver, divide the price of $1 face value of the 90% silver coins by .715 and you'll see what you're paying for the silver content. Today, not including any shipping, I can buy $1 face value in Franklin halves from one online site for $26.32. Dividing that by .715, I see I'm getting the silver content for $36.81/oz. At the moment, that's 80 cents over the spot price of silver. Not a bad deal, especially when I buy enough so that the shipping is free.

I don't have much to do with the so-called war nickels, coins made with 40% silver which include the Kennedy halves made from 1965 to 1971 and the Eisenhower "S" dollars made from 1971 to 1976. If I find a really good deal on them, I may buy some. For the moment, I'm keeping the ones I've collected from my change the last 40 years, but I'm not buying any.

Silver bullion coins

Although everyone's survival larder should contain junk silver coins, you may decide to consider silver bullion, too. If so, consider the Silver Eagle "dollar" coins made by the U.S. Mint. They contain one ounce of .999 fine silver. Though they are designated as dollar coins (because, by law, all coins issued by the government must have denominations on them), they are worth whatever an ounce of silver is currently going for which, today, is about $36. And, yes, I have some.

But there are two problems with Silver Eagles. First is that, like the new silver proof coins, they are not as recognizable to the general public as junk silver is and this *may* make them more difficult to spend in hard times.

The second problem is a more difficult one to deal with: Silver Eagles are now being counterfeited, in China among other places, and as they become more valuable, expect the quality of the counterfeits to improve.

Many people are also investing in silver bullion rounds (they look like coins) and bars made by private mints. I'm not. The trouble with them is that they are going to be more difficult to spend because they are unlikely to be recognized by the general public, and to sell them they generally need some kind of authentication. In the meantime, like the Silver Eagles, they are and will continue to be counterfeited.

If you're going to put money in bullion, make it separate from the junk silver coins that you can be sure are going to be spendable, if and when the world goes to pot.

Americans are always going to recognize dimes, quarters, and halves, and junk silver coins, especially those that have seen years of circulation, and they are going to be difficult to fake.

When to buy

The price of silver is high, just now, and though I wish I had laid in my stash when it was a lot cheaper, I'm going to buy about $10 face value each month for the next year. However, I believe there's a "correction" coming and the price will come down. And if the spot price goes below $33 an ounce, I'm going to buy a little more than $10 face value each month. How much more depends on how low the price goes.

So, how low do I think it might go? I think the spot price of silver will dip back into the $20 to $30-per-ounce range and there's a remote chance it'll visit the teens, one more time. But don't wait for that. It may not happen.

What about gold?

Gold is good. But the biggest problem with holding gold is that it's difficult to spend. Unless you're buying a large-ticket item or making a massive purchase of food, guns, ammo, etc., how do you get change? If a guy wants junk silver quarters for a few gallons of gas, I can easily fill my tank with some silver change. I can't as readily do that with gold.

Also, if you're like me and you've only got a little money to spend, start with junk silver. Right now, for $1500 I can get about $55 face value in silver or a 1-ounce piece of gold bullion. Tell me which one you think is more useful.

Silver will outpace inflation

With the recent bailouts, during which the Federal Reserve Bank poured about $11 trillion into our economy to bail out its Wall Street cronies, the value of the American dollar is going to decline faster than it ever has. There is no way that that amount of money, created out of thin air, can be introduced into our economy without creating inflation, and inflation is going to guarantee that, over the long run, your stash of junk silver will become worth more in Federal Reserve Notes. Inflation is not going to go away.

Theoretically, the rise in the price of gold or silver will, over the long run, stay in step with inflation. (In the short run, it doesn't.) But there are other forces which, over the long run, *may* make your stash of junk silver go up even faster than inflation and even faster than gold. This is what will make the premium you have to pay for your silver today less painful tomorrow.

One of the forces that will make silver's price rise is that silver is in demand because it has a multitude of industrial and consumer uses. Silver conducts heat and electricity better than any other metal. Because of this, it's used in the production of computers, cell phones, monitors, chips, automobiles, etc., and more uses are being found every day. Sometimes a lot is used, but usually it's very little. But even in minute amounts, millions of computers, monitors, cell phones, etc., add up to a lot of silver.

Silver is also valuable for use in the purification of water and air, and it's got antibacterial properties. It has uses for which no decent substitutes have yet been found. Modern civilization just wouldn't be the same without this precious metal. And because of the way it's used in such small amounts in so many industrial products, it's often not economical to recycle, so it's lost.

Foreign demand

With roughly a third of the world's population between them, both China and India are industrializing and both are trying to provide more consumer products to their citizens. One commentator has pointed out that about 10 years ago, the per capita consumption of silver in China was a mere $^{1}/70^{th}$ of that in the West. But now, they're catching up.

In the meantime, the world's supply of new silver has not kept pace with silver consumption. Since 1990, more silver has been consumed every year than has been produced. To make up for the shortfall, silver reserves have been depleted and the price of silver has increased — well ahead of inflation.

In the future, the world's two most populous countries are going to be eating up gobs of the metals as both their industrial bases and consumer demands increase.

And if that's not enough, China is *finally* allowing its people to own silver bullion. Until recently, private ownership of the metal was illegal. There are roughly 1.33 billion people in China and even if you take only a small percentage of that figure taking possession of silver for savings, numbers like that can do nothing but drive up the cost of this precious metal.

All of these reasons and more are going to drive up the demand on silver and, along with it, its cost, promising to make your silver stash more valuable to you in bad times. Δ

Notes

Notes